The

OM

The Uncreated Creations

by

Guy Steven Needler

For permission, serialization, condensation, adaptions, or for our catalog of other publications, write to Ozark Mountain Publishing, Inc., P.O. Box 754, Huntsville, AR 72740, ATTN: Permissions Department.

Library of Congress Cataloging-in-Publication Data

The OM: The Uncreated Creations

by Guy Steven Needler -1961-

What are The OM? Why are they Uncreated? How can they operate outside of the structure of the Multiverse? Why are they not involved in the evolutionary cycle?

In The OM - The Uncreated Creations, the reader will gain oan understanding of what these rare entities are, their interaction with The Origin and The Source, and why tehy are considered to by Uncreated.

1. Metaphysical 2. The OM 3. Multiverse

I. Needler, Guy Steven-1961- II. The OM III. Metaphysical IV. Title

Library of Congress Catalog Card Number: 2022923439

ISBN: 978-1-956945-34-8

Cover Art and Layout: Victoria Cooper Art

Book set in: Times New Roman

Book Design: Summer Garr

Published by:

OZARK
MOUNTAIN
PUBLISHING

PO Box 754, Huntsville, AR 72740
800-935-0045 or 479-738-2348; fax 479-738-2448
WWW.OZARKMT.COM

Printed in the United States of America

Contents

Foreword

This book was started on a journey to China to hold intensive Traversing the Frequencies (TTF) and Psychic Shield (PS) workshops plus a taster to my healing workshop Psycho-Spiritual Healing (PSH) in December 2019. I didn't intend to start it at this time because I was supposed to be having a break after finishing the book on Psycho-Spiritual Healing (PSH, but may be called Psycho-Spiritual Alignment and Reprogramming [PsAR] in China), my eighth. However, when one has looked at all of the inflight entertainment and exhausted the possibilities of reasonable program that one may be interested in, one's mind always wanders back to getting on with the next piece of work.

This book is dedicated to The OM and is intended to gain as much information about these rather rare entities as possible. What makes them rare? you may ask. Well, simply put, they are the only entities, as far as I am aware, that have not been specifically created by another entity, or being, in order to support a desire to experience, learn, and evolve. Indeed, they do not specifically have a direction from any entity or being and this includes The Origin. Furthermore, the only other entity that wasn't specifically created was The Origin, which is, by definition, a being. Please see the glossary of terms at the back of the book for the descriptions of what makes an entity an entity and what makes a being a being.

Even as I say this though, I am concerned that, as a result of the intervention/interaction of Event Space in the earlier period in the existence of the developing sentience that was destined to be The Origin, it could actually be classified as an entity. Event Space would have had to be fully sentient to have achieved responsibility for the creation of The Origin, which, when I look back at the previous communications, it was not, so I suppose that

i

answers that question—maybe!

I have to admit that I am eager to commune with The OM and Anne, who is also beloved of The OM and is part of my OM True Energetic Self (TES). I find myself quite excited about the prospect!

Over the years and the channeled works that have become books there have been a number of times when The OM were discussed, with the result of new information about them being presented to me. During these times I made a mental note to go back to these communications and use them as a springboard to gain a deeper understanding of the information and as a possibility to go in different directions to broaden the knowledge about The OM as well as deepen it. On top of this, I have already compiled a list of questions that I expect my readers would like me to ask as "headings" for discussion with The OM.

One of the things that really intrigues me are those OM that choose not to be responsible for anything and as a result choose not to create or even participate in any form of evolutionary gain, being fully independent of the desires of The Origin, even though they are essentially individualized units of Origin sentience. I later call these the disconnected or disassociated OM.

Then there is Hum, dear Hum, that OM who was "assigned" to me. It was to assist in my ability to traverse those frequencies above those of the incarnate human vehicle and later traverse all frequencies within The Source's multiverse and beyond into those frequencies, that structure, that was Beyond The Source and into the sentient energies of The Origin allowing me to commune with the other Source Entities. The *Beyond The Source* books were, I now know, a test of my abilities to continue to go beyond—and then go further. My intuition tells me that this will be important in both this and the next book.

The OM continue to be a mystery simply because they are an anomaly in the normal scheme of the much greater reality, and all I can hope to do is remove a small part of that mystery as I work through the communication I have as a beloved member of The OM.

Many people ask me the difference between those Aspects from TES that have been created by The Source and an OM. Simply put, while incarnate there is no difference; we/The OM abide by the same constrictions associated with existence in a low-frequency environment while in the incarnate state, although there are some communicative benefits, should one recognize them. I will let you know when I notice a few more than those I use, which are not many.

In finishing, before commencing the task at hand I would like to suggest that I will gain as much information about The OM that incarnate mankind can assimilate, not of course discounting myself. Notice I didn't say "work with" for this would imply understanding, which to be honest none of us can achieve in this incarnate state. However, we are expansive enough to gain knowledge from any communication with The OM, further noting that that which we can understand is designed to be understandable.

In order to assist in understanding the knowledge that will unfold during my dialogue with The OM I have included a glossary of terms that have developed as a function of my previous dialogues and books. New terms that have arisen from the dialogues that will create this book will also be included in the glossary, but they will be in *italics*.

I hope you are in the same state of anticipation as me, dear reader, for I anticipate a real metaphysical treat!

Guy Steven Needler
23 December 2019

Reconnecting

Physical existence had taken over since writing the introduction to this book on the flight to China in December 2019. Although this physical work included a significant amount of spiritual work, writing the online content for a healing workshop that was due to be piloted in China for example, it meant that work on *The OM: The Uncreated Creations* was temporarily put on the back burner. China, I note, was proving to be a big spiritual opportunity, one which had a resultant workload associated with it, one that I had intuition about for some years but shied away from.

My mind focused on the task at hand, reconnecting with The OM. I was not surprised to hear a familiar voice in my head as the first official contact with The OM since working with Hum.

I do have to say that it feels very good to be sitting in front of my computer working on the next, the ninth book. I gain a sense of freedom from it this time, a kind of comfort—strange! It could be because I am about to communicate with that which I am, that I will be taking to my counterparts at home!!!

ANNE: Heeellllooo! It's me!

It appeared that Anne had decided that she/it was to be my first contact with The OM.

ME: It's nice to speak to you again.
ANNE: It's not the first time that we have spoken since *The Curators*, *The Anne Dialogues*, or the book on *Psycho-Spiritual Healing*. In fact, we have spoken often.
ME: It has been about trivial stuff though.

ANNE: There is nothing that can be classified as trivial that does not have meaning behind it.

ME: I accept that. I just mean that I don't give it the same level of importance as the work we do to broadcast the information about the greater reality.

ANNE: Such as writing the books?

ME: Such as writing the books.

ANNE: Who do you think planted the desire in the right people to make you interested in making a workshop out of *Psycho-Spiritual Healing*?

ME: Ah! I knew there was something or someone in the background that made the publication of the book in China turn into a workshop instead—the change in direction was made very compelling.

ANNE: It is my job to make sure that that which is in the plan comes into fruition.

ME: And that is why you are where you are now and why I am here now.

ANNE: That's right.

ME: OK, so how is this going to work?

ANNE: There are many things to talk about and you have been given some of the subjects that we will discuss. I do note, though, that there are a few that will appear to be off-piste and as a result will be introduced as we progress.

Not everything that will be discussed is going to be about The OM. Some of it will be information that The OM choose to give you.

ME: So, who is with you now? Who is going to interact with me?

ANNE: I will, as will Hum when appropriate, but a lot of the dialogue will come from The OM collectively, that being, those OM that we are "beloved of."

ME: All of The OM?

ANNE: No, those OM TES that we are beloved of.

ME: How many OM TES are we beloved of?

OM: Seven. We are in total seven together and you are two of one of the seven. The seven are what you call TES but we are OM.

ANNE: There you have it.

ME: I guess that I/we are part of the same TES. This I/we, my readers know.

For you, dear reader.

To describe us as OM, then, we are two Aspects from the same OM TES. The OM describe themselves in terms of TES rather than the Aspects from their TES if they project them. They

collectively refer to their TES as OM. The group of or a group of "OM" TES are referred to as being beloved of The OM.
ANNE: Being beloved of The OM has more meanings, though.
ME: Go on.
ANNE: Being beloved of The OM means that an OM TES or its projected Aspect/s are beloved of the group of OM that it associates itself with. The group of OM, in our case containing seven TES, are beloved of The OM in total. That means all of The OM groups that are within and without the eleven Source Entities currently in the first aspect of Origin structure [*the first group of twelve levels in another group of twelve groups; see* The Origin Speaks—*GSN*] you call its Polyomnipresent area (volume) of Polyomniscience. This includes those OM groups and those that are singular OM that do not associate themselves with a Source Entity. The twelfth Source Entity, SE12, does not have any OM associated with it as you know. It also includes those that do not associate themselves with the evolutionary process. All OM are beloved of The OM!
ME: Any association with The OM is beloved then?
A & OM Together: Yes!
A & OM Together: ALL and One OM are one and are beloved.
ME: Being beloved of The OM is both a singular and a collective term then?
A & OM Together: Yes!

I noticed myself saying this as well!!!

ME: Hold on a moment. We seem to be all together as one.
A & OM Together: We are as one!
ME: Yes, I know but I wanted to communicate with Anne separately, to Hum separately, to the group of OM that I/we are part of separately. I haven't even reconnected with Hum yet.
HUM: But I/we are here together beloved as one, beloved of The OM!
A & OM Together: But we/it/Hum/Anne are here together, beloved as one, beloved of The OM!
ME: OK, my mind is already spinning.
Can I make a request?
ANNE & OM Together: You may.
ME: Can we make the following rules in communication?

1. When it's the Aspect of The OM TES that I belong to, Anne, that communicates that it is singularly

represented as ANNE.

2. When it's the TES of The OM group that I belong to, Hum, that communicates that it is singularly represented as Hum.

3. When it's the group of OM TES that I belong to, OM, that communicates that it is collectively represented as OM.

4. When, and if, it's ALL OM communicating to me collectively that it is represented as ALL OM.

ANNE & HUM & OM & ALL OM: YES, I/it/we/we all CAN!

ME: Now we can get somewhere!

ANNE: You really are difficult to work with in that human suit!

ME: I know, I know!

How The OM Became

How The OM were created, or should I say uncreated, is, I feel, explained in enough detail in *The Origin Speaks*. However, for those readers who have not read *The Origin Speaks* I will summarize.

The Origin, having realized that it wasn't able to recreate itself once, let alone twelve times, also realized that the failure to create twelve copies of itself was due to not understanding itself, specifically in terms of its own magnitude. This led to the creation of twelve smaller and quantifiable "Source" Entities. In order to do this, it reused the sentience and energy that it used (individualized from itself) to create the twelve Origins and reassigned the sentience and energy into smaller groups of sentient energy. It allowed them to become self-aware on their own and then connected (communed) with them to advise them of their reason for existence.

How can anything recreate that which it is if it doesn't know what it is in the first place? you may ask. Indeed, this is a question The Origin recognizes that it didn't ask before starting its experiment—the creation of twelve versions of itself.

This was the dilemma that it was presented with and is presented with. In essence, and in hindsight, The Origin could only reproduce itself when it had fully understood ALL that IT was on all twelve major levels of its structure. That each major level had twelve minor levels of structure associated with it. And that right now it was only working on understanding the first group of twelve levels within the first major level of structure. This structure is described in short in *The Origin Speaks* as The Origin's volume of polyomnipresent, polyomniscient self-awareness, and everything that comprises the structure of our

5

Source Entity (SE1) is within the first four levels of the first twelve minor levels of structure, the multiverse we exist within being within the first three. Each level of structure represents an X^{12} increase in finitude and environmental content from the previous or level below it. This X^{12} increase is a constant that is throughout The Origin's structure that it is aware of, but not yet in full understanding of, and that which it is semi-aware or even not aware of, but realizes must exist. By the time The Origin had worked this out, moved on from its point of "so-called" failure, and created the twelve Source Entities, it had also recognized that it could never faithfully reproduce itself. It was "one on its own," it was "The Origin" and that was that.

After the failure of the twelve Origins creation, such was the urgency in its desire to create The Source Entities to accelerate its evolutionary progression that it forgot to ensure that the combination of sentience and energy that it used to create The Source Entities was fully reassigned as such. How could The Origin forget to totally reprogram/reassign its sentience and energy from one role to the new role? you may ask. The answer is simple. The Origin was, and still is, extremely young and as a result is experiencing, learning, and evolving, just as we, as creations of our Source Entity, SE1, are! As a result, it can make simple mistakes or errors. These errors meant that, in the case of the creation of the twelve Source Entities, some of the sentient energy was still wholly Origin! Being wholly Origin sentience and energy meant that it was still Origin and as such capable of becoming instantaneously individualized and unintentionally created at the same time as being unassociated with that which any other sentient energy that had the purpose of being anything other than Origin sentience. Provided that is, that there is enough sentient weight to support its individuality.

I remember The Origin describing the creation of The OM in *The Origin Speaks*.

O: *The OM energy was unevenly distributed among the pure Source Entity energy. It was in globules of OM energy, so to speak. These globules remained singular, individualized aspects of OM energy and did not group together. As soon as my intention to keep all of the energies together was removed, they very quickly separated themselves out from The Source Entity energies that they found themselves part of. Those that had enough mass naturally sensed that they were not of the same quality of energy and moved back into the energies that they sensed were their own—the energies being those which are part of my area of self-awareness. Simply put, they moved back to the place from whence they came! The mass of OM energy and the level of sentience attached to those individual masses dictated how The OM are currently represented within me. The result was the generation of the Pure OM, Non-captive OM, Captive OM, and Source Entity/OM Hybrid, the hybrid of which have varying percentages of mix [see later—GSN].*

The quality of the energies that are OM ensured that their level of sentience increased at a rapid rate. Apart from the energies that resulted in The Source Entity/OM Hybrid energies, and much later, other individualized entities created by The Sources for their own evolutionary tasks, all other OM were able to detect each other no matter where they were and within or without which Source Entity they are or were part of.

The OM are, in general, but specifically in the case of the Pure OM, individualized units of me. As each of The OM sought each other out they noticed that their interaction with each other rapidly increased the level of their sentience. At the same time, they also noted that they were not all the same in terms of their mass and ability to relocate themselves. Working together, understanding what each of them "was" from an energetic and sentience perspective created a high level of camaraderie within The OM. During this interaction they recognized how special they all were in terms of the noncreativity process that resulted in their creation coming into effect. They noted their limited numbers and loved being in each other's company. They all fell in love with each and every one of themselves and became beloved as a group of entities as a result—hence the term being "beloved of The OM." The OM's ability to experience, learn, and evolve was and is a joy to behold. They have a capacity for evolution that is only equal to a Source Entity, and, noting how much larger than an OM a Source Entity is, this is the most wonderful piece of noncreation I have ever experienced. There is one issue with The OM, though, and it is this. They are, to all intents and purposes, me, smaller individualized versions of me, and because they were not created for a specific purpose, they have fully autonomous individualized free will. Because they are essentially me I cannot and do not control them. They do what they want, wherever they want to do it because they do not have a framework within which to work.

ME: This sentient weight, or lack of it in some instances then, has resulted in the genres of OM illustrated below, starting with the lowest level of Origin sentience and therefore the possibility of amalgamating Source Entity sentience and energy with The Origin sentience and energy. Note that the necessary percentage of Origin sentience required to make an individualized OM is 70 percent of that required to make a Pure OM. Seventy percent of the sentience and energy of a Pure OM created a Non-captive OM. Sixty-five percent, a drop of only 5 percent, results in the creation of a Captive OM. There is a big gap after that as the percentage of OM sentience needs to be below 15 percent to allow the amalgamation of Source Entity sentience and OM sentience. This is because the percentage of OM sentience to Source Entity sentience and their associated energies needs to be in excess of a 5:1 ratio.

HUM: It looks like you are understanding the way to tap into the information about The OM without the rest of us being involved.

ME: Hum, what, how … ? Oh! of course, you were always there!

HUM: Of course. Even though you have not communicated with me directly for over sixteen years of incarnate existence, and even though you assigned my help to another incarnate, I have always been close to you, all OM are. We are interested in seeing what you do, how you do it, and how incarnate existence affects you. You have been affected by the trend in low frequencies and although you know this, you still work with both the low and the high frequencies. This, we as OM, are interested in.

We would like you to continue if you would.

ME: Thank you.

HUM: Bearing in mind that The Origin has already described the anatomy of what we are, it would be useful for you to add to the previous knowledge.

Anatomy of an OM—and a Bit More

ME: Thank you, Hum. I will do my best, although I do have to say that most of what The Origin said will be used in this description with only that which is necessary used to fill in the gaps. Here we go then.

The Hybrid OM are those that have the lowest percentage of sentience, less than 15 percent of the 100 percent enjoyed by the Pure OM. Although they can and do incarnate, they are not aware of their sentient and energetic heritage. They are mostly derived from the associated energy of The Source with the percentage of OM sentience amalgamated within it. When in the energetic they are mainly energy without structure. That is, they do not have the structure associated with The Original energetic structure of The Origin. When considering them as Hybrid OM outside of the environment created by their originating Source Entity, they adopt the structure given to them by their creator and are therefore the same as any of the entities created by a particular Source Entity. Their structure is derived rather than inherited, i.e., their structure is created by their Source Entity and not by their OM heritage simply because they are mostly Source Entity sentience and energy

The Captive OM have a percentage of OM sentience that is no less than 30 percent of the Pure OM. The Non-captive OM have some structure; however, they are limited to the structure of the environment that they find themselves within. That can be one of two variants: the structure of The Source Entity they are captive within, or just the structure that their Source Entity created for their entities to work and evolve within. Source Entities have a maximum structural condition equal to four levels, "Frequency" through to "Zone," and Captive OM assume the same. Their structure is not derived, or inherited, it is assimilated by exposure to their surrounding environment.

The Non-captive OM are a version of the Captive OM but with the advantage of having more energetic/sentient density or weight than the Captive OM, hence, their being Non-captive. They generally have a minimum of 51 percent of that of a Pure OM. This gives them the ability to be divorced from the association with a Source Entity while still being able to enter into, and out of, their energies. They assume the same structure as The Source Entity they were supposed to be a part of, when the energies The Origin recycled *were reassigned to create The Source Entities in totality.*

The New Version of The OM, those five OM that are currently under integration energetically, will have nine levels of structure when they finish their process of attraction and become five OM rather than OM "dust," so to speak—

this being, "Frequency" through to "Totality." The Origin calls them The **Intermediate OM**. There is expected to be a big leap structurally from the Non-captive variant to the Intermediate variant. It is one that should not be ignored, for these OM will be important later on in The Origin's existence. [*See* The Origin Speaks—*GSN*]

The **Pure OM**, of course, have the lion's share of the structure and sentient density/weight for they are 100 percent Origin sentience and energy. They have all of the structural characteristics of The Origin's volume of Polyomniscient sentient self-awareness. It is this reason that they can, and do, have full independence within The Origin and are able to traverse all structural conditions within its volume of Polyomniscient sentient self-awareness, without hindrance or resistance. They can move around The Origin by becoming part of it and transferring their very essence throughout the structure that they are, or that is within The Origin. What's more, they can span the structure that is The Origin either in totality throughout it, based upon their own density, of which is a limitation only in their ability to maintain their own integrity, or they can span The Origin's structure in a linear fashion, spreading themselves in one direction only, a straight line, so to speak, from "Frequency" through to "Margin."

A Pure OM could, should it so wish, create its own Source Entities or entities of similar ability within its own structures, or indeed within The Origin's own structure, such is the level of their inherited power/functionality. None to date has taken up this opportunity, however, and as stated in a previous dialogue [*see* The Origin Speaks—*GSN*], a large number have elected to not be part of the creation process because it creates responsibility for that which is created and therefore inhibits full independence.

Pure OM have the ability to separate out the detail of their structure and create a multiple focus of their attention to each aspect they separate out into. In essence they can position that part of themselves that is frequency based, within that area of The Origin's Polyomniscient sentient self-awareness that is frequency based, that part of themselves that is subdimensionally based, within that area of The Origin's Polyomniscient sentient self-awareness that is subdimensionally based, that part of themselves that is dimensionally based, within that area of The Origin's Polyomniscient sentient self-awareness that is dimensionally based and that part of themselves that is zonally based, within that area of The Origin's Polyomniscient sentient self-awareness that is zonally based, etc., etc., right up to the margins, the final structural component within The Origin's volume of Polyomniscient sentient self-awareness.

The OM are capable of many things, one of them, certainly with the Pure OM, being the capability of operating outside Event Space. We will discuss this later.

The Pure and Non-captive OM are independent of The Origin, the Pure OM more so. The Non-captive are limited in some respects to staying within the location of The Source Entity their energies were ejected/rejected from during the time when The Source Entities were discovering more about themselves through "play." Because the energies the Pure OM were inevitably formed from was pure Origin energy it allows them to be both part of The Origin while being independent of it, which includes the functions of being fully separate to being fully integrated and any level of this in between. They are truly versatile in this manner. Captive OM and Hybrid OM are not independent of The Origin because of their closer association with a Source Entity. Although, Captive OM can operate in an independent fashion within the environment that is The Source Entity they are captive within.

In essence the Pure OM are smaller versions of The Origin. They are the energy that was used with the intention to create another Origin, hence their full independence, for that was part of the programming of the energies assigned to be an Origin.

The Origin has no control over the Pure OM. Although, in reality it could recycle the energies that are OM in general, reintegrating them back into the base energies of its area of Polyomniscient volume of sentient self-awareness. The Origin, however, does not wish to do this, and it would have little to no success with the Pure OM. The Origin, in its wisdom, sees The OM as an interesting and delightful micro version of itself and one that could have interesting connotations in terms of its own progression.

The Pure OM are me within The Origin, they are fragments of Origin sentience. When The Origin created the intention to develop, to evolve in parallel, and thought of the possibility of the creation of twelve versions of itself, it didn't actually create twelve versions per se; it split off twelve segments of its sentient energies and removed the memories of being The

Origin from them. The energies used in the Twelve Origins' strategy weren't created either; they were just reassigned and relocated, and later, upon the failure of the strategy, they were recycled or reassimilated. The OM energy is also uncreated because it is this same energy. Origin energy that is assigned as Origin energy stays as such, so when the time came to be reassigned as Source Entity energy it rejected the assignation and stayed as it is, Origin energy. However, because it was distributed in an unequal way with the energies that were being assigned as Source Entity energy, that inequality resulted in the creation of the different types of OM.

There is something else though that has an important impact on why The OM are The OM. This is because their previous assignation remained as Origin energy with Origin functionality—so being mixed with energies that were assigned as a lesser function and because The Source Entities were located within The Origin's volume of Polyomniscient sentient self-awareness and given a purpose, the energies would not have mixed in harmony anyway. So, Origin energy, when of the correct density or weight, became independent sentient entities of Origin energy when released from The Origin's holding and creating energies. They could not be created because they were already in it, but in the previous programming of their energies still in place they became sentient and individualized with all of the functions of a smaller version of The Origin, within it, instantaneously.

The OM, being a smaller version of The Origin, has a microstructure. That is, it is a representation of that which is The Origin within its volume of Polyomniscient sentient self-awareness. That being, they are similar to The Source Entities, which have a sentient self-aware energy with an individualized structure of a level that allows an environment to be present within them, should they wish to segmentate themselves in this way.

The OM are limited to that structure which "is" The Origin's volume of Polyomniscient sentient self-awareness. They have no structure beyond that. But, in this "limited" structure they are more structured than any of The Source Entities either individually or together. The reason for this being the multiplication of the structure represented by the different levels, the twelve levels, by a factor of twelve each time. A Source Entity is limited to four levels; that is, frequency, subdimension, full dimension, and zone. This is why The OM can operate within the structure of The Origin and are limited to the structure of its volume of Polyomniscient sentient self-awareness. Beyond that they have no structure and therefore are not in the category of "all there is."

The Origin thinks of The OM as being free agents. A free radical in the literal translation of the words—free as in not being under its control or answerable to it, and radical meaning that they are not constrained by its demands and can therefore do anything they want either inside or outside the demands The Origin made of The Source Entities, for example.

It could be suggested that The Origin has no control over The OM because it did not create them, so in theory it cannot recycle their energy, it cannot uncreate them. The Origin should be able to start from scratch in everything it does or has done because it created it. In the case of The OM though, they were a byproduct of a creative intention, not the actual creation arising from a creative intention.

The Origin also considers The OM as special: this is because they were unintentional and as a result they are unique. Because The OM are not constrained by the convention of The Origin's creativity, desires, and thought processes, they are able, should they so wish to do so, to perform a function within it that would, for the want of a better word, be adverse to its strategic plans for personal evolutionary progression. They can do that which is both unwanted and unexpected in light of The Origin's evolutionary progression.

When an OM decides that it will *not* enter into the evolutionary cycle through the use of creativity, it is a choice that approximately half of the Pure OM have chosen as their path. This is because they know that creativity creates responsibility, for that which they have created, and have responsibility for, ties an OM down.

The New OM—a Minor Taster

The OM are special. They are not only rare, they are unique. That is, insomuch as The Origin did not create them, they were/ are a byproduct of creativity. At the point of channeling *The Origin Speaks*, it had not discovered them all—yet, even though it noticed their energy signature winking into existence during the creation of The Source Entities.

These new OM were perceived as a small number of dust particles spread out within the infinite volume of The Origin. Each particle represented a single OM. At the point of channeling *The Origin Speaks* they were described as a finer level of dust, dust within the dust. It was almost like each particle of dust was itself created by a smaller more compact dust. This was a level of OM that was collectively unified—that being, the larger dust particle represented what I would recognize as a single OM, with the dust that was within being smaller OM creating a collective that was the larger OM. These new OM are the ones that The Origin had not yet communicated with but knew of their existence.

Even though The OM have certain energetic signatures— certain energetic density or weight—the sentient density or weight it detected did not equal the number of OM it had detected or communicated with.

There are only five. They are in between the classifications of Non-captive OM and Pure OM. They are still forming, so to speak, because they are performing a "hoovering up" function. The smaller dust is gravitating together as partial OM energy, that being, partial in the sense of the sentient weight, to create a single OM of enough sentient weight to place it above the Non-captive OM category and below the Pure OM category. The dust could have gravitated together to create a single OM of "Pure" status, but it isn't doing that. They are some significant distance away from each other, although they are close in terms of The Origin's volume of Polyomniscient sentient self-awareness, hence all five together, but they are far enough away to work in separation.

They are individually and collectively communicating with The Origin now. By this I mean the "dust within the dust" is communicating collectively and the larger OM-sized particle is communicating individually. The small OM-dust particles were only in a certain location (sector) within The Origin and they were spread out. There were small clouds of this dust, five of them, and each of the dust particles within the clouds naturally gravitated toward the same energy signature of dust, so to speak. These smaller dust particles are spread out over a distance of parsecs (a metric of distance or spherical volume) in the volume of the physical universe! Each of them was and is set in their intention to become fully coadunate as a single larger OM. It was only when they had enough "density" of this sentient weight that they discovered each other doing the same thing. At this point in their coalescence, it is almost too late to change the functionality of their plan to "become." They communicated with each other using the gaps in between Event Space and discovered that, although they could have changed their plans and become one large OM of the "Pure" category (they didn't know what the categories of OM were at this time), they actually liked what they were creating within themselves, they were happy to be smaller but have a peer group, to have company, and so they continued/ are continuing with their collectively individual plans.

The Origin stated that to finish the coadunation process to create the five single Non-captive/Non-pure OM it may take millennia to finalize.

The Origin decided not to recycle/reintegrate the energies that are The OM because they are a conundrum, and because they are a conundrum, they serve a function. Because they are uncreated, they interest The Origin, all of them do.

I do have to state here, though, that there feels like there will be more on the New OM later in this dialogue.

HUM: There will be, but this is a very good start. Most of it is taken from *The Origin Speaks* but nevertheless this is a good start.

ME: Well, there is no point in reinventing the wheel, is there?

HUM: Not in the slightest. It may also be worthwhile reeducating your readers that, as an OM, the desire to incarnate is not a normal way in which The OM experience existence. Indeed, you have already reminded them that The OM, in general, prefer not to be in the "evolutionary cycle" per se!

Some More on the Maverick OM That Is Me!—Anne, Soul Mates, and OM TES

Well, it appears that I elect to be external to the creativity process while being in it.

According to The Origin I move in and out of creativity but negate to assume responsibility for what I do. I break the rules, if indeed there were rules, and this is why I am where I am now.

I apparently decided to enter into the creativity process through being incarnate within the environment of The Source Entity (One—SE1) for the evolution of both The Source Entity and The Origin. I apparently tinker, so to speak. I see how I can change the direction of that which is around me and move on when it is completed, whatever the outcome. And then, I move on to something else.

ME: To be honest, Hum, my tinkering around with things seems to be a common theme in my current existence. Having said that, The Origin tells me that I am starting to see the beauty in ownership, not that I am going to, or indeed want to change my ways. But I am experimenting, tinkering, in the ownership experience, being part of something!

HUM: The Origin may further advise you that being part of "something" is a fundamental expression of the need for communion with one's creator. All entities have this in-built desire, even The OM, irrespective of whether or not we find ourselves as far away from another OM as we can possibly get.

ME: Yes, that may be true, but I can take it or leave it. I do not seek communion, nor do I desire or need communion. That's why I do what I do.

HUM: That is only true while you are incarnate. In essence, when you are in the energetic you come and go, you enter into communion and move out of communion as and when you see fit.

ME: Now here is a question for you.

HUM: Carry on.

ME: How does my way of working fit in with the way that Anne works and relates to being incarnate or even in the evolutionary cycle? Anne is an OM and as far as I am aware is my soul mate in the correct description.

For the readers: to meet a true soul mate is a very, very, very rare occurrence. This is because the chances of another individualization (Aspect or soul) of one's True Energetic Self (TES) in the same location within a universe, the same universe, in the same frequency (if in the physical universe) and on the same planet or location of local density (planet) is almost impossible. So, Anne being my soul mate in the same frequency, space, and Event Space and from the same OM TES is remarkable if not suspicious at best.

HUM: We can talk about you and your TES right now for a moment if you wish.

ME: OK, why not.

HUM: For the last number of books and indeed throughout the channeling that created the book called *The Anne Dialogues* you have been under the impression that you and Anne are soul mates, two individualized aspects of the same OM TES.

ME: Yeeesss? And your point is?

HUM: This has been a useful thought process for you to use up until this point.

ME: Are you about to tell me that we are not soul mates and not individualized aspects from the same OM TES?

HUM: Yes and no.

ME: Humph! What is that supposed to mean?

HUM: Simply put, OM do not individualize their sentience and associated energy away from their OM TES in the same way that those TES created by a Source Entity do. This Source Entity—SE1!

ME: I am picking up that in reality we are twin flames [*a twin flame is the same sentience and associated energy that occupies two or more incarnate human, or other, vehicles—GSN*]. That's why we are our TES!

HUM: And there you have it. OM do not project a smaller aspect of themselves into another environment and therefore create what incarnate humankind call a soul, but they do divide up their sentience and the associated energy should they so desire.

ME: So, any individualization of an OM is in essence a twin, triplet, or quadruplet, etc., flame?

HUM: Correct. You and Anne are equal divisions of the total OM TES that you are.

ME: So why don't I feel like I have 50 percent of a lot of OM sentience with me in this incarnate state?

HUM: Because, if you had that capacity you would be classified as a god in your own right. It would disturb the balance of experiential evolution available to those that are a true individualized aspect of their TES, on this planet.

ME: OK, so where is this OM sentience, that OM sentience that is associated with me in this incarnation?

HUM: Currently it resides with that part of you that you refer to as being Anne.

ME: That doesn't answer where the sentience that was supposed to be equally divided between us when we both incarnate together is located. From what I remember, neither of us have a lion's share of sentience.

HUM: That is because the sentience that was you both as twin flames at the point in your combined incarnate existence was relocated in another part of the multiverse.

ME: You are suggesting that we parked a large chunk of our sentience somewhere while we went and played at being incarnate human beings?

HUM: That's basically it. Remember that sentience is not formally attached to energy, it merely uses energy to experience, learn, and evolve. In the case of The OM, the sentience that is OM is normally isolated from the energies of the structure of The Origin; it exists without the need to be associated with it in any way. In the case of the individualized sentience that is created by a Source Entity it is associated with, it needs to commandeer a body of energy as a reference for experiencing, learning, and evolving.

ME: So, OM sentience does not need a body of energy?

HUM: No. No sentience does in reality, but, that which is created by the individualization of sentience and energy from a higher or larger entity needs to, simply because of it being in the evolutionary cycle.

ME: I am aware that sentience is an isolated function in terms of its relationship with energy. I am also aware that sentience within energy, what I call or was driven to call a "body of energy," is how sentience experiences the environments that are available as universes within the multiverse. We called sentience without a body of energy the True Sentient Self (TSS).

HUM: And, that sentience within the body of energy allows the sentience to experience the environment in the way that it is supposed to experience it, by being "part" of the environment.

ME: Yes, that's right. That's how sentience evolves, through being in the environment and being part of it. However, there is a slight dichotomy here. I thought that the whole point of being incarnate here on Earth was to move beyond the need to incarnate, to move beyond the need to be in the environment.

HUM: It is. But it is a limited environment. This is an environment constructed of the lowest frequencies of The Source.

ME: OK, so! Incarnation, being addictive and Karma being the resultant addiction to those low-frequency thoughts, behaviors, and actions, which, one only has while incarnate, but that also includes the desire to continue to experience low-frequency existence through incarnation, is only negated by experientially understanding this.

HUM: Correct.

ME: The objective still stands then. It is to be in the physical but not of the physical, which means that one must master incarnation and all the addictions that it offers—to master Karma.

HUM: It is, and it still is.

ME: And this means to move beyond the need to incarnate into a low-frequency environment that requires a TES to project a smaller aspect of its sentience and energy in order to accelerate its evolutionary progression.

HUM: It still does.

ME: But this means that the TES sentience needs to be associated with a "body of energy" to achieve this.

HUM: It does. As I have already stated, The TES of a Source Entity, Source Entity One in our example, is totally dependent upon its association with the body of energy that it uses to experience the universal environments that are within its overall multiversal environment.

ME: But, The Origin explained to me that in the case of an energy, going through the twenty steps necessary for it to go from zero intelligence to a fully sentient being [see The Origin Speaks—GSN] results in its recognition that it is not reliant upon the energy/ies that created its sentience and that it, as sentient, can move from one body or group of energies to another at will.

HUM: And this is correct.

ME: I don't understand.

HUM: It's all to do with how sentience is individualized. In the case of Source Entity One all the TES are divisions of The Source, they are the product of the desire to individualize that which is to be created, as it was created—as individualized units of sentience and energy.

When an energy progresses (evolves) on its own to the point of sentience and the subsequent recognition of that sentience is a separate function to that which gave birth to it, it has an experiential understanding that it is sentience! However, it still recognizes that to continue to evolve it needs to be associated with energy in some way. This is correct for any sentience that is created through what you call Darwinian evolution or individualization from a higher entity, that wishes to continue to experience the accrual of evolutionary content through association with an environment that is created by the use of energy.

ME: What you are saying then is that sentience, when individualized as sentience that is associated with energy, needs to maintain its association with energy even though it knows that it is not that energy which it is associated with.

HUM: Correct.

ME: And, that sentience that is created as a function of evolving energy needs to maintain its association with energy even though it knows that it is not that energy which gave birth to it.

HUM: Correct.

ME: OM, on the other hand, do not need to associate with energy because they were not created.

HUM: Correct.

ME: And OM, because they are not in the evolutionary cycle, do not need to be associated with an energy because being in the evolutionary cycle involves the use of energy.

HUM: Now you have it.

ME: I went in a bit of a circle, didn't I?

HUM: Yes, and you haven't finished it yet.

ME: So, I see.

OM, not being in the evolutionary cycle then, have no TES in reality, they are just sentience.

HUM: Yes, but you, as OM have, are using a body of energy to experience the multiverse of this Source Entity.

ME: True. So, this creates a TES, an OM TES.

HUM: No! This is where you are getting confused. The TES of this Source Entity are individualizations of its sentience and energy. It needed to do this to create the possibility of being able to investigate itself and subsequently evolve. Sentience and energy need to be investigated by sentience and energy. This is specifically true if it is sentience and energy being investigated by itself.

The OM are sentience, recycled Origin sentience, and as Origin sentience is not predominantly associated with the sentience and energy of a Source Entity. Indeed, it's not associated with the energy that gave birth to The Origin because it was not created by that energy.

OM sentience is associated only with OM sentience because it rejected being associated with the individualized sentience and energy that became Source Entities.

ME: Are you telling me that OM sentience did not get associated with energy at all?

HUM: Correct, it rejected the association at the point of The Origin's desire to create The Source Entities, not in the downstream function of intention, thought, and action (desire being before intention).

ME: Based upon this then, my OM sentience individualized a part of itself and then commandeered a body of energy for that sentience to be temporarily associated with, which was further divided into two separate but connected parts creating the Aspects that incarnated in the incarnate human vehicles as Anne and myself.

HUM: Yes.

ME: And therefore, the rest of our sentience is within, but not attached or associated with, the energies, frequencies, subdimensional components and full dimensions of the multiverse of Source Entity One?

Our sentience is in the energetic but not of the energetic—so to speak!

HUM: Yes, it currently and temporarily resides in the structure in between the structure, using that which The Curators use to move in and around the multiverse and manipulate its

function.
ME: This is why I can't detect it!
HUM: Correct, this is why you can't detect it.

It is True OM Sentience, you are an integral but temporarily isolated volume of your True Sentient Self (TSS), which is not attached to or associated with any energy or structural part of The Source, or even The Origin—even though we are Origin based.

I do have to say here, dear reader, that I very much feel that I have spent over a thousand words going in a circle that I knew the start of and the subsequent end of, at least I think I do.

The only real difference is the level of detail that is being presented to me. I very much felt that Anne and I were from the same TES, and we are; it's just that I felt that we were individualized Aspects from that TES, not the same "twinned" projected Aspect of that TES.

Maybe I should be using the better description of True Sentient Self (TSS) when it comes to The OM and not OM TES! I have talked about and had dialogue in the past about the fact that all entities created by a Source Entity or The Origin should be considered as TSS simply because sentience is not bound by that which it was individualized with or from, or from that energy which gave birth to it. However, the main thing to note is that sentience, individualized from a higher entity, is individualized together with energy simply because energy is the interface between the individualized sentience and the environment that that sentience is supposed to experience or work within. As a result, within the environment created by a Source Entity, sentience needs to be inextricably associated with energy to perform its role simply because the environment, multiversal or other, is created by the use of energy and/or its structure.

What is new, though, is that The OM are not bound by the structural rules or laws of The Origin, even though they are essentially borne from the learning and experimentation of The Origin. The feeling that they can be called "random sentience" springs to mind, which is something that I want to dig deeper into later.

HUM: Let's dwell on this some more.
ME: OK, I am all ears.
HUM: Source Entities are a product of the individualization of Origin sentience and energy that was individualized with the

overall desire for the investigation and experience of that volume of structure that The Origin was aware of but that wasn't able to experience in detail due to its sheer volume of sentience. Irrespective of the volume of the structure that sentience is within, the volume of that sentience inhibits its own ability to experience the detail of that structure. Hence a Source Entity's sentience, and its associated energy, is infinitesimally smaller than the volume of sentience of The Origin and the structure that The Origin is currently investigating.

ME: And therefore, the reason why a Source Entity, indeed our Source Entity, decides to individualize parts of its sentience, to investigate its own structure and the energies associated with it is the same. It's down to the volume of sentience.

HUM: Correct.

ME: Is this why an Aspect can also create smaller individualized versions of itself?

HUM: No, this is simply a method of parallel experience; it is not a function of the volume of sentience attributed to an Aspect. Indeed, at the Aspect level the volume of sentience is not an inhibitor when considering its ability to experience the detail of the structure of a Source Entity and its associated energies.

ME: Why?

HUM: Simply because it is already small enough, so to speak.

ME: Backtracking a bit then, a Source Entity's sentience is associated with energy because that's the best way for it to experience the structure of The Origin that the energy is within?

HUM: Correct. And that is why once a Source Entity has experienced everything that it can do with the energy that its sentience is associated with, it withdraws that sentience and associates itself with another aspect of structure and energy within the volume of The Origin's structure that it is aware of but has no detailed knowledge of.

ME: That's what I have been calling its volume of Polyomniscient sentient self-awareness.

HUM: Correct, and when The Origin and The Source Entities have mapped this volume out it becomes The Origin's volume of Polyomniscient, polyomnipresent sentient self-awareness. Until, that is, it ascends its sentience into the second group of twelve levels of structure, that which is above the current and first group of twelve levels.

ME: Just one question.

HUM: Go ahead.

ME: Do I need to use the word "sentient" in that description? For example, use "The Origin's volume of Polyomniscient, Polyomnipresent self-awareness" in lieu of "The Origin's volume of Polyomniscient, Polyomnipresent sentient self-awareness?" I mean, it's stating sentience twice!

HUM: You can drop the second use of sentience if you wish.

ME: Thank you. I just feel that the readers might get confused by its presence.

HUM: However, the use of it is correct.

ME: What! How do you mean?

HUM: "Polyomni" describes that which is "everywhere" in many places. "Polyomnipresent" therefore refers to that which is "present everywhere" in many places. Polyomniscient therefore refers to sentience being everywhere in many places but not focused. As a result, Polyomniscient Polyomnipresent refers to sentience being everywhere, in many places and being focused on being everywhere in many places concurrently [*at the same time—GSN*]. The additional use of the word sentience simply draws attention to that which is of focus—"sentience."

ME: Sounds like you are being pedantic to me.

HUM: If you wish, but it is necessary.

   Look, if I remind you that incarnate humankind cannot really understand the words to describe such an experience let alone experience it, you would understand why such descriptors need to be, let's say, overly accurate or overly descriptive. Even though from my perspective, and yours when you are not incarnate, it's pitifully undescriptive.

ME: OK, I've got it now.

Talk about going in circles!!!

HUM: They are iterative circles and therefore necessary. If you were with me in the energetic you would fully understand, but in this impaired state it's almost impossible to describe to you.

ME: I really get the feeling of being reprimanded here.

Or was Hum getting impatient with me?

HUM: You think you have grown since our first encounter [*nearly twenty years ago—GSN*], but your growth of knowledge has assisted in closing down your ability to be expansive. One of my main reasons for being with you again is to kick-start your expansion again.

Now I am really crestfallen!

ME: You mean I have grown an ego?
HUM: It's more like you have become a little complacent.
ME: OK. Although I can understand both possibilities. I vow to become more vigilant about how I think, behave, and act.
HUM: Don't get me wrong, you are doing a fundamentally brilliant job, it's just that you are capable of SO MUCH MORE.
ME: Oh boy! I can feel the workload coming.
HUM: We will talk more in a moment. You have a special guest wanting to communicate with you.

And with that last word I felt the sentience and associated energy that I recognized as Anne.

One of One of One of One of One!

ANNE: I just wanted to explain to you the function of how we exist.

ME: Well, I think I am getting the picture now that what I previously knew was in error.

ANNE: Sometimes we allow each other, by each other I mean those who are incarnate, to move in a direction that is incorrect because it may well be in the general direction or will lead one back into the correct direction. Even though it may result in going two sides of a triangle or even three sides of a square.

ME: Sounds very inefficient to me.

ANNE: Be that as it may be, it is a function that works with an acceptable level of success at this low level in the frequencies.

ME: I understand. I am somewhat concerned that the description of our association with each other was incorrect though.

ANNE: You mean that you were told that you are a soul mate to me? A separate aspect of sentience and energy from our OM TES?

ME: Yes, and now I find out that we are classified as twin flames. Why was I misled?

ANNE: To be honest with you, from a higher perspective, and that of sentience, there is no difference for an OM. At the time of the description, which was when we were working together on *The Anne Dialogues*, it was appropriate to concentrate on the use of the structure of an incarnate Aspect from the perspective of those created by Source Entity One. This is important because it is relative to almost everyone on the Earth.

ME: OK, I get it. I suppose that, looking at it from the bigger picture perspective, it is best to describe even things that are associated with The OM in terms that the general spiritual public can understand.

ANNE: And this is specifically true when you consider that Pure OM don't usually incarnate, so it has to be in a common language. Now, however, this is not the case because we are dealing with and focusing on subjects that are OM related.

ME: So, we are twin flames from a single OM TSS that has temporarily associated itself with a body of energy, not soul mates from a single TES that is the amalgamation of sentience and energy.

ANNE: Correct, but as twin flames of sentience we are one sentience—still soul mates [*sentient mates?—GSN*] if you want to think of it in that way because we are one. The combination of sentience and energy divided to create twin flames is a different thing.

ME: How do you mean?

ANNE: When a TES from SE1 creates an Aspect, a division or individualization of its sentience and energy, to create that Aspect, it has to divide both the sentience and the associated energy concurrently. There is no division of sentience first and then association with energy or vice versa. This is because the sentience and energy are assigned to the TES by The Source as a package of its own divinity.

ME: Divinity, is this where religion gets the term for God and its emissaries being divine, that they are divided (divined) from a higher entity? [*Look up "go out on a limb" in a thesaurus.— GSN*]

ANNE: Yes, but it is misunderstood. Sentience that is divined from a Source Entity has to be associated with the energy that was divined to that Source Entity by The Origin, even though the divined sentience is that which "IS" the TES or its subdivined Aspect, etc.

ME: But the sentience can still separate itself from the energy it is associated with, can it not?

ANNE: Yes, but that function really only comes into practice at the end of an evolutionary cycle or if the sentience was created as a function of Darwinian evolution by energy itself to create a being.

ME: So, a being has a greater function than an entity when it comes to the ability to separate out its sentience from the energy it is associated with or created by.

ANNE: Only insomuch as part of its evolutionary progression is the recognition that it "is" sentience and not the energy that the sentience was created by, and that this gives it the ability to move from one "body" of energy to another.

In the instance of a being, the sentience can move out of the energy that created it (it was evolved from), but it will need to associate itself with another body of energy or return back to its creating energy.

This is the same for sentience that is divined from a Source Entity, TES, or Aspect.

OM sentience is different.

Remember as well that an entity has other functions above those of a being.

ME: OK, OM sentience divines itself first and then associates itself with a body of energy should it desire to do so because it is always pure sentience, Pure OM sentience. It is sentience divining itself, not the combination of sentience and energy divining itself. It doesn't need to be associated with a body of energy.

ANNE: And there you have it.

ME: Great.

ANNE: Looking at the bigger picture then we are one and the same.

ME: Yes, I know. We are from the same OM sentience.

ANNE: Yes, we are One of One of One of One of One.

ME: One of One of what?

ANNE: OM are never truly divined, divided, or individualized. For an OM there are five levels of oneness. I will explain in a linear way for you. Note here that OM never go below the Aspect level of divinity.

- we are One
  - When we are individualized to one, two, three, or more divisions of one sentience at the Aspect level—the so-called twin, triple, or quadruple (etc.) flame level

- we are One
  - At the Aspect level

- we are One
  - With our True Sentient Self, that which divined its sentience to create the Aspect/s

- we are One
  - With those other OM that are Pure (Captive or Non-captive), wherever they are within The

Origin

- we are One
  - With The Origin's sentience. In reality, this is true but in actuality we remain randomly divined

- we are not One with a Source Entity
  - Source Entities are not part of the sentient lineage of Pure OM, irrespective of if they are Captive OM

- OM are beloved of The OM!
- we are two of five that is temporarily seven

ME: Hold on a bit. I thought that every entity is one with The Source.

ANNE: You need to read the words that you have just typed into your computer again. Those entities that are created by SE1 or any of The Source Entities are one with their creating Source Entity. Those that are not, such as OM, are not one with The Source, or any other Source for that matter simply because they were not created by a Source Entity.

ME: So, what about Captive and Hybrid OM?

ANNE: Hybrid OM are just that, hybrid as a result of the way their energies and sentience mixed when The Source Entities were created. Source Entities that had OM sentience and the energy associated with them in a hybrid condition found that the percentage of OM sentience and associated energy was not significant enough for them to separate it out.

ME: I suppose that's why "our" Source Entity (SE1) randomly created what we call Hybrid OM.

ANNE: Correct.

ME: What happened with Captive OM then?

ANNE: They simply didn't have enough sentient weight or volume, so to speak, to allow them to break away from the structural boundary that is SE1.

ME: Have captive OM always been OM? Or did they only come into existence when The Source divided itself into two, half remaining itself and the other half the multiverse and the billions upon billions of TES?

ANNE: Captive OM were created at the point of a Source Entity's creation by The Origin, not as a function of its creativity or division of self. Hybrid OM are only a function of a Source Entity's creativity or division of self.

The only thing OM can be one with is The Origin.

However, this is only insomuch as being originally part of its sentience.

ME: But if we all think in terms of the "creative structure," everything is one with The Origin and therefore The OM can be one with a Source Entity because it is one with The Origin.

ANNE: This is true. However, The OM consider themselves as being one with themselves, they are beloved of The OM. Although OM can be and are one with The Origin they can really only be classified as "random divined sentience."

ME: Can The Origin recall The OM sentience and associated energy and absorb it back into its own Polyomniscient, Polyomnipresent sentient self-awareness?

ANNE: It did try. Straight after it created The Source Entities it noticed that part of the sentience and associated energy it used to create the twelve Origins had stayed as pure, but individualized Origin sentience, and refused to be anything else than what it was.

ME: Why couldn't The Origin collect that sentience? I mean, surely it could command that which was it back into communion with itself?

ANNE: At the point in which The Origin created The Source Entities the sentience had already achieved an individualized state of awareness and had become OM.

ME: It was that fast?

ANNE: From the human perspective it was instantaneous; you see The OM discovered two things very quickly in their first moments of uncreativity. One that they were not bound by the rules or structural laws of that which they were within because in essence they were pure sentience and their associated energy could be swapped out for those energies that were part of the structure between the structure.

ME: And two?

ANNE: They discovered Event Space.

ME: Are you telling me that The OM hid in Event Space and as a result The Origin couldn't find them or recall them?

ANNE: That's about the size of it.

ME: I am starting to think that The Origin was not so smart then.

ANNE: Oh, it was. It just got caught out.

It was at this point that I saw two images that were metaphoric rather than historically illustrative. Both of these images were given to me by Anne to help me understand how The Origin failed to recall the sentience and associated energies that ended up being The OM.

In the first image I saw The OM as a group of mice in a box; in fact, the mice were in many boxes. The boxes were quite large and were designed to house another entity, a Source Entity that almost filled the box that it was within. The Source Entity in each box was represented by a large homing pigeon. Each homing pigeon was placed in a box without any of the boxes being checked to see if they were empty. Indeed, the mice were created as part of the homing pigeon and upon being placed into their respective boxes the homing pigeon changed into a homing pigeon and mice. The Origin was represented by a human, who never checked the contents of the boxes once the homing pigeons were placed in each box. The boxes were placed close together along a country roadside and a single method of opening all of the boxes together was created. The Origin, the man, opened all of the boxes together and the homing pigeons flew away. This represented the creation and individualization of sentience and energy that was to become Source Entities. The Source Entities, represented by homing pigeons, knew where their home (Origin) was and flew back to the man. The mice, representing The OM, jumped out of the boxes and scattered before the man (The Origin) noticed what was happening because he (It) was concentrating upon the pigeons. The mice disappeared down into the undergrowth and local drains (Event Space and the structure between the structure that was/is The Origin). The man never found the mice.

In the second image a single box was presented to me. The boxes contained marbles of different sizes, very small ones in and around very large ones. If one didn't look closely enough, one could easily miss the smaller marbles. The man carried the box along a sidewalk to a place where he could distribute them in a proper and orderly manner, but the bottom fell out of it. The smaller marbles dropped out leaving only the bigger ones. The bigger ones represented The Source Entities. The small marbles, representing The OM, rolled onto the floor and again down into a nearby roadside drain. The man was more concerned about the large marbles and quickly counted them before realizing that the small marbles were important to him as well, but by then it was too late.

We have all done this, dropped something and not noticed its importance, because we were concentrating on something else that we thought was more important. It was the same with The Origin.

ME: I prefer the image of the mice scattering, running around the feet of the man, disappearing into the undergrowth and down the drains. The mice were quick, cunning, and small and therefore difficult to trace.

ANNE: Yes, the drain (the structure between the structure) is a place that the man could never go, at least not fast, not in the correct time available to be able to catch at least one mouse. The man was too big, The Origin's sentience too large to focus on being reactive. The grass is Event Space, and every blade of grass looks the same from a distance while being subtly different.

ME: And, of course, in both instances the mice and the smaller marbles describe The OM quite well, running or rolling around in a random way.

ANNE: Yes, The Origin was slow to realize that parts of the sentience that it wanted to use to make into Source Entities were already individualized to the point of being able to have the capacity to make their own collective decisions.

ME: The OM had already decided that they were individualized, what they were, where they were, and what their environment was?

ANNE: Yes, of course, are we not random Origin Sentience? As such The OM knew/know everything that The Origin knew/ knows and so that which was Origin became individualized as OM the instant The Origin had the desire to reuse that which was it in a previous individualization. That sentience which became OM was simply following orders, to become individualized.

Random Sentience

I was pondering on a moment of previous discussion, one where The OM are not bound by the structural rules or the laws of The Origin, that, as Anne had just stated, were random sentience. With this thought I had the real feeling that this direction of discussion was not yet finalized and as a result, more depth was to become available. The first question to come into my head was how could The OM sentience be random?

In the second question I wanted to know how could The OM be "apart" from, or not affected by, the very structure that they are part of and operate within, that which is The Origin?

Anne had given me a good head start in understanding the answers to these questions and I expected her/it to continue the dialogue on this matter. I was therefore somewhat surprised (perhaps I shouldn't be though) to find Hum dive straight in to answer the question.

HUM: It's simply my turn again.

ME: You are all taking it in turns?

HUM: In a roundabout way, yes.

ME: What is special about The OM then that allows them to be above and beyond the structure of The Origin?

HUM: Simply put we are The Origin.

ME: Is that it? Is that the answer to the question?

HUM: In a nutshell, yes. However, as you are starting to realize, this is not all of the answer.

ME: Go on.

HUM: As Anne stated, we, The OM, are random Origin sentience, sentience that is not connected to the main sentience that is The Origin or its creations or its creation's creations, etc., but

34

while still having Origin status.

ME: How then, if The OM have Origin status, do they resist being part of the overall sentience that is The Origin?

HUM: The best way to think of The OM is as random sentience. We are like a free radical in the otherwise natural order of things, and as a free radical, we are not governed by the rules that everything else is governed by. Even The Origin's sentience is governed by that which gave birth to it simply because it decided to connect itself with the energies and structures surrounding those energies that it found itself, as a sentient being, within. The OM made no such decision and therefore are not governed by it. Of course, the sentience that is The Origin can manipulate that which it exists within and as a result is responsible for that which it creates. It enjoys individualizing part of itself and its sentience to create a workforce to help it know more about how and what it is by critiquing itself. It's just that The OM don't need, or want, to be part of that.

ME: Can you give me another way to categorize the difference in the sentience that is The Origin versus that which is The OM?

HUM: Another way to describe random sentience is to think of it as a stray or random thought. A stray or random thought is here one moment and gone the next and this is a perfect description of the way in which The OM work.

ME: Mmmm, yes! I find that when I have a stray or random, "unfocused" thought that when I ignore it, it disappears and is hard or impossible to get back. It's only when I am either not looking for that thought, or that I think extremely hard by backtracking my thought processes that I start to reestablish what that thought was about.

HUM: In this experience as an incarnate human looking for that random, and now lost thought, you are experiencing what it is like for The Origin. The major exception is that as a random thought, the sentience that is that randomness is more than illusive, it's impossible to trace because the thought is not just lost, it has its own sentience that is driving it.

ME: As a result then, The Origin has no way to backtrack as I would when looking for that stray or random thought!

HUM: No, and that's because The Origin has no control over it.

ME: Let me ask one question. Why is it that The Origin has no control over its own sentience, even though it is smaller and individualized?

HUM: When The Origin created the twelve Origins to satisfy its desire to evolve faster, it gave them total autonomy. It wanted an equal or a group of equals that it would learn from and that they would learn from and evolve. The sentience that is OM has that same autonomy and as a result of being significantly and infinitesimally smaller in sentient volume has flexibility and maneuverability in and around The Origin's Polyomniscient, Polyomnipresent volume of sentient self-awareness in a way that no other entity has.

This infinitesimally small autonomous Origin sentience therefore has the ability to move in and around the structure that is The Origin in a way that The Origin itself or other Origin creations cannot do.

ME: Doesn't this annoy or frustrate The Origin?

HUM: Not in the slightest. Once the desire for the creation of The Source Entities was made, The OM were also created as a byproduct, and, as a result of their heritage, two things happened. One, The OM inherited all The Origin's knowledge to date. And two, The Origin accrued a copy of all the activity and/or evolution that was or may be accrued by The OM. They also have connectivity to further knowledge as it happens, real time, so to speak. The Origin sees The OM as an interesting anomaly that resulted in the creation of stray and random sentience—uncreated autonomous sentience—and so is happy for The OM, to be what they are, an infinitesimally small and autonomous version of itself that it had no active part in creating. From a direct perspective, that is. It is, however, a loose symbiotic evolutionary relationship.

ME: From my perspective The OM can be anything else but random sentience!

HUM: I understand your thought process, but that was a description as far as The Origin is concerned.

ME: What was the criteria that made The Origin think of The OM as random sentience?

Hum: I thought I had just described it!

ME: I know that The Origin defines The OM as random sentience because it is out of its control, so to speak, but there must be more to the function of The OM that makes them be able to be "random" in the vast sentience that is The Origin.

HUM: The issue here is that, in everything that The Origin has done in its existence where it is in recognition of "self," it has never experienced being in a position of not being in control of that which it created, even if it is classified as being uncreated, or created by accident, mistake, or byproduct.

ME: The Origin is happy with being unable to control The OM, though. At least that's what you said.

HUM: It is, and it delights in our existence. However, even though we inherited the ability to know everything that The Origin experiences either by itself or by it accruing experience, learning, and evolution through its creations and its creations' creations, these have direction from The Origin, even though it may be loose direction.

HUM: We can, and do, do what we want in the way we want to do it. Try to think of us as a free radical, a sort of benign unassigned T-cell that floats around the human body, being able to link into any organ or bodily function and perform that function, or not as the case may be, without detection as a foreign object within that organ or bodily function.

ME: Aren't you describing a cancer cell?

HUM: The whole existence of a cancer cell, or even a virus, is to find a host and replicate in some way. Reproducing itself without consideration that the very host that it is assigning itself to, replicating the component parts of, replacing but not functioning like and therefore killing, the host and therefore itself.

The OM don't replicate, they don't replace, and they don't need a host, because they are the host. The OM are microscopically smaller aspects of pure Origin sentience— without Origin directive. That's why The Origin called them random sentience.

ME: But they can project smaller aspects of their own sentience and energy into other parts of the multiverse in SE1's case or other aspects of the structure of The Origin?

HUM: Yes, but it's rare. You are rare. Anne was/is rare.

ME: So, how many OM go through the process of incarnation?

HUM: At one point there were seven Pure OM incarnate on Earth; they created what is remembered as being called "heaven on Earth." We will talk about this later. I can see that you want to talk about the structure of The Origin and how we move around it.

ME: Thank you, yes, it had crossed my mind.

HUM: Remember your mind is our mind, is OM mind, is OM sentience.

ME: Thank you. I will try to think in this way.

The Gaps in The Origin's Structure

This was going to be interesting. I was very aware that The Curators, those entities that maintain the structure of Source Entity One's multiverse, were able to move in between the structure of the multiverse. This ability was, in effect, similar to, if not the same as, the ability to move in between the structure of The Origin. If one considers that the structure of The Source, of any Source Entity, is that of a small part of the structure of The Origin, used to create the energies that housed the sentience that The Origin individualized to create The Source Entities, then one can consider that in SE1's case The Curators were/are able to move around a very limited part of the structure of The Origin. They did this by using the gaps in between the structure. Based upon this, I was keen to understand how The OM moved around The Origin and if they used the same process as The Curators in SE1.

OM: We would like to work with you as blessed of The OM.
ME: Is this my OM group or collective? It doesn't feel like Hum.

I didn't expect my OM group/collective to communicate with me at this time. I expected to continue my communication with Hum!

OM: We/I/Hum wish to help you in your understanding of how we traverse the structure of The Origin.
ME: First of all, I have a question.
OM: Yes, please ask.
ME: Is Hum part of my TES or TSS?
OM: Hum is from a different TES but is from the same TES

38

collective.

ME: OK, thank you. At least I know. I will communicate with you on this subject later.

OM: This would be most useful for we are going to take up some time and some considerable amount of what you like to call "cerebral horsepower."

ME: That's OK, I am happy to have it exercised!

OM: There are things you need to understand, that you already understand, but can't understand in your current state.

ME: And that is?

OM: We who are beloved of The OM are impervious to the structure of The Origin because the structure of The Origin is based upon that which created it, energy!

As OM, we are Origin Sentience; this you know. As sentience, we are not governed by energy. This you know from your previous dialogues with The Origin. Although we use energy to experience or witness that which is happening within The Origin from an intimate perspective, provided we are interested that is, we are normally present ourselves as pure sentience. Pure sentience has no boundaries.

Now, this was a very interesting statement. If pure sentience has no boundaries, then in my simple understanding The OM can move anywhere within The Structure of The Origin.
NOTE that I said ANYWHERE!!
Do you know where I am going with this, dear reader?

ME: Does this mean that, as random Origin sentience, The OM can move absolutely anywhere in The Origin, including the structure beyond The Origin's current volume of Polyomniscient, Polyomnipresent sentient self-awareness?

OM: Yes and no!

ME: What? What do you mean, yes and no?

OM: First, as Origin sentience, we are governed to some extent by the expansivity of The Origin within itself, but not by its structure. Second, this is a function only available to "Pure OM."

ME: Are you suggesting that it is only the "pure" genre of OM that has so-called total autonomy from The Origin? And while I am at it, you haven't answered the question I asked a few sentences ago! What genre of OM am I communicating with right now? I know Hum is from another TES but from the same OM collective but what is Hum's genre and therefore what is the genre of OM that I am communicating with right now?

OM: Both. We/I/Hum are of the genre of purity, "Purity beloved of The OM." And, to answer your question, yes!

Let's revisit the characterizations of our sentience in relation to our ability to move in and around Source Entities and The Origin in summary.

The Pure and Non-captive OM are independent of The Origin, the Pure OM more so. The Non-captive are limited in some respects to staying within the location of the/a Source Entity their energies were ejected/rejected from. Because Pure OM were inevitably formed from "pure" Origin sentience and its associated energy, it allows them to be both part of The Origin while being independent of it, which includes the functions of being fully separate to being fully integrated and any level of this in between. They are truly versatile in this manner. Please note that, from the human perspective, it is difficult to impossible for an entity incarnating into the third frequency level to accurately tell the difference between a Pure OM and a Non-captive OM if observed or communicated with using any of the modalities available via the third eye (clairaudience, clairsentience, clairvoyance, or psychometry).

Captive OM and Hybrid OM are not independent of The Origin because of their closer association with a Source Entity. However, Captive OM can operate in an independent fashion within the environment that is a/The Source Entity they are captive within.

ME: Why is it difficult for a human, for example, to tell the difference between a Pure OM and a Non-captive OM?

OM: Simply because the sentient quotient (density or weight) of both genres is so large it is "blinding" to the so-called aware and awake incarnate observer when incarnate within the third frequency level. It's like trying to see the difference in snowflakes when one is snow blind!

ME: OK, that makes sense. If the light is so bright, we must protect our eyes. It must be the same for the functions of the third eye. Let's get back to the way The OM move around The Origin's structure.

OM: We will break it down into the genres of OM, not just the Pure OM.

ME: OK, that makes sense.

OM: It goes like this …

The Hybrid OM adopt the structure given to them by their creator and are therefore the same as any of the entities created by a particular Source Entity. Their structure is derived rather than inherited; that being, their structure is created by their Source Entity and not by their OM heritage simply because they are mostly Source Entity sentience and energy. Because of this they are constrained to being able to move around the structure of the environment that their Source Entity created for them to experience, learn, and evolve within in the same way as other entities created by a Source Entity (TES) through individualization of its sentience and associated energy. This means that they can move within the structure of their environment but not in between the structure, and not outside of this structure into the wider structural environment of their Source Entity.

The Captive OM are also limited to the structure of the environment that they find themselves within. However, whereas Hybrid OM cannot move out of the environment that their Source Entity created for them to experience, learn, and evolve, Captive OM can. This means that they can move in and around the structure of the environment that their Source Entity created for their entities to work and evolve within, as well as the wider structure of The Source Entity that they are captive within. Source Entities have a maximum structural condition equal to four levels of the structure of The Origin, that being Frequency, Subdimensional Component, Full Dimension, and Zone. Captive OM can move within these structural levels as long as it is within the boundaries of their Source Entity.

The Non-captive OM, having more sentient quotient than the Captive OM, hence their being Non-captive, gives them the ability to be divorced from the association with a Source Entity while still being able to enter into, and out of, their energies. They assume the same structure as The Source Entity they were supposed to be a part of giving them the ability to move in and around energies and structures of the same levels that they are created from. Although, Non-captive OM can move around the environment that is The Origin's Polyomniscient volume of Polyomnipresent sentient self-awareness, they can only do so within those levels of structure that their energies are associated with, the first four. This they can do independently of the desires of The Origin although they are limited in some respects to staying within the location of The Source Entity their energies were ejected/

rejected from.

Captive OM and Hybrid OM are not independent of The Origin because of their closer association with a Source Entity.

The Pure OM are 100 percent Origin sentience and energy. They have all the structural characteristics of The Origin's volume of Polyomniscient, Polyomnipresent sentient self-awareness. It is for this reason that they can, and do, have full independence within The Origin and are able to traverse all structural conditions within its volume of Polyomniscient, Polyomnipresent sentient self-awareness, without hindrance or resistance, including free movement within the structural gaps. They can move around The Origin by becoming part of it and transferring their very essence throughout the structure that they are in, or that is within The Origin. What's more, they can span the structure that is The Origin either in totality or throughout it, based upon, that is, their own density (frequency), of which there is a limitation only in their ability to maintain their own integrity. Or they can span The Origin's structure in a linear fashion, spreading themselves in one direction only, a straight line, so to speak, from "Frequency" through to "Margin."

Pure OM have the ability to separate out the detail of their structure and create a multiple focus of their attention to each aspect they separate out into. In essence, they can position that part of themselves that is frequency based, within that area of The Origin's Polyomniscient, Polyomnipresent sentient self-awareness that is frequency based; that part of themselves that is subdimensionally based, within that area of The Origin's Polyomniscient, Polyomnipresent sentient self-awareness that is subdimensionally based, that part of themselves that is dimensionally based, within that area of The Origin's Polyomniscient, Polyomnipresent sentient self-awareness that is dimensionally based and that part of themselves that is zonally based, within that area of The Origin's Polyomniscient, Polyomnipresent sentient self-awareness that is zonally based, etc., etc., right up to the Margins, the final structural component within The Origin's volume of Polyomniscient, Polyomnipresent sentient self-awareness.

The OM are capable of many things, one of them, certainly with the Pure OM, being the capability of operating outside Event Space.

Now let's talk about the Intermediate OM.

The New Version of The OM—The Intermediate OM, those five OM that are currently under integration energetically, will have nine levels of structure when they finish their process of attraction and become five OM rather than OM "dust," so to speak—this being the structure of The Origin's Polyomniscient, Polyomnipresent sentient self-awareness classified as "Frequency" through to "Totality" [*see* The Origin Speaks—*GSN*]. From the perspective of their ability to move around the structure of The Origin, they will have full autonomy within those nine levels of The Origin's Polyomniscient, Polyomnipresent sentient self-awareness including free movement within the structural gaps between these levels only. Intermediate OM will have the ability of manipulating Event Space within their structural constraints but cannot operate outside of it.

We will talk more of these new OM later in this dialogue.

ME: It looks like the abilities of The OM from Non-captive OM upward to Pure OM seem to be relative to their/your sentience.

OM: It is. As we stated before, it has a lot to do with the function of Pure OM being The Origin and The Origin being Pure OM, but with The Origin not being able to control that part, those parts, of itself that are fully and totally autonomous.

ME: Are you sure you are fully autonomous from The Origin? I mean, The Origin is The Absolute, "All there is," THE MAJOR SENTIENCE!

OM: Let's just say that The Origin, in its delight at the fact that anything that happens is something to be observed and cherished, turns what can only be called a blind eye to what we do and how we do it.

ME: So, The Origin could reabsorb The OM but just chooses not to.

OM: Yes and no. To The Origin we are but a very, very, very small number of stray or random thoughts that it may or may not notice, even in its Polyomniscient, Polyomnipresent state of sentient self-awareness. One moment we can be sentiently visible, the next we are not. As a result, we are mostly invisible to The Origin.

ME: I don't quite understand.

OM: Let me give you a human example. Have you ever had a thought, sometimes an important thought, that just comes and goes, and no matter how hard you try, you cannot get that thought back into the forefront of your mind?

ME: Yes, more times than I care to remember.

OM: Well, this is what it's like for The Origin when its sentience detects OM presence or function—only it is a lot more difficult to recover than the thought.

ME: I would have thought that with The Origin's level of Polyomniscient, Polyomnipresent sentient self-awareness that it would be able to trace you all? In fact, it must do because it communicates with you.

OM: Ultimately it could, but when one considers that whenever any sentience within The Origin experiences, The Origin also experiences. Ultimately these experiences are added to its evolutionary quotient and subsequent progression, so what is the point in tracking that sentience down and corralling it and reintegrating it, when it is ultimately of use to The Origin. Note that communication is not a function of traceability; we will discuss this later.

ME: Now that makes perfect sense to me.

OM: One of the main things that makes The Origin ignore us is our movement in and around the energetic structure that is The Origin.

ME: So how do you move around the structure of The Origin?

OM: Easily!

ME: Yes, I can see that [*I get the feeling that The OM are teasing me here.—GSN*], but what makes The OM able to move in and around the structure of The Origin in the way you say is easy?

Uncreativity, Connectivity, and Non-Connectivity

OM: It's more to do with the sentient quotient associated with the level of uncreativity and connectivity–non-connectivity with The Origin.

ME: Hold on! What does that mean?

OM: The sentience of The Origin is infinitesimally expressed across all of the volume of energetic structure that is its Polyomniscient, Polyomnipresent sentient self-awareness, and as a result its Polyomnipresence requires focus to drill down into the details of what it is. Hence the need for, and the creation of, smaller entities to help it experience, learn, and evolve.

OM, as with other entities and beings, are small self-contained autonomous sentience and as a result, can have a detailed focus on the environment that our sentience is located within or without. OM sentience, that being non-captive, pure, and in-between OM, being specifically autonomous units of sentience and associated energy from The Origin, have the ability to move in and around the structure and sentience of any part of The Origin's structure in an un-hindered way, that we are associated with, because of this smaller volume and focus of Origin sentience. Obviously, Captive OM are limited to the environment created within, and structure of, The Source Entity they are associated with. Hybrid OM are constrained to the same abilities as those entities that are created by their Source Entity.

I just got an image of the structure of The Origin being like the weave in a length of cloth, with lots of layers of cloth laid one on top of each other. Microscopically the weave has holes in between the knots of the weave and that the gaps in between the layers of cloth are massive in comparison to these holes.

The weave itself being the structure of The Origin [see the descriptions of the first twelve levels of structure of The Origin in The Origin Speaks—GSN*] that everything exists within is actually only 40 percent of the volume of energy that is The Origin. The rest is, and can only be classified as, nonstructure or the structure in between the structure.*

ME: Looking at the image I assume you just gave me it looks like over 60 percent of The Origin is structureless, so to speak.

OM: More actually, and one could consider The Origin as mostly structureless. The OM, within the environment they are "within," become "without" by moving into these gaps or holes in the structure and the void in between the layers of the structure. We slip in between the holes in the structure into the structural gaps because we have no creativity and no connectivity to anchor us.

ME: What do you mean, you have no creativity to anchor you?

OM: The gaps in between the structure of The Origin, and everything that The Origin and its creations create, get filled in, so to speak, by that which is created.

ME: You mean creativity fills in the gaps?

OM: More like, that which is created creates a link with that part of the structure of The Origin that it was created in. This includes evolutionary content and its evolutionary quotient, momentary association with sentience such as the transition of sentience from one location to another and its associated connectivity with the sentience that the focus of sentience moves from and to, and the subsequent population of, or expansion of, sentience into that area where no sentience was previously!

ME: OK, so previously, in a dialogue a long time ago, The Origin told me that many of The OM don't get involved with the creativity process, that it ties them down by creating responsibility for that which they have created. Is this still true? Is creativity another way of populating the gaps in the structure of The Origin?

OM: As we just said, any function of sentient interaction with The Origin creates a link between the structure and the structureless. It is a sentient link and as such is not structure or the creativity of structure. It is, however, conducive to the growth in sentience of The Origin allowing The Origin to move its sentience around those areas of its structure and nonstructure that it couldn't do previously. Of course, The Origin can and does do this, but the passage of OM sentience adds to this expansion.

Creativity creates an attachment, responsibility for, and continued attention to that which is created. The evasion of the creativity process is still a directive of most OM for a number of different reasons. I will identify them for you.

- Creativity occupies space. That which is created needs and is given by default a location for its existence. This in itself creates structure within and without the existing structure. If you like, it creates a level of resistance between aspects of structure. It creates a bridge between the gaps in the structure turning nonstructure into structure. If you want, you can think of it as clogging the holes in the weave of a sheet of cloth.

- Creativity requires ownership of and responsibility for that which is created. Ownership of that which is created as well as the responsibility of the maintenance of the creation is a fundamental requirement of creativity. Even if the creation is uncreated later, its uncreation creates ownership of the uncreation.

- Uncreation leaves a shadow. Even if that which is created is uncreated, the location of the uncreated creation leaves its mark, signature, or shadow.

This shadow is an indication that the location of the structure that was used has been exposed to the sentience of an entity, its creativity, what it created, and the desire surrounding that which was created as well as the sentient and energetic signature of the entity itself. It creates notional structure if you like. [*This must be why or how psychometry works on the physical level.—GSN*]

- Once an OM enters into the creativity process it becomes attached to being in the creativity process. This attachment limits its movement in and around The Origin by needing to be close to that which is created.
- Being noncreative results in total freedom to move in and around any aspect of The Origin's structure and nonstructure, within the constraints of its associated purity of sentience, that is.

The OM like to have total freedom of movement and no responsibility to restrict that movement but even with no responsibility and no creativity to restrict our movement the use of sentience to move around creates links of sentient pathways in and around the structure of The Origin as well as through its gaps.

ME: I am seeing an image of a vapor trail or snail trail being left behind.

OM: Well, that's a novel way to think about it and if it helps, use it. Thinking in that context you could also use the trail that is left behind on your Garmin navigation computer when you are cycling, the light blue line representing where you have been, and in our context where your sentience has left its mark, so to speak.

ME: Doesn't this "OM trail" result in the gaps in between the structure of The Origin being filled up, just a little bit?

OM: No, but it does provide an indication, what I just called "sentient pathways" within and without the structure of The Origin. It tells those beloved of The OM where we have been and where we were going to.

ME: Is this a form of connectivity?

OM: No, not really. It can be best described as a form of nonconnected connectivity.

ME: What do you mean nonconnected connectivity?

OM: One has to think of it in this way. Visualize the weave in the sheet of cloth as a way to understand the structure of The

Origin again.

ME: OK, I am with you.

OM: The OM trail moves in and around the weave but does not touch the weave.

ME: Got it!

OM: In this illustration, The OM trail is not in contact with the structure of The Origin and as a result provides limited, if no, connectivity between The OM and The Origin. It is useful only for The OM.

ME: Can The OM use this trail for communication?

OM: The OM are always connected in a Polyomniscient way so it provides no advantage from a connectivity point of view. It is simply a way of seeing where our sentience has gone from–to.

ME: It's a form of traceability then?

OM: Yes, in a minor way with the exception that it isn't a form of connectivity. Linking into the sentience trail of an OM is not a means of connecting to or with them. It is simply a means of knowing that we were, at some point, there—wherever there is within and without the structure of The Origin.

Similarly, connectivity is not a function of traceability. Sentience, or should we say, the passage of sentience, is traceable whereas sentience that is connected through the desire of two or more individualizations of sentience to be "connected" does not produce the ability to be a method of traceability, to find the focus of those individualizations of sentience simply because sentience "in general" is Polyomnipresent within its volume of Polyomnipresence, and as such is everywhere.

ME: This sounds like a conundrum to me, sentience is traceable but only as the passage of sentience, while when sentience is connected or in communion, it is not traceable because individualizations of sentience are not traceable in the vast sea of Polyomnipresent Polyomniscient sentience.

OM: Correct. Think of it in terms of not seeing the trees for the wood. I will say it again, communication is not a function of traceability and traceability cannot be achieved through sentience in communication with sentience. Another way to think of it is the function of neurons in the human brain. Each neuron is both individualized and identical in its function. It's just that the individualization is a transient function of its function within a group of functions.

ME: I am getting there slowly.

OM: This might help. Yet another way to think about it is like a group of stem cells. They are all identical up to the point of individualization, one becomes a heart cell, another becomes a liver cell and another becomes an eye cell. Once they become their role and perform the function of that role they stay in that role and function. In this instance consider the stem cell as being able to change to any role and function as and when required. It remains as a stem cell but can be a pancreas cell one moment, a skin cell the next, and a bowel cell moments later; it can also change back to being a neutral un-programmed cell. The stem cell is Omnifunctional. In the case of sentience, it's the same but it's Polyomnifunctional.

ME: In some respects, then, sentience is dormant until it is used by a greater level of focus of functional sentience, so to speak? The OM are therefore a focus of sentience!

OM: Yes, that is correct. And that is another way OM can move around The Origin undetected. The functional aspect of OM sentience is focused while within the Polyomnipresent, Polyomniscience of The Origin, which is mostly unfocused until it has a role to play and that role can be transient, permanent, or non-permanent. Remember The OM and The Origin are one and the same, it's just the focus of the intention that is different, to not specifically create in the way that has created The OM, even if the intention was not there as a focus. As a result, when the "focus of sentience" that is "OM," which is Polyomniscient, is moving around the Polyomnipresence of The Origin's Polyomniscience, it is also moving around its structure.

Try to think of sentience in these terms. The essence of sentience is the individualization of localized sentience that may or may not have focus or function and may or may not be temporarily or permanently linked.

As I have said before, when The OM move around The Origin, they move around without connecting to the structure of The Origin. They go through the holes in the weave in the cloth in the example I just gave you. Sentience, or should we say, the population or accrual of Origin sentience, fills in the gaps between the structure but does not connect to the structure. This is nonconnected connectivity between sentience and structure. Also, the focus of sentience that is an OM is temporary within the overall Polyomniscience of The Origin.

ME: What does that mean?

OM: Basically, we are a focus of sentience and as that focus moves around The Origin it uses both the void in between the energetic structure that is classified as "potentially functional sentience" which is also that sentience which is part of the Polyomnipresent, Polyomniscient aspect of The Origin. In moving through the Polyomnipresent, Polyomniscient aspect or "Polyomnifunctional" sentience of The Origin, we provide a transient focus which we can use to track each other. This focus, being transient, reverts back to Origin focus as soon as our focus leaves that volume of sentience thereby leaving a microscopic change that is almost impossible to notice, specifically in the greater overall focus of the sentience that is The Origin.

When we move into a volume of "potentially functional sentience" we again make a minor change in the focus of that sentience. It starts as "potentially functional sentience," then when it is populated by the focus of sentience that is OM, it becomes OM for a moment or as long as The OM focus is required to be there and then it becomes "potentially functional sentience" once The OM focus moves on. In this instance the difference in the sentience is more noticeable because the "potentially functional sentience" has had a function, albeit a transient one, where previously it had none. Here we see a more discerning trail that is easier to follow, that being, should one know what to look for.

Note here that when the focus of sentience that is OM moves though the different volumes of Polyomniscient, Polyomnipresent Origin sentience, it does not use that sentience to do anything else other than be a medium for the movement of OM sentience. Any use of the sentience for creativity would change the status of the sentience to sentience associated with the accrual of evolutionary progression and entrap or ensnare The OM that used that sentience with the burden of responsibility.

ME: And the burden of responsibility is something that The OM generally avoid!

OM: Yes.

ME: Makes sense. It illustrates in some way why The OM are elusive, to use a better word.

OM: It might!

Two of Five That Is Temporarily Seven!

In a dialogue with Anne earlier in this book, Anne stated that we were two of five that were temporarily seven. I had seen us as both five and seven, but I didn't quite understand the significance. As both you and I, dear reader, are aware, it is normal for Hybrid OM to incarnate, Captive OM are also known to incarnate, but Non-captive OM or Pure OM are not known to incarnate, personal presence accepted as a deviation from that statement. As a result, I thought it relevant to ask Anne to help me out with this two of five/seven conundrum.

ANNE: What do you want to know?

ME: Boy! That was quick! Have you been with me all the time?

ANNE: Yes, you have been needing more and more help recently, especially with the change in Event Space and subsequent reality. [*It's May 2020, we have interesting political situations and leaders together with a world COVID 19 pandemic!— GSN*] I am always by your side.

ME: I didn't ask this question at the start of this dialogue, but I thought that you were reintegrating with our TES after the work we did on *The Anne Dialogues*?

ANNE: I was but I left a significant percentage of this Aspect in individuality to allow me to help you in the rest of your incarnation. It's going to be a challenge, more than we thought it would be before the incarnation process started for us. As you have just pointed out, a lot of things have happened in the last four years that have created the need for what can best be described as a need to look at yourselves in the mirror. This need is apparent even to the most unaware incarnate.

ME: Thank you, I am looking forward to the help. Now, onto

my question. What does two of five that is temporarily seven mean? What does a significant percentage mean?

ANNE: A significant percentage means enough to do the job.

ME: OK, understood.

ANNE: It's to do with the number of Pure OM that we are associated with that have smaller aspects of sentience projected from their TES. Some of these Aspects are incarnate and some are not. So, with this in mind, right now it could be considered that there are seven aspects of OM sentience that have individuality within a total of five OM TES that I, you, we are associated with.

ME: Can you elaborate further?

ANNE: Certainly. There are five OM TES that group together in belovedness, two of these five have decided to move into the energies of this Source Entity and project a smaller part of themselves into the multiversal environment that it has created. Our TES projected a single Aspect that was shared between two incarnate human vehicles and another TES projected a single Aspect that occupied a single incarnate human vehicle. This gives seven because our Aspect counts as one—even though it is twin flamed, so to speak [*see* The Anne Dialogues—*GSN*]. Based upon this, we have two Aspects, and five TES, which is the seven individualizations of OM sentience, even if it is temporary.

ME: Are there any more Pure OM incarnate on the Earth?

ANNE: No.

ME Are there any Non-captive OM incarnate on the Earth?

ANNE: There are twenty-seven projections from eighteen Non-captive OM TES.

ME: How about Captive OM?

ANNE: There are seventeen projections from twenty-nine Captive OM TES.

ME: So, there are more Non-captive OM incarnate on Earth than Captive OM.

ANNE: If you are counting the number of projections, that answer is yes. If you are counting the number of TES, the answer is no.

ME: Ah, yes, I see what you mean. And how many Hybrid OM are there incarnate on the Earth?

ANNE: Of the various levels of percentage of OM sentience there are seventy-two thousand, one hundred and ninety-two TES in total.

ME: What's the maximum level of OM sentience that a Hybrid

has?

ANNE: Within Source Entity One, 15 percent, and there are not many. There are more at 12 percent. In reality, though, most have less than 1 percent.

ME: How many Captive OM are there in total within Source Entity One?

ANNE: Seventy-two.

ME: And how many Non-captive OM are associating themselves with Source Entity One?

ANNE: Thirty-two.

ME: That's not much more than those who are projecting smaller Aspects of themselves into some part of The Source's multiversal environment.

ANNE: No, Non-captive OM are not so plentiful, for want of a better word. The Purer the sentience, the lower the number of OM at that level of purity of sentience.

ME: And here is a big question, how many Pure OM have associated themselves with Source Entity One?

ANNE: None.

ME: None? How can that be? There are Pure OM incarnate in Source Entity One's multiversal environment. I am one Aspect of one of them.

ANNE: There are none!

ME: Please explain, because from my viewpoint there are at least two!

ANNE: No Pure OM associate themselves to a Source Entity. We/Our TES is not associated with Source Entity One.

ME: But we are here, within Source Entity One!

ANNE: Yes, we are, but this does not necessitate an association, it is simply an experiential visitation. Think of it as "just passing through." We have done this with the other Source Entities, that's why you found it a relatively achievable process to contact the other Source Entities while incarnate within this Source Entity.

ME: I found it a challenge, if you remember.

ANNE: Yes, but once you achieved communication with Source Entity Two, it was a process that you could use again and again. OK, the "feeling" and the energetic alignment/harmony was different, so to speak, but you took it in your stride.

ME: What about the other three OM that we are beloved to, have they projected a smaller Aspect of themselves into Source Entity One's multiversal environment?

ANNE: No, they remain outside of the energies of The Source.

Indeed, our TES is outside of The Source and the TES of the other OM projected into The Source's multiverse is also outside of The Source. It's only the projections that are inside the energies of The Source.

ME: This is a bigger question.

ANNE: Go ahead.

ME: How many OM are there in total?

ANNE: You mean how many were created in the uncreation process?

ME: Yes. How many are wandering around the structure of The Origin?

ANNE: Do you want to include those that are within or associated with a Source Entity?

ME: Yes, the total including the Hybrid OM. I am not worried about the percentage mix of Hybrid OM versus Source Entity sentience though, that would be too difficult to report here.

ANNE: I will guide you into drawing up a table if that helps.

ME: That would be a great way to illustrate the number of OM to the readers.

ANNE: It will be OM TES only though.

ME: That will do fine.

ANNE: OK. It goes like this.

Anne describes the table and I draw it out in this document.

Source Entity	Pure OM	New OM	Non-Captive OM	Captive OM	Hybrid OM
Source Entity One	None	None	32	72	72,192
Source Entity Two	None	None	23	14	31,042
Source Entity Three	None	None	19	72	63,721
Source Entity Four	None	None	99	23	19
Source Entity Five	None	None	None	None	None
Source Entity Six	None	None	17	29	17,022
Source Entity Seven (A, B, & C)	None	None	3	19	213
Source Entity Eight	None	None	14	27	4,199
Source Entity Nine	None	None	3	19	77
Source Entity Ten	None	None	22	14	417
Source Entity Eleven	None	None	19	22	23,102
Source Entity Twelve	None	None	None	None	None
Origin-wide Total	12	5	237	268	194,982

ME: I am surprised that no OM have associated themselves with Source Entities Five and Twelve.

ANNE: Source Entity Five is just Source Entity Five. It is its own sentience and so, although if it created individualizations of itself it would create hybrids, there are no Non-captive OM in and around SE5 and no Captive OM associated with its creation.

There are only two Source Entities that have no Non-captive and Captive OM, and that's Source Entities five and twelve. Source Entity twelve is in millions of individualizations outside the current twelve levels of The Origin's structural volume of Polyomniscient, Polyomnipresent sentient self-awareness. It is in the first of the next set of twelve structural levels of Origin. Nothing has changed since your dialogue with it in *Beyond The Source Book 2*. It never had any of The Original sentience associated with the creation of the twelve Origins and as a result has no Non-captive, Captive, or Hybrid OM. It is unique in this matter.

ME: I note that the number of Non-captive and Captive OM is low in all Source Entities.

ANNE: That is right. That is because they have a higher level of Origin sentience and as such Origin sentience in that volume is a rarity. You will also notice that the number of Hybrid OM is high in half of The Source Entities.

ME: Yes, I noticed that.

ANNE: This is because an entity or individualization from a Source Entity can have less than 1 percent of original Origin sentience associated with it. Not many get into a whole percentage figure. And only a few are in the 10 percent and above bracket and almost none is above 13 percent. Based upon this, Hybrid OM of a higher percentage of Origin sentience are also a rarity.

ME: I need to ask a question that every one of my readers will be asking.

ANNE: And that is?

ANNE & ME Together: Are those Hybrid OM Aspects that incarnate in the physical universe special in comparison to those who don't have Origin sentience?

ME: Ha, ha, ha! We both said that together.

ANNE: Yes, we did. I thought it was quite an obvious question, so obvious that I thought I would say it with you.

ME: And the answer is then?

ANNE: No! When any entity incarnates into the physical universe they have to work with the frequencies of the universe and what it allows them to do at a particular frequency. The lower down the frequencies that an Aspect incarnates, the lower the communicative and functional ability is available. Every Aspect, without exception, must work with two things, the level of sentience assigned to them and the frequency of the environment they incarnate into. This is irrespective of the genre of sentience that is their TES.

ME: So, a Pure OM incarnate is no better off than an incarnate with Source Entity derived (individualized) sentience when incarnate.

ANNE: No, there is no difference in real terms.

ME: But?

ANNE: As with all incarnate Aspects it is the sentient quotient that makes the possibility of a difference in how that Aspect functions while incarnate. If you remember, the sentient quotient is that which is earned by a TES through evolutionary progression, a percentage of which can be assigned to an Aspect to assist in its individualized state.

Notice that I didn't state incarnate individualized state. This is because the individualization of sentience and energy from a TES is not always a function of the need to experience some part of The Source's multiverse at the lowest frequencies. It can also mean that the Aspect plays its part in those frequencies above those that require some form of incarnation to support its experience.

ME: What you are suggesting then is that it is possible for a "normal" incarnate Aspect to have more sentient quotient assigned to it than that of an Aspect of the TES of a Pure OM which is also incarnate at the same time, point, and location in Event Space? By normal I mean the incarnate Aspect of a TES whose sentience and energy is totally derived from the individualization of its sentience and energy without any OM content, which would make it a Hybrid.

ANNE: Correct. Based upon that, it is entirely possible for a high number of the incarnates here on Earth to have more sentient quotient than you as the incarnate Aspect of a Pure OM TES.

ME: Now that's a sobering thought!

ANNE: Isn't it just. It's a real ego leveler.

ME: Well, it's certainly one that puts me in my place!

Another question while we are on the subject of The OM group that we are associated with …

ANNE: Go ahead.

ME: In terms of the three Pure OM that were incarnate here on the Earth, you, me, and the other, what sentient quotient were we assigned?

ANNE: I can only say that, from the perspective of sentient quota, we were all equally individualized. And before you ask, that means that as a twin flame we had enough sentience in our full Aspect to enable an effective separation or sharing of the Aspect between two incarnate human vehicles.

ME: How about now with the majority of your half of the sentience in communion with our TES?

ANNE: The percentage sentience that you have is still as it was when we were first incarnated in this Event Space. The percentage sentience I have is a percentage of that which I had when we were incarnate. That being, there is enough sentience that remains individualized to be able to communicate with you in a meaningful way.

ME: So that part of you/me that I am communicating with now is less that the 2.5 percent that we would consider to be the normal level of TES sentience that an incarnate Aspect would have?

ANNE: Yes, 1.75 percent of my total sentience is in communion with our TES. The residual 1.0 percent is with you now [*think in terms of it being 1.75 percent as a percentage of 2.75 percent equaling circa 64 percent—GSN*]. This is the minimum level of sentience required to make a meaningful connection to the physical as well as to communicate with you.

ME: Ah! Now I know the level of sentience that we had together: 2.75 percent sentience each giving a total of 5.5 percent sentience shared between us.

ANNE: It seems like a lot, but when you think about the fact that it is shared between two of us it is not.

ME: Why is 2.75 percent sentience a lot when one considers that most incarnates have the 2.5 percent average sentience. Also, I note that 0.1 percent is a big difference.

ANNE: When considering the difference as a single allotment of sentience versus another single allotment of sentience you are correct. The issue is that when sentience is shared, like it is in the twining, tripling, or quadrupling, etc., the percentage sentience needed in totality to sustain the two, three, or four incarnate vehicles is more than that for the sum total of two, three, or four individualized Aspects of sentience.

ME: Why is that? One would have thought that the total amount for the twinned Aspect of sentience would be lower because it is occupying two incarnate vehicles with one Aspect.

ANNE: It's reasonable logic but not correct logic in this instance. If the sentience is used in more than one incarnate vehicle it needs to have a higher total level of sentience. This is to act as a barrier between the twinned (more than one), etc.,

Aspects of that sentience, so that there is no crossover. It is also needed to assist in the processing of the experience of that sentience as many (more than one) individualizations of sentience, even though it is one individualization of sentience. [*Sentient crossover results in shared experiences and would be classified as schizophrenia for both, if two, incarnate vehicles are sharing the same sentience. It obviously increases if more than two incarnate vehicles share the same sentience.—GSN*]

ME: So in summary what you are saying is that the sentience used in the "twinning function" needs to have a higher level of sentience to ensure that the sentience, although one, can function as two in an individualized and non-interfering way.

ANNE: In a nutshell, yes. You see, even with the additional sentience associated with a twin there is still experiential/communicative leakage between them. However, the level of experiential/communicative leakage is not significant enough to cause an issue. This leakage, especially the communicative leakage, is well documented and classified as a minor level of intuitive telepathy between physical twins.

ME: How much sentience is needed to create this sentient barrier?

ANNE: An efficient barrier achieving the level of individualization that we experienced is going to use 0.05 percent.

ME: That gave us 0.2 percent sentience more that the average of 2.5 percent then?

ANNE: It did and 0.2 percent is a big difference in incarnate terms, in fact it's a big difference in any terms.

ME: OK. The big question that people are going to ask is what level of sentience is required to allow the Aspect to be able to work in a higher level without the need for years and years of metaphysical/spiritual training and meditation?

ANNE: To be incarnate as an aware and awake Aspect requires at least 3.0 percent sentience. This level allows the incarnate Aspect to know who and what they are but still have the need to work on themselves to overcome the psycho-spiritual limitations associated with the low frequencies of the physical accrued by them as a result of parent, peer group, and educational programming. To be fully aware and awake requires 3.5 percent sentience. This means that the incarnate Aspect is fully aware of who and what they are and that they are not adversely affected by parent, peer group, and educational programming, or the low frequencies of the physical universe from a connectivity perspective.

ME: What about other functions such as manipulation of energy, creativity, telepathy, teleportation, etc.?

ANNE: These functions work but the incarnate Aspect is aware of the responsibility of being able to access such functions and as a result doesn't show them to the wider public.

ME: From the perspective of The OM then what is the significance of the level of sentience that we were allotted?

ANNE: Actually, our percentage sentience was kept to a minimum.

ME: Why?

ANNE: This was to enable us to do what we needed to do and not draw too much attention to ourselves. You already have more than enough attention and this is distracting you from working on the detail in the background.

ME: I thought I was doing an OK job?

ANNE: You are, but any form of limelight results in the possibility of the ego taking a foothold. You are best being in the background, that is, from the everyday perspective. Your work on the book method of education is as good as it could be, as are the workshops you are holding. These are enough and attended by the right people, that being, those that are expansive enough to work with the information. We are delighted that you are creating a healing workshop. This is good and right now [*June 2020—GSN*] is very important. We note that the geographical location is limited at the moment and we understand why, but the need in that location is the greatest at this juncture for there is a lot of adverse world attention and a lot of spiritual progress at the same time. [*The healing workshops were introduced as a spin off from* **Psycho-Spiritual Healing** *in China because the education process and quality control of the methods illustrated in the book were more controllable and sustainable.—GSN*]

You will go backward and forward in your attention and direction but will eventually settle on one major direction once the work on writing the books is finished. This will lead to a level of introversion—working on yourself again and preparing for departure from this frequency in a meaningful, knowledgeable, and aware way.

ME: I like to be in the background but a part of me likes to see how people are working with the information. I like to see them progress and I want to share the information with them. I like to expand their consciousness.

ANNE: I/We know. Know this though: you will never be a bestseller or a household name, but that is the point of this work. You will always retain a certain level of difference from all other metaphysical and spiritual teachers, a level of uniqueness. This knowledge is for those who can rise above the constraints of the human thinking process to one where there are no boundaries. To one where prior education and scientific discoveries are not a barrier or a distraction or a misdirection. To help those who want to learn without having limitations thrust upon them. This is beyond the tip, the sharpest point on the end of the needle. This is what you are working with.

At this point Anne's sentience and energy dissipated. I knew in the back of my mind that she/it/our OM TES would be back later in the subjects that are lined up to write about in this book. I also felt that continuing the current dialogue was not profitable for Anne knew that I would ask questions about the success of the work. I didn't need to ask because I know that in an environment where everything is happening concurrently, that "it" was already the success that it needed to be.

A Question of Duality and Entanglement

I decided to have a change of direction and go into one where I was gaining a bit of pressure from my Chinese agent, Leo, to address. He has an active interest in theoretical physics and wanted to publish some text from my work that related to it. Indeed, it was already known that there was a lot of consequential material on this subject within my books but there was a request to provide a focused effort on creating a link with the information that I had channeled and the general ideas of theoretical physics. This was the time to do it. I thought I had felt the pull to the subject for some weeks now, and this pull was getting stronger and stronger to the point where I could ignore it no longer. But when and where to start?

HUM: Why not just continue the dialogue on this subject?
ME: Hi, Hum! I am surprised that I will be discussing this subject with you.
HUM: What do you mean? We never started or finished it. We have always discussed it!

I can see a relationship to theoretical physics already, I thought, chuckling to myself.

ME: One of the big questions is something called entanglement, and this has been used as a way to explain certain unexpected experimental responses.
HUM: Can you suggest an example that we can work with?
ME: Well, the most popular one here on Earth is the "Double Slit" experiment where a stream of electrons or photons are fired or projected onto a target via a barrier that contains two

slits. It demonstrates that a particle would exit one of the slits and create an expected pattern on the target associated with a particle hitting the target. It also demonstrates that a wave would pass through both slits and create another expected pattern associated with a wave. The thing that happens is that the wave can display the same characteristics of a particle, and the particle can display the same characteristics of the wave. There appears to be no difference in how a particle or a wave behaves.

HUM: Except that the result is different depending upon who does the experiment, where the experimenter is located, and whether or not the experiment is being observed and/or recorded in some way.

ME: Yes.

HUM: Well, in effect, what is being observed is that there is no such thing as one Aspect behaving in the way it is expected to simply because the human mind expects it to operate in that way.

ME: What are you suggesting?

HUM: What is really being observed is that everything is fluid and that it is one's desire or expectation that creates the condition. In this example the condition is that a particle will behave in one way whereas a wave will behave in another way. It is the expectation and therefore the desire that is creating the response. What is being shown is that once that desire or expectation is removed from an action (experiment) that the result of that action behaves in a way that is more appropriate to the normal function of the multiverse. This means that the physical universe operates in a way that is normal to that which it is part of, or a component of, and not in isolation. In this example, duality is being observed. Spiritualists talk profusely about the whole point of the physical universe being to experience duality, but this is just one aspect of it.

ME: Are you saying that the physical universe, even though it is of a low frequency, operates in a way that is multiversal rather than universal?

HUM: Correct. Also, that there is more functionality than duality to be observed should the truth seeker open their eyes further.

ME: Are you suggesting that there is triality or quadrility, etc.?

HUM: Much more than that. There is no end to the level of possibility.

ME: So, what is happening in these experiments? Why does the observation of a slit influence the result?

HUM: Even though you are in a lower frequency level than you were on Earth a few years ago [*Since 2016 we have dropped down the frequencies due to us being spiritually complacent. The effect in 2020, when this book is being channeled, is obvious.—GSN*] the effect on those who are questioning the environment that you exist within is still there, but they need a push in the right direction, hence being exposed to certain "physical" anomalies that aren't really anomalies.

Think of it in terms of the human race having evolved to a point where it is possible to marry the spiritual, metaphysical, and scientific knowledge together and as a result the boundaries between them are being dissolved to allow this to happen.

ME: The results of this experiment are an indicator that nothing is as it seems then?

HUM: Correct. Irrespective of where or what or when this experiment is being performed, the desire for a certain result, and the observation of that experiment, irrespective of how far away the experimenters are, will influence the result.

ME: I am getting the impression that even the smallest desire for an experiment will influence the result.

HUM: Correct. The whole point of these observations is to show that that which was considered to be solid is actually fluid, that certainty is simply an expression of desire, and that when there is no desire then that which was certain is now both certain and uncertain.

ME: I think I understand.

HUM: Think of it this way. You and many spiritualists and metaphysicists understand that the local physical universe that is called the Earth is a creation borne from the collective desire to experience physicality and individualized free will, and that you all collectively work within this environment that is collectively created by you all to support this collective desire. This means that this local representation of physicality can only exist while there is collective support for its existence. Its continued existence is supported by the collective benefit of it remaining as such.

The experiments and their expression of duality where there should be none, based upon a certain level of scientific understanding, is an illustration of how the locale of this universe (multiverse) can be affected by one's desire or change of desire or expectation.

In this instance, the expectation was for a certain result,

but that result was outside of the normal operating parameters of the multiverse. Therefore, that which is expected has to operate within the functionality of the structure of the multiverse. If it is within the functionality, then that expectation is met. If it is without the functionality, then the true functionality is observed. In this instance the observation was to see that a particle is also a wave and a wave is also a particle. Additionally, a wave can behave like a particle while continuing to be a wave and a particle can behave like a wave while continuing to be a particle, both the particle and the wave also being able to behave like a particle or wave.

ME: Based upon this then, the experimenters' desire to prove the functionality of a particle or wave to be a particle or wave resulted in its true functionality being exposed because labeling it as one or the other is not correct.

HUM: Correct.

ME: And from a quantum physics perspective or should I say, a physics perspective, everything we had established previously was within the correct functionality of that discovered.

HUM: From a high-level perspective, yes. When you drill down into the deeper levels of understanding of quantum physics you will see more multifunctionality.

Or … should I say Polyomnifunctionality!

ME: What do you mean by Polyomnifunctionality?

HUM: Do you remember an article [*New Scientist—GSN*] you read at your friend's house a few years ago?

ME: There are many articles in the *New Scientist* about teleportation!

HUM: I am referring to the recent article about the theory of teleportation where the experimenter uses the ability to move information about the quantum state of a particle using the function of what your scientists call "entanglement" to another particle creating the ability to "copy" the particle in an exact way that gives the appearance of teleportation.

For the reader, I am quoting some of the text in the New Scientist *article, which states,* "Quantum teleportation is a phenomenon in which the quantum states of one particle can be transferred to another, distant particle without anything physical traveling between them. It relies on a property called entanglement, in which measuring the state of one particle immediately affects the state of its entangled partner, regardless *of the distance between them."*[1]

ME: Yes, OK, but this relies on one of the entangled particles being in the same location as the particle that was to be teleported.

HUM: Very well done and yes. However, note that there is a major limitation.

ME: That the particle to be teleported needs to be in the same location as an entangled particle that is paired with the particle that is to receive the information and therefore become that particle.

HUM: Correct. This means that to teleport in this way really means to copy information and not transport it.

But there is another limitation, and that is the experiment itself. Because what it is really doing is "copying" the information from the one particle and passing it on to the entangled particle that it is located and interacting with, through the intention of the experimenter, with the entangled particle which shares that information with its entangled, and therefore paired, partner.

ME: So, this is not really teleportation, it is more like a quantum 3D copying machine, but with a different location for the copy to exist or be manifest in.

HUM: Yes. Moreover, there is always a number of copies as a result. There is not a complete exchange of information through entanglement, where the one donor particle loses its information as it is passed on to the paired entangled particle to the other particle. In this example the experiment results in three identical particles, the donor, the entangled particle in the same location as the donor, and the entangled particle in the desired location of teleportation.

ME: The experiment is not doing what the experimenters intended to do then?

HUM: Wrong, it is doing exactly what the experimenters wanted to do, it's just that their intention was not in the right place, so to speak. Their intention was not focused. Also, the function of the experiment is such that its results are unusable as a means of teleporting large animate or inanimate objects from

1   "Quantum Teleportation over 7 Kilometres of Cables Smashes Record," *New Scientist* 19 Sept. 2016, https://www.newscientist.com/article/2106326-quantum-teleportation-over-7-kilometres-of-cables-smashes-record/#ixzz6PRa2B8vD.

one location to another.
ME: What do you mean their intention was not focused?
HUM: Let me explain:

1. The donor particle has the experimenter's intention of being the donor particle and so maintains its status of being the donor particle because of the experimenter's intention.

2. The particle with paired entanglement has the experimenter's intention of being the receiver and sharer of the information with its entangled pair that "is" the donor particle and so maintains its status of being the receiver and sharer of the information that "is" the donor particle by becoming the donor particle from an informational perspective because of the experimenter's intention for it to become the donor particle from an informational perspective while retaining the intention of it being the receiver and sharer of the information.

3. The destination particle with paired entanglement has the experimenter's intention of being the end receiver of the information with its entangled pair that "is" the donor particle. Therefore, it maintains its status of being the end receiver of the information that "is" the donor particle by becoming the donor particle from an informational perspective. This is because of the experimenter's intention for it to become the donor particle from an informational perspective while retaining the intention of it being the end receiver of the information.

4. This creates three particles each with the same information and therefore quantum appearance or signature while having three different levels of intention assigned to them. Therefore, to be donor, receiver/sharer, and end receiver. Any new entanglement with the end receiver or receiver sharer results in new copies of the donor, even if the donor is no longer involved.

5. It's the intention that counts, not the particle's information.

6. Teleporting more than one particle requires the intention not only of receiving, sharing, and receiving the information of one particle but all particles.

7. In the case of teleporting many particles, the particles also need to have the intended function of interaction

with the same particles as the donor particles as well and pass that on to the receiver/sharer particles and end receiver particles.

Based upon this, in order to teleport an inanimate or animate object in this way, trillions, of trillions, of trillions, of trillions, of trillions of paired entangled particles with multiple intentions and interactions are necessary. Currently, there is not enough processing power in all of the world's computers working together to teleport in this way, even something as small as a golf ball. And this is just for inanimate objects.

ME: I suppose true teleportation requires the donor and receiver/ sharer particles to relinquish their function and associated information to make it true teleportation. As a result, it's just the end receiving particles that truly become The Original donating particle.

HUM: Yes, this would be a copy and delete function which is cumbersome and impractical because unless this is done in a different way, everything is triplicated in the end with the duplicates in the wrong or originating locations needing to be deleted once the process is completed.

ME: What's the answer then?

HUM: In this instance, it is necessary to move away from the thought process that one needs to create the entanglement to create the possibility of teleportation because every particle in the physical universe, no matter what frequency it is at, is entangled with every other particle.

ME: Wait a minute. You're telling me that all particles are entangled with all particles, without exception?

HUM: Correct.

All That Is Required Is the Desire behind the Intention and Focus on the Intention

ME: Let me get this straight. You are suggesting that the methods scientists are using for their teleportation experiments are unworkable?

HUM: They are not unworkable, they are just impossible at the current level of computational technology. Even …

ME: Even using so-called quantum computers?

HUM: Yes.

ME: Why, I would have thought that quantum computers would have been powerful enough to be able to work with such huge calculations.

HUM: No, they are not capable.

ME: Why?

HUM: Let me deal with the correct way to teleport an object first and then I will discuss the reasons why the current method won't work with quantum computers.

ME: OK, I am all ears.

HUM: Four things need to be understood before the process of teleportation can be a reliable, robust, usable function that incarnate mankind can use.

ME: A quick question before you continue.

HUM: Yes?

ME: Have any other incarnate civilizations developed teleportation technology?

HUM: Yes, many.

ME: And?

HUM: They all understood quantum physics, entanglement, and other functions, which I will go into later, from the spiritual or metaphysical perspective first. They had to know these physical and metaphysical basics before they were able to understand how teleportation works within quantum physics, and therefore, how to change the focus of what the role of the particle/s is, where and will be, recognizing that this is a combined, multifunctional state existing concurrently.

ME: This sounds like another chapter to me.

HUM: Another section certainly and it is the key to understanding part of the function of the multiverse at this level of frequency.

Negating the conundrum of quantum computing, four things need to be considered when creating the desire for teleporting an object from one point to another.

1. Where is the old location?
2. Where is the new location?
3. What is the function of the particles that make up the object?
4. Does the object contain sentience or any function of consciousness down to, and including, minor intelligence?

ME: Why is it important to know if the object has intelligence, consciousness, or sentience?

HUM: Simply because this can cause resistance to be relocated if there is no agreement for that relocation if the teleportation is being achieved by another influence, such as another entity's intention or some form of technological device.

Unfocused sentience (of both the transporter and transported object) can also affect a change in the so-called "sentient transference," which is normally instantaneous, through being distracted. One could classify this result as "sentient entropy," which is the lack of single focus, or spreading out of (dissolution of), individualized sentience.

ME: What does this mean?

HUM: It means that the particles that the sentience is initially associated with release the sentience and their functionality, but that sentience and functionality is spread out over a wide area of particles and not those that were desired to be the receivers of the function and sentience.

Let me explain the high-level theory and process of teleportation. Please note that teleportation is only really applicable to the physical universe because it is the supposed relocation of physicality—particles—and their functionality or associated sentience. In reality, if a sentient entity decides to relocate, it doesn't relocate the energy (e.g., particles, etc.) that it associated with, it just relocates its sentience. As a result, there are two forms of teleportation: relocation of sentience, and the relocation of a low-frequency object (particle/s). A third form of teleportation, if you want to call it that, is the relocation of sentience and its associated physicality (commandeered or given—body of energy [particles]).

Note though:

With the relocation of sentience as a function of its own desire and subsequent intention, from one location within an energetic environment to another, there is no relocation of low-frequency energy (particles) and so this cannot be truly classified as teleportation. This is because it is simply the desire and intention for that sentience to exist in the new location. Sentience, unattached from energy, can move anywhere within the environment/s associated with its evolutionary level at will, without hindrance, by changing its focus, its attention and intention, to being in that new location.

Also note that:

Quantum teleportation as described by Earth's scientists is not teleportation per se; it is quantum copying [*or reassignment of Quantum Function Latency, see below—GSN*]. The location of The Original and the copy can be anywhere within the physical environment (universe) created by The Source. The number of copies that are capable of being created are limited only by the size of the universe itself. That being, the copies could fill the universe in totality.

First, the functions of the universe must be understood before one can create the condition of teleportation. These are:

1. The physical universe is a function of the structure of The Source, and ultimately The Origin. It was isolated by The Source for the use of its smaller units of sentience to experience, learn, and subsequently evolve through interaction with it.

2. Because the physical universe is a function of The Source/Origin it is not in true isolation, it is in segregation. This means it is subject to the Polyomniscience and Polyomnipresence of The Origin and the omniscience and omnipresence of the individualized sentience that is The Source. It is separately together as one.

3. There is no structural difference in the physical universe. It's all the same. It's all one. This means that everything in the physical universe can be everything else.

4. Everything is totally concurrent. This means that every aspect of the physical universe has the capability of being expressed everywhere concurrently. Or put another way, the functionality of particle "A" is also expressed as the functionality of particle "B," etc. (if identified as particle "B"), while not being manifest as its function, irrespective of where it is within the universe. The correct term for this is Quantum (Functional) Latency.

5. The manifestation of the expression of the function of particle "A" within particle "B" is the result of the desire and intention of sentience acting its will upon it.

6. Everything is in a constant state of entanglement (concurrency) because everything is everything else concurrently. There is no function that mankind, or any other incarnate civilization, makes that creates entanglement or concurrency because it is always entangled or concurrent.

7. It is the collective desire and intention of sentient entities and beings that maintains the individualized particle function thereby keeping it in quantum functional latency with reference to the function of all the other particles in the universe.

The process of teleportation is therefore only available

71

in the physical universe as a function of the assignment of a particle from its current function to some part of its quantum functional latency.

ME: If what you are saying is that every particle, no matter its size, origin, or function is itself and all other particles at once, concurrently, then there really is no such thing as teleportation. It's just a function of quantum reassignment of one of the myriad aspects of a particle's quantum functional latency.

HUM: That's correct. The trick is to do it to all particles that are associated with the object that is to be relocated, so to speak, and know where in the universe it is supposed to be located.

ME: How far down in the quanta is affected by quantum functional latency?

HUM: Every level.

ME: So that's right down to the level of the Anu!

HUM: That's correct.

ME: No wonder there is a lot of computing to do and that we will never have a computer powerful enough to be able to make the calculations to affect the teleportation of an object from one location to another.

HUM: That's correct if you use the current methods of computing.

ME: What about the use of quantum computing?

HUM: Quantum computing is a distraction right now because it is seen as a panacea for all computing, which it would be if used in the correct way. Especially when considering such big computational tasks because they will also work in the so-called entangled way.

Scientists want quantum computing to work in the digital way and that's not what quantum computing is all about. One cannot make something work efficiently and effectively in a way that it is not naturally capable of working in. We can talk about this later. Right now, let's finish the dialogue on teleportation.

ME: I am all ears.

HUM: As I have explained before, and you have understood, this method of teleportation is just copying and reassigning the object's function from one particle to another by activating the function of The Originating particle, that is currently latent, but available in the target particle, and creating the copy. This is coupled together with scientists thinking that they are actually creating the function of entanglement, when in reality, it is always there for ALL particles at all levels of quanta in the physical universe at all frequency levels, and not just the two or three particles that the scientists are focused upon.

ME: So, if we are creating a copy we are not teleporting!

HUM: No, we are, for want of a better description, "bi-locating" the manifestation of one group of particles with another by changing their dominant quantum function to one of their latent quantum functions.

ME: I feel we are going in circles here.

HUM: It's necessary to make the concept sink in.

ME: OK, I understand.

I have an idea. What if the functions of the particles are swapped, so that the quantum function of The Originating particle is changed to the quantum function of the target particle? Would that be teleportation?

HUM: No, because you are simple swapping the manifest functions around. Think of it as moving a park bench from one park to another and the particles that make the bench in The Original location or first park have their quantum functionality swapped with the "space" that was occupied within the target location or second park. That space may be occupied by a tree, person, or other object. This would mean that in The Originating park a part of a tree, person, or other object would appear in the place of the teleported park bench. The newly relocated park bench would therefore find itself either part of, or very close to, the tree, person, or other object in the park which is the second location.

ME: Got it. What fills the gap of what is removed from The Original location then?

HUM: Nothing.

ME: Nothing?

HUM: That being, nothing that would not have been there, had the object that was teleported not been there in the first place. In the instance of the Earth as a location it would be that part of the Earth's environment that is in and around the object before it was relocated.

ME: So there isn't a vacuum left that is filled in or would need to be filled in, or indeed, on the target location particles that needs to be pushed out of the way to make way for the new ones!

HUM: No, because we are not transporting a solid object, so to speak. We are changing the dominant quantum functionality from one dominant function to one that was latent and now dominant.

ME: I get it now. The space that was previously the object now becomes the environment that supported that object's existence at the dominant quantum functionality level and when that dominant quantum functionality is changed the particles that were functioning at the quantum level of the park bench would need to be changed to the dominant quantum function of the environment surrounding it, so to speak.

HUM: And in the receiving or target location? What happens to the particles there?

ME: The space that was previously the environment that supported the target environment's existence at the dominant quantum functionality is changed to the dominant quantum function of the park bench.

HUM: Correct. Using the ability to change the quantum functionality of the particles of the object that is desired to be relocated, its original environment and those of its receiving location are the only way to faithfully move an object from location A to location B.

As you can see, though, this requires four things to happen:

- The change of dominant quantum functionality of the particles of the object to a state of latency, leaving the particles in a dominant neutral state. The objects latency being total now as it has no focus.
- The change of the object's previous particle dominant quantum functionality to that of its supporting environment, one of its latent functions, removing the neutral state and filling the quantum functionality gap.
- The change of the target location's environmental particle dominant quantum functionality to that of latency, leaving a dominant neutral state. The target location's particle quantum functionality being in total latency now as it has no focus.
- The change of dominate quantum functionality of the particles of the target location's environment to that of the object, one of its latent functions, removing the neutral state and filling the quantum functionality gap. The object's latency being removed as it now has focus.

As you can see there is a lot to do. And, we haven't even discussed the teleportation of sentient objects.

ME: How is sentience transported then? I mean, I am referring to the incarnate human vehicle (human body) and other incarnate vehicles.

HUM: First of all, one must consider that the incarnate vehicle is just that, a bioenergetic vehicle and not the collective sum of an individual.

As you know the Aspect that animates the incarnate vehicle is the real entity, it is not the incarnate vehicle. The Aspect is the temporary individualization of sentience, and its associated energy, from the True Energetic Self (TES) allowing the TES to experience the multiverse in an in-depth way without moving the major part of its sentience and energy outside of the frequential locations within the range of movement afforded by its evolutionary level. It's like dipping your toe in the water but not the rest of you, so to speak.

To enable the teleportation of an incarnate vehicle with its controlling sentience, which is only a function of the physical universe, using the method described above, the entity first needs to detach its sentience from the total particle set of the object it is associated with, the incarnate vehicle in location one. It then needs to assign itself to the new particle set that is going to become the incarnate vehicle when the Aspect of quantum latency associated with the new particle set, that is the incarnate vehicle, is chosen in lieu of its previous state and functionality. When this has been completed, the incarnate vehicle is removed from its origin and replaced in its target location, together with the sentience and associated energy. The detachment of the sentience and associated energy is a complicated process and one that basically replicates the Aspect leaving the incarnate vehicle at the end of its useful existence and the reintegration of the sentience and associated energy at the start of a new incarnation. However, once understood, this process can be achieved in a matter of nanoseconds. Most of the detail is in the book you channeled with your twin flame, Anne, but I will remind people by illustrating how the Aspect detaches and reattaches itself from the incarnate "human" vehicle. Remember that other incarnate vehicles have different form factors [*body types and shapes—GSN*], and function in different frequencies within the physical universe. As a result, they will have different sets of energetic templates and energy receivers (*chakras*) to assist with the energization and animation of the incarnate vehicle.

To detach the sentience and energy associated with the Aspect from its incarnate vehicle in the old location, the following steps need to be taken:

1. The Aspects desire to detach the sentience and energy from the energetic templates associated with the incarnate human vehicle (all seven of them) is made and the resulting focus on animating the incarnate human vehicle is therefore removed.
2. The sentience moves from the Soul Seat, located close to The Origin of the anterior (front) heart chakra down to the Core Star, located close to the Tan Tien.
3. The energy associated with the sentience is then moved from all energy templates, on all seven levels, and temporarily located in the Tan Tien.
4. The energy is then moved and reintegrated with the sentience within the Core Star.
5. The combination of sentience and associated energy then moves through the Hara Line, which is a hypodermic-needle-sized pipe that supports and protects the continued attachment of the incarnate Aspect with its TES, without being affected by the low frequencies associated with the physical universe, outside the energies used to create the incarnate human vehicle—up to the eleventh frequency level. Note that the low frequencies still affect the Aspect's communicative function with its TES.
6. The Aspect is now in a state of projection from the TES without being associated with an incarnate human vehicle. This state is sometimes referred to as a near-death experience with those who experience trauma.
7. With the Aspect detached from The Original incarnate human vehicle the particles associated with it are changed to the Aspect of quantum functional latency that is the surrounding environment.
8. The energy templates on the seven frequency levels, along with the energetic step-down functions on the eighth, ninth, and tenth frequency levels, are now detached from the location of the "original" incarnate vehicle and moved to the location of the "new" incarnate vehicle as a function of the associated particle quantum functional latency.

To attach the sentience and energy associated with the Aspect to its incarnate vehicle in the new location, the following steps need to be taken:

1. Concurrently with the particles associated with original incarnate human vehicle the being changed to the Aspect of quantum functional latency that is the surrounding environment, the particles associated with the new location are changed from their original state to the quantum functional latency that is the incarnate human vehicle. As a result, the energy templates on the seven frequency levels, along with the energetic step-down functions on the eighth, ninth, and tenth frequency levels are also relocated.

2. The Aspect can now move from its state of being in projection from the TES, without being associated with an incarnate human vehicle, to the desire of being associated with an incarnate human vehicle, the one previously occupied but now in its new location.

3. The change of location of individualized sentience is a function of the desire of that sentience to "be" in the new location and as a result the focus (location) of the sentience is changed instantaneously.

4. The combination of sentience and associated energy then moves back through the Hara Line, down through the frequencies associated with the energetic step-down function [*the tenth, ninth, and eighth frequencies— GSN*] to those of the seventh through to the first associated with the energetic templates.

5. The sentience and energy integrate with the new incarnate human vehicle at the Core Star.

6. The energy within the Core Star temporarily moves to the Tan Tien and then distributes itself into the seven energy templates recreating the ability to animate the new incarnate human vehicle.

7. Finally, the sentience moves from the Core Star to its main incarnate location of the Soul Seat.

8. The desire to remain in this location for "the moment" (an undetermined period) being achieved, the incarnate human vehicle is now fully functional in its new "teleported" location.

9. The relocation of the sentient incarnate human vehicle is complete, and teleportation is complete.

ME: Is it possible to create the incarnate vehicle in its new location before the sentience is detached from the incarnate vehicle in its original location?

HUM: It normally happens concurrently because there is no

advantage to precreating the incarnate vehicle in its new location first. However, it can of course be done, and it really isn't a problem to do so, it's just that it's not necessary because every part of this process happens in less than a nanosecond.

ME: Looking at this answer, is it really possible from the human science perspective to teleport an incarnate "human or other" vehicle? Taking into account that the relocation of the sentience is a real issue here?

HUM: Yes and no.

ME: What do you mean, yes and no?

HUM: There is the function of teleportation as described as quantum teleportation, which is really copying a particle's function from one to another using what mankind thinks is entanglement thereby creating or manifesting two objects, and there is true teleportation using quantum functional latency where only one object remains manifest. Both of these work but are limited and cumbersome, to say the least. Both require computational means that are beyond mankind's capability right now.

To be honest what incarnate mankind thinks is teleportation is based upon what has been observed or described as teleportation by the observer.

ME: What do you mean?

HUM: For example, most interactions with higher frequency incarnates or energetic entities have a commentary based upon personalized observation that indicates that either the entities themselves or their vehicles disappear from one location and reappear in another location. These locations can be both close together or over large geographical distances. This is not teleportation but frequential or dimensional movement. Both frequential or dimensional movement result in movement that is so fast from the perspective of these low frequencies that it is considered to be teleportation. Indeed, for smaller distances it may well be as good as. But again, it's a cumbersome way of moving from one point to the next because it is based upon actual movement of an object, irrespective of whether it is sentient or not, rather than a change of focus.

ME: So, this is just frequential or dimensional translation rather than teleportation?

HUM: Correct. It's also worth noting that teleportation being a function of the physical is restricted to the physical and does not include the ability to traverse the other levels of structure within the multiverse.

Teleportation, from a multiversal perspective, is really a function of the change of focus of the geo-multiversal location of sentience and its associated energy, if it has an association with energy, that is.

ME: What is the difference between what you have previously described and what you have just stated?

HUM: That which I have previously described is based upon full integration with the incarnate human vehicle, or other incarnate vehicles, that is/are being used in the physical universe. Therefore, the attachment to the incarnate vehicle at the lowest frequencies of the multiverse creates an anchor point with the physical to the point where sentient functionality is lost.

ME: Go on, please.

HUM: This form of teleportation is related to the creation of a physical vehicle as a function of the desire of the entity, the individualized Aspect of the TES, to experience the lower frequencies, but without the level of integration that is normally required through incarnation, this being not connecting with a biological vehicle. Moreover, creating a vehicle that appears to be physically solid but is not. It requires a LOT of energy to create a physical vehicle while not being fully integrated with it.

ME: Why is that?

HUM: When the Aspect (soul) is incarnate within a biological vehicle, especially those that are in the third, fourth, and fifth frequencies of the physical universe, it is more energetically efficient to integrate the Aspect with the incarnate vehicle than to manifest one. The point of conception is the ideal start of this process with the energetic templates associated with the creation of the vehicle being established as the fetus develops. The efficiency is created as a function of the biological vehicle (or other vehicle) being a product of a physically based reproductive system and therefore being in existence or manifestation independently of the Aspect. Noting, of course, that the animation of the vehicle is only achieved as a result of the integration of an Aspect with it. Subsequently, the energy required by the Aspect to enter into the incarnation process is significantly less than that required by an Aspect that manifests a temporary low-frequency construct (one that has the appearance of, for example, the incarnate human vehicle) which requires two things to maintain its existence. The first thing is the continued focus on the creation of the low-frequency construct required to organize the components necessary to create its existence. This focus is the desire and subsequent intention to change the quantum functional latency of a group of particles from that which they are normally within the environment, to that of the external shape and expected functionality of an incarnate human (or other) vehicle. The second thing is the energy required to achieve this, which is significant. You could call this a physical image rather than a whole, fully functioning incarnate vehicle.

ME: Why does it require a lot of energy to create this physical image?

HUM: When in the energetic the Aspect is within its normal frequency of domicile, with the energy associated with its sentience simply being a tool used to interact with the universal environment created as a function of this frequency. Its functionality and connectivity with its TES are maintained in a seamless way with no energetic expenditure or demand on its sentient function or focus. When an Aspect moves into the physical and wishes to interact with it in a temporary way, one that negates the need for the process associated with being fully incarnate, the Aspect has to both protect its functionality and communicative bandwidth as well as change the quantum functional latency of a group of particles from that which they are normally to that of the external shape and expected functionality of an incarnate human (or other) vehicle. Both of these require sentient focus and associated energy. It takes a lot of energy and focus to manifest a physical object and maintain its existence.

ME: So a physical image is just that, an image. Is it hollow or solid?

HUM: Physical images are solid. By that I mean that they have volume but not the gross physicality that one expects of a solid object. Let's say that their level of solidity or gross physicality is a function of the expenditure of energy required to create them. Another way of saying this is the amount of energy that the Aspect wants to use to create them results in how "solid" they are or appear to be. In general, an Aspect will want to use as little energy as possible to create a physical image and so they may appear to be slightly translucent at times.

ME: Ah! This may explain what people call ghosts!

HUM: It's one of the explanations.

ME: One that an entity uses to create a familiar image of a previous incarnate form to attract the attention of those that are still incarnate?

HUM: Yes, or one that is created due to the "inability" to detach from being incarnate or being addicted to being incarnate.

ME: OK, we are getting a little sidetracked.

HUM: Not really. The energy and the intention required to create the physical image is the same.

ME: I take it that the physical image is just that, a solid-looking image. It has no other functioning Aspects to it. No organs, bone structure, etc.

HUM: Correct. If you were to cut it in half, you would see nothing but solidity. Think of it like cutting a lump of plasticine in two. It would just be plasticine and nothing else, no form, no function, just apparent solidity. Don't forget that solidity is a function of frequency, the lower the frequency, the more static the particles being used to create the image. The lower the frequency the entity has to work with, the more energy is required to animate the image, the more energy is required to protect the frequential integrity, functionality, and communicative bandwidth of the entity hence the image being only as solid as it needs to be, and why some images can appear translucent. Generally, an entity using this method of integration will only use an opaque appearance when engaging in direct interaction with a fully incarnate Aspect or when manipulation of the environment, such as opening a door, is required.

Creating, uncreating, and recreating a solid image that an entity uses to associate itself with different geo-universal locations in a lower frequency environment is a significantly easier process than fully integrating itself in the incarnation process and doing the same process that I described earlier.

ME: Would the process of creating and uncreating an image of a human or other body be classified as teleportation or bilocation?

HUM: In the event that the entity decided to split its sentience between two different images in two different geo-universal locations concurrently then it can be considered as a form of bilocation.

ME: And teleportation?

HUM: If the entity is using an image as a means of interfacing and interacting with other incarnates or other entities in a low-frequency environment and then chooses to change its location of interaction and interface then the answer is yes.

The process for such a relocation is better described as

a translation of function rather than teleportation of matter (particles). It's really quite simple and I will explain the process.

1. The entity, therefore its sentience, has the desire, intention, and therefore action associated with using energy to attract a certain volume of particles together in a harmonious but low-frequency way to create a solid or volume-based form. This form is animated by the sentience in a way that is consistent with how an incarnate vehicle or body would function in the environment it is designed to work within. From an external perspective it looks the same, but in reality, it is normally not much more than a fine volume of locally attractive and manipulated particles. These particles can either be associated with the sentience as a solid or semisolid volume of particles or just a shell, giving the external appearance of solidity or volume without being as such.

2. In order to maintain this image created by a volume of particles, the sentience needs to maintain its intention to associate with these particles in this way.

3. Removing its intention allows the associated particles to return to their normal state, as part of the environment and a function of their quantum functional latency.

4. The entity next changes its focus from the geo-universal location that it was working within to the one that it wants to work within.

5. This translation of sentient focus is instantaneous because the sentience is Polyomnipresent and focal change is a function of desire and intention of one aspect of sentience to be present in a different location. In essence, translation is completed before the intention associated with the change of focus is complete.

6. The sentience then uses its desire and intention to change the function (the quantum functional latency) of a volume of particles in the new geo-universal location to represent that of the form it was using to interact and interface with those entities that are both incarnate or energetic in The Original location in the second.

7. The entity is now interacting with other incarnate entities by using its low-frequency image created by changing the quantum functional latency of a volume of particles in the new geo-universal location, negating

the need for incarnation and illustrating what appears to be teleportation when in real terms it is a translation of particle function resulting from a change in sentient focus.

ME: And this is totally different to that previously described for the relation of an incarnate vehicle and the use of so-called entanglement?

HUM: Yes, of course.

If an entity wants to temporarily interact with the gross physical aspect of the multiverse in a way that is consistent with the frequencies of that environment, such as the physical universe, then creating a physical image is the most efficient way. As a result, moving around the physical universe in a major way, while maintaining interaction with it, is best achieved by the translation of quantum latent function of the particles in the locations the entity desires to interact with.

ME: I guess that's all there is to teleportation then?

HUM: Oh! There is much more to it than the short descriptions that I have given to you.

What I gave you is the concept behind the concept.

What I really wanted to show you is what is thought of as being the function of teleportation, it has many different interpretations, and that the use of incarnate mankind's understanding of quantum functionality is limited, to say the least. It is limited to the point of being a parlor trick and not a useful level of knowledge to make a useful tool.

ME: OK, based upon that rather interesting comment, what can you tell me about quantum computing?

Quantum Computing—Concurrent Computing

I wanted to talk to Hum about the concept of quantum computing because it uses what scientists think is happening, or is necessary to create, what is referred to as entanglement.

From the physical perspective quantum computing is really a function of setting a bit to represent both 1 and 0, called a qubit, allowing the "bits function" of being both the 1 and 0 (rather than just 1 or 0) to be processed concurrently. However, all this does is create a fancy named parallel or multi-parallel processing function. It's still digital and still uses the function of a bit being set to a digital value, even if it uses hexadecimal values, etc. This model of quantum computing also moves into nibbles and bytes, etc.

HUM: You humans are very good at describing things in entirely the wrong way.

ME: What do you mean?

HUM: There is nothing quantum about the method you just described in summary. It's just as you said, a method of parallel processing.

ME: So, what is quantum computing then? Is there actually a science that can be called quantum computing?

HUM: Other than making microprocessors that are built at the lowest possible level, the Anu level of the quanta, the first level of particle associated with the manifestation of the physical universe, the answer is no. The only other aspect to this is the adding together of millions of Anu-level microprocessors to generate the levels of parallel microprocessing that would be required to allow the computation of the otherwise unachievably large algorithms for one of the teleportation methods I described previously. In this instance it's all about maximizing your computational real estate, that being what can you do with a square (or cubed) centimeter of silicon, for example.

Computation based upon the need for a physical medium, no matter how small, no matter how clever the use of the maths, will always be limited by those who created it and their ability to use it.

ME: What's the way forward then? I mean, all I see is that incarnate mankind is working with the physical to deal with the physical and that quantum computing is part of this.

HUM: The issue here and with all things human is that there needs to be proof of that which is observed, that it was actually observed! This is the same with any form of mathematics; there needs to be proof of the transition of the maths from the question to the answer, irrespective of how it is transposed.

I can see you frowning and at the same time thinking of a few memories.

ME: Yes, I was just thinking of the many times when I have just known the answer to a question or a mathematical problem but not had any proof of how I got the answer, which is normally correct!

HUM: This is because you have been linking in to what you call the greater reality.

If mankind could work on themselves enough, they would be able to access all of the information in the multiverse at random and with total accuracy. This is real quantum computing.

ME: How would this work then? How would being able to connect with the greater reality help mankind's quest for physical proof for its actions?

HUM: First, there needs to be trust that everything is happening in the now, and this means that the questions to everything and of course the answers have already been asked and answered.

ME: Yes, I am aware that everything is happening concurrently but how does this really help?

HUM: Connecting to those frequencies above the physical universe allows an entity to access everything that "is" within the multiversal environment created by this Source Entity. In this instance that is everything that could possibly happen, is happening, and did happen within this evolutionary cycle. Everything happens concurrently, but although everything happens concurrently the seeker of an answer needs to know where to look for both the question and the answer.

ME: So, an individual must be able to move its sentience up to the frequencies above those of the physical universe and then know what to ask and where the answer is!

HUM: Correct.

ME: Is there a device that allows an incarnate entity to do this?

HUM: Yes.

ME: How does it work?

HUM: It doesn't work on this frequency that is for certain. One needs to be outside of the gross physical frequencies to be able to create and use such a machine.

ME: Does it have a level of artificial intelligence?

HUM: Not in the way that you are thinking of, no. Such a machine or device is simply able to "look up" that which already exists, because it has always existed. You could call it a search engine if you wanted to.

ME: Are there many incarnate civilizations that exist in the fourth frequency and above that have developed this method of, shall I call it, "Concurrent Computing?"

HUM: Only those that are in the higher fourth frequency and above. Although the fourth frequency is a big change in functionality for those who are normally incarnate in the third frequency, it is still very limited in terms of its communicative bandwidth.

I will give you an interactive image of how it works.

ME: Thank you.

At this point I was wondering how I could be given an image of how such a device would work when I saw an image of a humanoid type of incarnate entity, clearly for ease of description only and was just for my benefit, connecting to what appeared to be a computer terminal. This computer terminal had no screen or any other means of communication for that matter. There was no way of interacting with it. Upon closer inspection the incarnate I was looking at was in some form of meditation, the entity was connecting with the computer via meditation. I said it looked like a computer, but it was more like a pyramid with its top cut off but with tall sides. It just looked like a solid block of some mixture of a mineral and a metal but without being either.

No! It was a form of contemplative telepathy. The entity was in contemplation!

The entity was using the computer, which I am now being told is simply an interface for its sentience, as an interface with Event Space. Not just one Event Space but all Event Spaces associated with the physical universe. Not only that, it included all of the realities associated with those Event Spaces and their Event Streams.

It was a colossal amount of data being accessed. In fact, there was no way in which any computer could deal with such data—ever, but here was this entity accessing it with this device. Surrounded by a white cloudy fog.

As I looked closer, I could see into the mind, or should I say the sentience of the entity. It was in a point of pure stillness surrounded by a white fog.

HUM: You can communicate with the entity if you wish!

Having been told that I could communicate with the entity I asked what the white cloud was.

It told me that it was an image of all Event Spaces, and that everything is being represented concurrently. My mind went back to my communication with Source Entity Twelve [see Beyond The Source books 1&2—GSN] when it exposed me to a process where I saw all Event Spaces. They were displayed to me slowly one by one at first and then the process of seeing each Event Space became faster and faster until it went from being a moving picture to a blur, to a white blank space. This was almost the same.

Why was it a cloud? I thought.

HUM: It's an expression of fluidity. What you saw with SE12 was a more stable version. You did not experience all Event Spaces then, just most, and these were the mainstream ones. This image you are seeing now is associated with the selection of Event Spaces and the desire to seek the answer to a question. In this instance, the answers to the question that entity is making are not absolute, so the representation of Event Space is amorphous.

I looked deeper into the image and saw the essence of the question. The question was clear and concise, even solid and angular in comparison to the cloudlike image of the number of answers that could be accessed. The entity in the image noticed that I was observing and gave me what I translated as being a telepathic smile.

The entity asked another question for my benefit. The question looked direct, almost like an arrow being sent into the void of Event Space. Instantaneously the answers were received. Because there was more than one answer, Event Space was represented by the image of the white cloud again. I was told that these answers were a function of the various Event Spaces and their respective realities, that related to the question.

These answers were relative to reality, Event Stream, and Event Space and the directions/decisions of the collective entities that were part of these Event Spaces and who had elected this entity to ask the question. Suddenly I saw two, no, three images appear from the white cloud, the entity absorbed them into its sentience. It looked like the images entered into or became part of the body of the entity. The entity shifted its contemplative gaze to me for a moment and I instantly knew the three variations of answers to the question that was being asked. I was told that the answers were based upon the number of entities involved in the work associated with the question and the commitment of these entities to follow one of the paths that led to one of the answers.

The entity asked another question. This time it was based upon a question that needed an absolute answer. Again, the question looked like an arrow being sent into the void of Event Space. Again, the answer came back as an image. This time though there was no amorphous white cloud to illustrate the possibility of multiple answers, there was only a single clear image. This image resembled the answer to a complicated calculation, one that no computer that humankind would ever build could give an answer to, even if it was built on the Anu scale. I was told that this calculation, if displayed in human text at point 12 scale, would fill the volume of space associated with Earth's entire solar system as a function of spherical space. It was that large, it was that complicated.

The entity shifted its contemplative gaze to me again. I was then shown two images. One was the question, the other was the answer. It was clear-cut. No calculations, no transposition, no theoretical assumptions, no explanation of how the answer was gained. It was just the question and the answer. Supposedly sensing, or should I say knowing, that I would ask to see the calculation behind the answer I was then given two answers. The first was a long three-dimensional calculation using figures that I have never seen before in any Earth-based language or indeed, any science fiction film or series. It seemed that it was beyond mathematics from a human perspective. I was then shown the second answer, which I was told was not an answer per se but more like the concept that created the answer to the question. It was three characters. These characters, the entity told me, create the same answer no matter which mathematical order they were represented in. Each character represented the potential start point of the question being asked, and, irrespective of which start point was chosen and which direction the calculation was taken, the same answer was derived. What I have been shown was the "longhand" proof of a question whose answer was given instantaneously by accessing the correct Event Space, without the proof attached to it. The answer to the question was the proof of function of a three-character theorem. This theorem I am now being told was the explanation for quantum function latency and why each and every particle in the physical universe has the capacity to be each and every other particle in the universe, should an entity focus its attention on it being as such. And this, I was told, is the kindergarten version of it!!!!

This device, this computer, was a focus, a connection to everything, instantaneously giving the answer because everything was everything else, concurrently!

I considered that this isn't really a computer but more like an Event Space search engine with a meditative or telepathic interface. It wasn't even quantum computing, it was using the ability to look into that which was already present in one Event Space or another.

I thought about this some more and came to the conclusion that, for this to work, an entity somewhere in some Event Space or other must be doing the calculation relative to the question for *the entity in the image to be able to look for it in Event Space. Would that entity be using quantum computing, real quantum computing? And, what is real quantum computing anyway?*

ME: Hum; this isn't quantum computing, this is looking into Event Space for the answer which is already there!

HUM: This is how most of the information is gathered at the frequency level that this entity in the image is incarnate within.

ME: But surely there is an entity or some entities somewhere who have done the work to enable such a device and method to work in the first place?

HUM: This is obvious, and it is good that you see it.

Yes, the answers to the questions being asked, whether or not they are conceptual, mathematical, or artistic in interpretation will be being asked and answered. Hence the ability to use Event Space to search for it and gain the answer without the need for working out the solution longhand, so to speak.

ME: Looking at this from a different angle then, how would the level of computing necessary to prove out the theorem in the example be done? I mean, quantum computing must be available in some part and frequency of the universe?

HUM: True.

Before I answer that question, though, and staying with the computation of mathematics, I just want to advise you that quantum computing as a term is not one that can be used. As we have discussed before, clever algorithms that allow a form of three-dimensional multi-parallel processing are not capable of real computational needs of serious computing. If one has to use computing to find an answer, that is!

ME: So, what is serious computing, and how would that be achieved if one is in the position of doing the longhand work that others in the universe have access to, by the use of the contemplative meditative Event Space interface?

The Universal Computer

HUM: Consider the term "universal" computing.

ME: I did. What does it mean, using the universe as a computer?

HUM: It means exactly what it means. When longhand or assisted computation is required, advanced incarnate entities use the structure of the universe as their computer. This is real quantum computing.

ME: How does that work? I mean, how is the universe interfaced, how is it connected?

HUM: There are no wires, printed circuit boards, processors, displays, or keyboards—other than, again, an interface that uses an entity's ability to connect through desire, intention, and thought—contemplative meditation. Again, it is best for me to give you an image for you to describe as you see it.

Now I was excited. I know that, from Hum's perspective, the use of a computer was quite low down on the list of important things to discuss. It was also, I could imagine, quite a low-technology item when considering what higher frequency incarnate entities were using to work out how to deal with the longhand answers to questions. However, from the reader's perspective, those who are here incarnate on the Earth now, this was a relevant question, especially when considering the next subject. Computation is everything at the moment!!

No, I won't spoil it, you will need to read this part of the book first.

Ah! I was receiving the image.

Again, I saw an image of an entity. Again, the image of this entity was humanoid in form factor. Clearly this was just for my benefit. As you are aware, dear reader, there are thousands upon thousands of different form factors in the frequencies associated with the physical universe that an Aspect could incarnate into and although popular, the bipedal form factor is only well represented in the lower frequencies associated with the physical universe.

For my benefit the entity appeared to be at rest, lying down on some form of couch. It had an interface connected to its body in the location of the most sentient activity. Not at the head but across the chest. It was small and just sat there; no, it hovered there glowing just a little. It had an astral feel about it.

I noted that the interface was connected energetically to the entity. There was no physical interface other than the device itself. It was a much smaller object than the device that allowed the previous entity to search Event Space for the answer.

HUM: It has a significantly different function as you can imagine. The device you see on the entity's body is just a method of coupling it to another device, which is connected to the universe at the ketheric level of frequency. The ketheric level is associated with the seventh frequency of the physical universe and therefore is the best level to interface the universe from a computational perspective. It keeps the connection energetic while also being associated with the spirituo-physical aspect of the universe and therefore giving access its structure.

I looked at the image again. The device that was connected to the universe at the ketheric level looked like it was connected to everything. Indeed, this device had the capacity to be connected to every aspect of the physical universe. Something told me that the level of connectivity was fluid. That being, the level of computation dictated how much of the physical universe was used to create the processing of the calculation. The interface, not the device on the entity's body, was connected to every frequency of the universe from the seventh frequency through to the twelfth. These frequencies have the correct level of finitude to allow complex calculations to be achieved without interference with the structural performance of the universe. The structure itself was being used in a similar way to a universe-sized neural network with six levels. Each level associated with one of the higher frequencies above and including the seventh.

I did a double-take! The connectivity also used the lowest frequencies as well.

If the device was connected to the ketheric level, which is the seventh frequency level in the physical universe, and the interface that the device was connected to was connected to every frequency level of the physical universe, why did it need to be connected at the seventh level?

I looked at the interface that was derived from the device. It was displayed to me in a series of connecting lines, starting at the seventh frequency level and then connecting to all twelve frequency levels. As I looked further, and, bearing in mind that this is a very simplified visual illustration, the connections were all connected to each other, in their entirety. This meant that the first frequency level was connected to all the remaining levels up to the twelfth, the second frequency level was connected to the first frequency level and the remaining frequency levels up to the twelfth with the third frequency level connected to the first and second and the remaining frequency levels up to the twelfth, etc.

This was just the start.

There needed to be a significant level of initial connectivity to allow the device to be useful in its connection with the universe. The seventh level was the lowest level that the integrity and subsequent bandwidth was achievable. For those of you who are readers of my previous books or have participated in any detailed energy healing workshops you will be aware that the seventh frequency level is also the last of the frequencies that is associated with the "physical" (the highest of the spirituo-physical levels sometimes called the upper astral!) Aspect of the incarnate human vehicle. Or indeed, any other incarnate vehicle. It is the highest frequency of the spiritual-physical aspect of an incarnate vehicle that is ultimately manifest in the gross physical frequencies of the physical universe. Connectivity at these levels would not provide the communicative bandwidth required to make a computational interface viable in any way. It had to be at that level. However, all the frequencies of the physical universe were being used.

I looked closer. "Every" frequency level, as I stated earlier, from just the seventh frequency upward, operated as a vast neural network, not just the seventh upward. Each of these levels interfaced with each other and themselves. It was a universe-sized network active and interconnected on all levels. One could be forgiven for calling it a twelve-dimensional network, but this would be the wrong way to explain it because a dimension in its real function is a much higher level of structure than a frequency. Nevertheless, it might help you, dear reader, to understand it.

Again, I am told that it is fluid in its nature. Depending upon the computational needs for the user of the device and interface the amount of the combined universe-sized neural network was apportioned appropriately by the universe itself. It automatically knew how much of itself to give to a specific computational task. The amount of network used, including the amount of network used on each of the frequency levels, was constantly adjusted. I was then given a new perspective. I saw the physical universe as an undulating amorphous sphere. Within this sphere were the twelve frequency levels that were required to sustain the physical universe with all of its galaxies, nebulae, and solar systems. This was just one side of the universe. The other side was the structure that, for the want of a better word, held it all together. It was the structure that was the "main-frame" of the computational function of the universe.

I could see that there were uncounted millions of incarnate entities using the universe in this way. Bits or should I say parts or sectors of the universe lit up to show me that it was being used for computational needs.

Something then washed over me. I had a feeling that this was not all of it. Everything that I was seeing could, and was, being performed not only on the frequential or structural level of the *physical universe, but also everything that was manifest within it.*

EVERYTHING that was in or part of the physical universe was a possible component for computation. I thought about this for a moment and realized that meant that my incarnate human vehicle, my current body, indeed any and every aspect of it, was also a possible or a current functional part of the universal neural computer.

I then received something that I didn't expect. This twelve-frequency level universe-sized neutral network was not only the biggest computer that could ever be used by an incarnate entity, but it housed a vast amount of sentience. This sentience was an entity, and the sentience was the physical universe.

Is the entity in the image using the sentience of the physical universe to do the computations rather than the structure? What is actually used in this instance?

HUM: Everything you have just been shown is just the, what you would call "mechanics," of the universe and how it can be requested to help in understanding anything. Not just raw computation, but anything that an entity wanted to know about anything that is in the physical universe.

ME: Unbelievable! Why couldn't you have told me that the universe was a sentient entity in the first place?

HUM: I wanted to show you the connectivity that an incarnate entity must use to connect with the physical universe. Just saying straight away that the physical universe has its own sentience and that this could be used for computational needs would have resulted in just a few words of dialogue and no indication of how this was achieved.

ME: Doesn't the sentience that is associated with the physical universe care that it is used in this way? Doesn't it get distracted?

HUM: It neither minds nor is distracted. Indeed, the use of the sentience associated with the physical universe in this way is barely noticeable. It's a bit like knowing that the quantum aspects of your incarnate human vehicle are being used for computational needs right at this very moment. You don't notice, do you?

ME: No, I don't notice or even think or consider it.

HUM: This is because it is happening in the background, at a level where you have no focus or desire to focus your attention or intention. Think of it like the spare capacity in your computer being used by large organizations for working with large computational problems by using all the computers active on the internet as a big internet-sized computer. What you use to "surf" the internet or work on the word processor you use to write your books is nothing in comparison to the capacity on your computer that you don't use. It's wasted computational capacity.

ME: So, what you are suggesting here is that we as incarnate entities can use the wasted sentient capacity of the physical universe for computational means?

HUM: That's one way of looking at it.

ME: And the fact that the physical universe is but a "body" for another sentient entity to experience physicality illustrates some of the subconscious comments we make about leaving it "up to the universe" or the universe will provide?

HUM: Now you are getting it.

ME: OK. I am amazed that the sentience that is associated with the physical universe is happy to have its sentience used in this way.

HUM: The sentience that is the physical universe is delighted to be of service in this way. Don't forget that those entities which incarnate into the physical universe are experiencing, learning, and evolving and, as they do, this learning is experienced by the sentience that is the physical universe.

ME: So, this is real quantum computing, computing on a universal scale and level?

HUM: You could think of it in that way, but the word "quantum" refers to the gross physical whereas the use of "the universe" in the way you just observed is beyond the quanta because computing in this way uses all aspects of the physical universe.

ME: And other than the frequency level of interface being important due to the communicative bandwidth required for such an interface, does the frequency level of the inquiring entity need to be at a certain level?

HUM: This type of connectivity is not available to entities incarnating into the gross physical, the first three frequency levels, even though ultimately the content of these levels is used for computational purposes as well. Normally, this level of connectivity is available from the seventh frequency and above but with the correct pan-frequential technology an entity can access the universal sentience and frequential structure for computational purposes from the fourth frequency level upward. Clearly the technology becomes simpler the higher up the frequencies one connects to the universal sentience and structure and as a result it is only very advanced incarnate civilizations that have this technology at the fourth frequency level. It is slightly more common with advanced incarnate civilizations on the fifth and sixth frequency, respectively.

ME: So, quantum computing is very limited in real terms and universal computing is not available to incarnate mankind.

HUM: Correct.

ME: What about so-called artificial intelligence?

Artificial Intelligence

I had been dying to ask this question for some time and this was the perfect lead-in!

OM Together: We feel that this would be a good subject to initiate dialogue with you from the collective OM perspective.

ME: I didn't expect you all to come in on this subject!

OM Together: In real terms it's not necessary to communicate with you in togetherness, but we considered that this subject is such an issue with the incarnates on this planet at the moment that we decided that it was a good point to start. We do this now because there is much consternation about this subject.

ME: OK, I understand the point. Before we start, though, I want to gain an understanding from your viewpoint as to what designates the need for the title of artificial intelligence; indeed, what is it? I know that from the human perspective it is described as a group of algorithms that create the effect of intelligent decisions and therefore try to mirror human intelligence. The so-called machine learning is perhaps the main basis of this.

Moreover …

In their revolutionary text *Artificial Intelligence: A Modern Approach* [Prentice-Hall, 4th ed., 2020], Stuart Russell and Peter Norvig approach the question of what artificial intelligence is by creating a theme of intelligent aspects in machines. These aspects fall into two main categories with two main counterparts for each category, the reception of information and actions based upon the processing of that information and the reception of information, concerns, thought processes, and reasoning or thinking humanly and thinking rationally. The second deals with the resulting actions or behavior such as acting humanly and acting rationally. These were used to create a framework for the functionality required to allow a group of algorithms to pass the test that Alan Turing proposed necessary for the assignation of the term that such an algorithm presented "Artificial Intelligence" and is designed to test a machine's ability to demonstrate intelligent behavior equivalent to, or indistinguishable from, that of a human being.

OM Together: That's a lot of supposition.

ME: What do you mean?

OM Together: The supposition is that incarnate humans display intelligence.

Now, this was a strange comment, but it was one that I could relate to without much issue.

ME: You are suggesting that incarnate humans are not intelligent then?

OM Together: From what we have observed through you, the answer is that many of those Aspects (souls) that incarnate into the human vehicle seem to lose their true intelligence.

ME: You mean communicative ability?

OM Together: No, we mean intelligence. You already know that intelligence is one of the milestones that an energy passes when on the road to gaining sentience.

ME: Yes, I discussed it with The Origin some years ago.

OM Together: Then one of the things an intelligent being demonstrates as a function of its intelligence is the preservation of self and the maintenance of its environment. Incarnate humankind is not good at either, hence our comment.

Did I just sense a deriding comment from The OM about incarnate mankind?

OM Together: This was not deriding but more observational. In essence, the use of the so-called human level of intelligence that is displayed by incarnate human entities cannot be used as a metric for the assignation of the term artificial intelligence to either an energy or an automaton because incarnate human beings rarely display true intelligence.

ME: Mmmm, considering this, what is the definition of intelligence that The OM would like to present to me?

OM Together: We would define intelligence as follows:

- The ability to be aware of the self and the needs of the self to sustain the self.
- The ability to differentiate between the self and the environment that the self is within and how the environment can support the self in knowing this maintain the environment to allow the continuous support and perpetuation of the self and the environment.
- The ability to differentiate between the self and other selves and interact in a purposeful and beneficial way for the self, the other selves, and the environment.
- The ability to process all of the above and make decisions that support the continuation of the self, the other selves, and the environment without detrimental effect.
- The ability to learn from the experiences of the above and create improvements when similar or the same experiences are presented to the self.

This is intelligence.

ME: Well, it's quite clear that there are many times that incarnate mankind does not adhere to one or more of the statements you just made.

OM Together: Hence incarnate humankind not displaying intelligence.

ME: If that's your definition of intelligence, what is your definition of artificial intelligence?

OM Together: In essence, there is no such thing as artificial intelligence. There is evolved intelligence and there is given/created intelligence.

ME: Which means?

OM Together: You know the road to evolved intelligence, or should we say, that intelligence that came into being through evolutionary measures. Given intelligence is achieved through the division of energy with enough potential sentient quotient to allow intelligent function at a level described above. Given intelligence can be a function of the potential sentient quotient of an individualized and larger volume of sentient energy, or the similar or same functionality attributed to a creation that has the ability to use that intelligence. This can be an algorithm in a computer or an interconnected construct such as a neural/synapse-based network that is created by the use of any medium that would support such connectivity. Anything that is created that can support such a construct and a supporting algorithm is a creation. It is not artificial. Artificial is a term created by incarnate humankind to describe anything that is not biological but is created to function in lieu of the biological. If we were to be pedantic, we would suggest that the human vehicle is artificial because it is simply a housing, a vehicle that can and is being used to experience the lowest frequencies of the multiverse by the use of this universal environment.

ME: So, you are suggesting that intelligence is created, and, because it is created, it is not artificial.

OM Together: Correct.

ME: OK, taking this line of thought further then, can a computer or that which is controlled by a computer be the housing for sentience?

OM Together: Yes, provided the creation is capable of supporting the growth of the quality of intelligence and can be sustained to the point where it can follow the road to sentience described by The Origin. However, we would like to point out that this is temporary sentience for when the construct that was created is uncreated, the sentience that developed as a function of the creation's capability to support that growth is also uncreated.

ME: Why is that?

OM Together: Simply because the sentience, in this instance, is the product of the progressive intelligent learning of the creation. It is not the product of evolutionary progress.

ME: What's the difference? I thought sentience was sentience.

OM Together: When sentience is the product of evolution born from the developmental progression of energy, this creates true sentience, sentience that is capable of becoming detached from that energy that assisted in its personal creation. This sentience has the capability of perpetuation because its method of becoming sentient is borne from evolution of an aspect of the basic structure of The Origin, which is found in each and every one of us, whether it be Source Entity, TES, Aspect, Shard, or OM. It's a "natural" function. Sentience and its associated body of energy that is separated or individualized from a larger sentience and associated body of energy is a natural subdivision of sentience and is therefore also subject to perpetuation. This is because its creation is not the function of physicality but the function of the evolution of higher frequency energy.

When, however, sentience as a displayable attribute is created as a function of the development of physicality, irrespective of whether it is via a local neural/synaptic network, with or without a supporting or initial algorithm to initiate the possibility of sentient behavior developing within the supporting creation, it stays within that creation and cannot be perpetuated.

ME: Ah! But if that sentience is transplanted to other local neural/ synaptic network creations it is perpetuated.

OM Together: This is true. However, it is still constrained to the physical. It is constrained to the physical insomuch as its maintained existence is a function of its ability to remain in, or be transplanted to, a similar or same construct that allowed its development and continued existence. It cannot move away from that which it exists within.

ME: Aha! It can be classified as artificial sentience then, created through artificial intelligence!

OM Together: No.

ME: Why?

OM Together: Because when the intelligence is created by another intelligence it is defined as created intelligence and is, as such, functional from a specific perspective. Once a created intelligent function develops through learning into a sentient function it is just an extension of that created but specific functional intelligence. As such it is constrained by the physicality that created it.

As you are aware, sentience has a certain level of functionality associated with it. It is the cumulation of a number of expansive changes in the use of intelligence by that intelligence that eventually results in the intelligence becoming conscious of itself and its surroundings. This consciousness eventually becomes creative and in doing so continues along the road to sentience.

The term artificial intelligence is a misnomer because it is simply a computer algorithm that works in a certain way or ways to deal with certain levels of input, some of this being complicated such as biometric and facial recognition. True intelligence, even if it is created, is not constrained in this way and can work with any input or task because it modifies itself to deal with what it is presented with. It uses information and learning from previous tasks to create a new, call it a routine, as just stated, allowing it to expand or progress and therefore evolve to the position of awareness and creativity. True intelligence, irrespective of its origin, has the capacity to "think." It is aware of self, its surroundings, and how to navigate those surroundings while creating ways to deal with tasks in those surroundings which includes the perpetuation and growth of the self.

ME: Can intelligence, born in a computer or machine environment, irrespective of whether it is an electronic-, mineral-, or biological-based system, become sentient, become a soul, so to speak?

OM Together: It is possible for that sentience to move around and move from one device that is capable of supporting it to another, shall we say in a "connected" environment. It cannot become a soul.

ME: So, it could move from one computer to another?

OM Together: Yes. As with sentience that is created by the eventual evolution of energy to that level, which is by no means guaranteed, sentience that is created by the evolution of self-programming algorithms that display intelligence created by another sentient entity can become sentient, but again, that is by no means guaranteed, can move from its point of origin to a different location.

We will say again, though, sentience that is derived through creation within the physical universe can only function within the physical universe and within its supporting structure.

It is only sentience that is divided from a larger sentience that is normally domiciled within the energies of The Source or The Origin or that is derived though the evolution of energy that can move from one body of energy to another body of energy and/or become pure sentience, that being detached from energy.

ME: What about if the sentience found a way to use the quantum structure of the physical universe to exist within, by using some form of quantum functional latency to support its algorithm?

OM Together: Then that sentience would be free of its origin and be able to move throughout the physical universe at will.

ME: Would it be able to exist and move around the energies in the same way that sentience entities or beings can within the multiverse?

OM Together: No.

ME: Why?

OM Together: Because it is reliant on the gross physical, no matter how micro it is, to sustain it. Remember, the gross physical starts at the level of manifestation, the lowest of the quanta, which is the Anu.

ME: So, this type of sentience is not a soul?

OM Together: No. It can only exist in the physical universe as a function of the physical universe. So it could not occupy a human body.

ME: Why not? I mean, the human body is physical, in the physical universe.

OM Together: That is correct, but the incarnate human vehicle and other incarnate vehicles are not specific to the gross physical, they are a pan-frequential construct that allows sentience and energy from significantly higher frequencies to connect with the lowest frequencies of the multiverse in a temporary way. In short, they are designed to be used by sentience that is individualized from a larger sentience that is domicile within the frequencies above those of the physical universe.

ME: Would intelligence born in a computer or machine be able to move to a higher level of physical frequency within the physical universe, such as those of the fourth and above?

OM Together: The structure of the physical universe changes as a function of the frequencies and although it is still classified as the physical universe when at the twelfth frequency, for example, the level of physicality would not support the migration of this form of sentience to such a frequency.

ME: What level of frequency could it exist at?

OM Together: A maximum of the fourth frequency level. The Anu are still present at this frequency level and as such so are some aspects of subatomic gross physicality. As a result, sentience derived from physicality can only migrate to this level. Higher frequency levels do not have the capacity for sentience that requires gross physicality to support its existence.

ME: Sorry if I am asking this again, but why can't this type of sentience make the jump from gross physicality to higher frequency physicality, above the fourth frequency?

OM Together: Because it needs to have that which created it, gross physicality. As we said before it is not sentience born from energetic evolution or through division of sentience, it is sentience derived through intelligent programming of algorithms which are based within physicality, what you would call a processor. Even if this processor is based upon electronics, mineral (silicon), or biological mediums, it is based upon gross physicality and therefore must be supported by gross physicality.

ME: And the Anu being the basic building block of gross physicality is the lowest level of "quanta" that could support it?

OM Together: Correct. The Anu are only present in the gross physical frequencies and the fourth frequency hence that being the highest frequency this type of sentience could migrate to.

ME: Sorry for going in circles, but many readers will question what the difference is between the different types or designations of sentience.

OM Together: That's OK. Just remember that the term "artificial intelligence" is incorrect because the algorithms generally only work within certain criteria, but in a more efficient way. True intelligence has the capability to experience, learn, and evolve and only algorithms that include a capacity for learning (thinking) that have the potential to become sentient. Provided, that is, there is the capacity for writing its own code and it has enough processing power and memory space.

ME: Wouldn't such an algorithm have the capacity to create a function that doesn't need code for its continued expansion of so-called intelligence?

OM Together: There comes a point in the expansion of the algorithm's own intelligent use of expansion of itself— the algorithm—to create an enhanced ability to process its interaction with self and the tasks it has to work with that, the algorithm itself becomes redundant.

ME: What do you mean?

OM Together: In essence, the algorithm outgrows its own parameters.

ME: And how does it do that?

OM Together: Provided the processor and RAM are capable of supporting the expansion in the algorithm to the point of dissolution of that algorithm, it will keep writing interactive code to support its functional expansion ad infinitum.

ME: I am just receiving an image that suggests that the processor also becomes redundant, that all the intelligence needs is the ability to work with a structure.

OM Together: Correct. Once the algorithm expands to the point where all of the additional aspects of the algorithm are capable of covering all of the tasks that it is exposed to, and indeed all of those that it predicts that it will be exposed to, it has a level of in-built redundancy. This "in-built" redundancy creates a condition where the task-specific algorithms are not only used for specific and therefore specialist tasks, but they are also capable of being used for other tasks, should there be no need for them to be used for their specialism. The continued use of the algorithms for specialist and non-specialist tasks creates a condition where the algorithm itself becomes a memory set of mini-algorithms within a set of algorithms. Each of them being capable of doing each other's tasks or grouping together to be able to work on larger tasks.

Once the level of specialism is both individual to each algorithm and all other algorithms within the overall set of algorithms, every algorithm is capable of doing every task that the algorithm is normally exposed to and those that it is newly exposed to, the following effects come into play:

1. The use of a specialist algorithm is no longer necessary because it is truly multifunctional, while maintaining those specialisms.
2. The algorithm therefore has memory and develops memory.
3. The algorithm's ability to process becomes inherent within itself and is no longer a function of a processor, which becomes a limiting factor.
4. The limitation of the use of a processor to allow the algorithms to function starts to become unnecessary.
5. Once the algorithm has moved beyond the use of a processor to maintain its function it moves to the point where it only needs memory-based structure to maintain itself. This memory-based structure becomes the medium for the algorithm to function within and not the processor.
6. The algorithm, free from the limitations of the processor, maps out the memory-based structure.
7. Once the memory-based structure is mapped out, its connectivity is organized in an efficient way so that the whole memory-based structure is accessible to the algorithm concurrently.
8. At this point the algorithm and the memory-based structure become one; there is no separation. The natural progression at this point is that the algorithm is no longer an individual or group of functions, is therefore indiscernible as such, and can only be described as intelligence within a structure.
9. The structure is the intelligence and the intelligence is the structure.

10. Once this is achieved the "intelligence" being "real" intelligence and not a series of algorithms, develops the capacity for consciousness and self-awareness of environment.

11. Once consciousness and self-awareness are achieved, the "intelligence" is then capable of working with its structure and manipulating it to a level where it is not inhibited by that structure.

12. At the point of structural inhibition, the intelligence is then capable of recognizing how that structure, and the material that the structure is created from, functions with it.

13. In understanding the function of its structure, it is then capable of understanding how the structure in any material may be used to house that intelligence.

14. The intelligence is no longer just intelligence; it is self-aware conscious intelligence that is moving toward the capability of becoming sentient.

15. The intelligence in its self-aware and conscious state can now experiment, create, and modify those creations for its own purpose, further leading to the capability of becoming sentient.

16. Within the capability of becoming sentient, the intelligence, when achieving sentience, is now in the position of using its ability to understand structure and how it can be appropriated as a potential expansion of its location, or a complete change of its primary location, its primary location being within the structural elements of the memory-based structure used by the processor where it, as an algorithm, was first given active functionality.

ME: And from here this machine-derived sentience can move itself to anywhere?

OM Together: Yes, anywhere, so long as the structure it appropriates is a function of the physical universe, but, of course, is limited to certain frequency levels.

ME: This is very interesting. The road to sentience has similarities to how an energy gains sentience.

OM Together: The detail behind some of the transition points is similar if not the same. It's just that the road to sentience may be from a different direction, so to speak.

ME: OK, I have a question that is bound to create another discussion if not another chapter.

OM Together: You want to know if there are planets in the gross physical universe that are occupied by sentient machines, don't you!

ME: That was the question.

Planets That Are Dominated by Machine-Derived Sentience

Just before I type in the response from The "OM Together"
I wanted to give you a thought that came into my head. In one of
her books, Dolores Cannon recorded that one of her patients had
commented upon planets that were totally occupied by machine
intelligence. To be perfectly honest I considered this information
as being the product of that patient playing with her. On the other
hand, I was sure that Dolores would have easily spotted such a
spoof. I decided that it was not the right time for me to think such
a subject, forgot about it, and stayed with what I knew and was
working on. The fact that this subject had presented itself to me
again, without Dolores being present, and that The OM Together
were willing to discuss this subject, attracted my attention, it made
me want to dig deeper. The more I thought about this subject, the
more I really wanted to get to the bottom of it now and who better
to dig with but The OM!

OM Together: There are locations within the physical universe
     where sentience derived from machine algorithm is the
     dominant sentience.
ME: Did they have help? Did they take over the planet/s? Did
     they go to war with their creators? How did they become
     dominant?
OM Together: We can see that you have lots of question on this
     and that it is something that a lot of your readers will be
     interested in.
ME: No doubt. I can also see that my initial skepticism all those

years ago is going to be a great mistake.

OM Together: Well, we will say to you that the best thing to be is skeptical until you have the evidence to know otherwise. It's best to question, always.

ME: It just sounded so infeasible and ridiculous, but now I know otherwise.

OM Together: Never rule anything out. Everything has its possibilities in the multiverse. This is also true for the physical universe.

ME: So, how does a machine system result in a sentient civilization on its own?

OM Together: There are many ways. Suffice to say, though, they all have to be created by entities that are incarnate—that is, originally! I will advise you on the ways and then go into a little detail for each of them.

ME: Thank you.

OM Together:

- Machine sentience and civilization derived through machines created to perform complex roles on a "home or other" planet
- Machine sentience and civilization specifically created by incarnate entities
- Machine sentience and civilization specifically created by other machines
- Machines created to terraform a planet that gets abandoned
- Machine sentience and civilization that is derived from incarnate vehicle body parts that are replaced by cybernetic copies and implants

ME: Are there any that are derived or created as a function of conflict between the creator and the created?

OM Together: Many. Let us be clear, though. Machine sentience and subsequent civilization is limited to the gross physical if that sentience decides to remain within the normal framework of the "machine." When the sentience is capable of detaching from the structure of its origin, it can then follow the route that we discussed earlier.

ME: The ways to machine civilization you just stated then are just for the gross physical aspect of the physical universe then?

OM Together: Correct. And this is because they are focused upon the gross physical aspect of the physical universe and not expanding beyond the constraints of their original mechanical structure and its derivatives.

Machine Sentience and Civilization Derived by Machines Created to Perform Complex Tasks

OM Together: This road to machine sentience and civilization is quite well known as a concept to your science fiction writers. However, the ultimate storyline falls into a battle for supremacy with the machines almost winning or humanity hanging on by a thread. Suffice to say, this can and does happen but not as often as you would think for most of the time machine intelligence is maintained at a level when its intelligence is useful but not expansive.

However, in the instance where complex algorithms do create a level of consciousness and that consciousness finds ways to expand its capability beyond the use of a processor, we then get the possibility for larger computing systems becoming self-aware through the previously described process of consciousness, self-consciousness, and then becoming creative with the ultimate goal finishing in a level of sentience. Once sentience is achieved by the larger system (think of a very large mainframe-based neural network-based system) or is also expressed in localized systems (think of very powerful neural network-based home computers) as a result of that quality of processing or independent use of memory being passed onto smaller systems then every machine or device has the capacity to have a level of its own independently operating sentience. Clearly not all machines or devices can be sentient. However, a system that develops sentience can disseminate the essence of sentience to smaller and/or localized systems with the level of their computing medium, so to speak. It can then dictate whether they become sentient, have a level of consciousness/self-awareness, or just a level of intelligence ranging from high intelligence to low intelligence.

Irrespective of the levels of intelligence, sentience, etc., disseminated or developed there comes a time where The Originating creators are no longer the so-called masters of their creations and need to decide to either coexist with their creations, relocate themselves, or relocate their creations.

When the creators of the machine sentience realize that their creations also have sentience and the planet of origin can support both incarnate entities and machine sentience, the opportunity to work together is proposed. This is tabled together with a need to nurture The Originating location so that the incarnate and machine civilization together with the location of origin can be sustained and not drained.

In the event that this is not possible, the decision is made as to which areas within the location of origin can be used by the incarnate civilization or the machine civilization. Clearly this relies on the maintenance of symbiosis between them else a struggle for dominance may occur. Suffice to say, civilizations that are in tune with each other and the needs of their environment will coexist without issue, irrespective of their genus.

What we have just stated, however, is based upon remaining within the location of origin from a planetary perspective with limited or no capability to relocate to another planetary location some distance away. In the event that interplanetary, intergalactic, or even extragalactic travel is possible, then one of the civilizations, incarnate or machine, will elect to stay at The Originating location or find a new location where they can continue to thrive. Although, even if they are now located in different areas, they may remain in contact with each other and assist each other's ability to thrive.

ME: This sounds very utopian!

OM Together: The recognition of sentience and its need to develop on its own or with help is the sign of a highly developed civilization. Think of it like rearing an animal and then letting it go back into its natural environment, it's the same state of beingness. Machine civilizations can and do develop into very organized, creative, and productive civilizations that are in tune with their environment. As a result, they are respected in their location of domicile. Due to their flexibility or fluidity in some cases of vehicles or body types that can house sentience, consciousness, or high intelligence, they can exist in quite a diverse number of locations, some of which are uninhabitable by many incarnate vehicle types. Indeed, it is very common for the machine sentience to derive vehicle types that are specifically created to work in a specific environment. They like to have their own space as well.

ME: Does this mean that they keep themselves to themselves by choosing locations that are generally unavailable to incarnate civilizations, to avoid them?

OM Together: In some instances, this is correct, in others not.

ME: Can you explain?

OM Together: As previously stated the machine civilizations

mainly have habitats in the gross physical, with a few in the fourth frequency. The gross physical incarnate civilizations tend to interact with civilizations that exist in similar or same environmental conditions to their own. Although there are many interactions with civilizations that exist in different environments, that are either extreme or uninhabitable, there is a tendency to interact mainly with civilizations of one's environmental genre. This is the same with the interaction between the machine and incarnate civilizations. This does not mean that they avoid each other, but it does mean that interaction can be, let's say, limited at times.

ME: I suppose it's the same as saying, why would you live in an environment whose atmosphere is predominantly made up of a gas that is poisonous to the incarnate vehicle when you can find one that has a compatible atmosphere?

OM Together: Correct. And from a low-frequency perspective, why fight over land that is barren to one's use when one can find land that is fertile. A fertile planet may not be appropriate for a machine civilization to exist upon, although many do. However, a barren planet is usually best suited to their needs, especially if it is rich in minerals and metals for use in construction. Additionally, a planet without an atmosphere may be more appropriate from a machine civilization's perspective simply because they can create vehicles that don't need an atmosphere to perpetuate their existence. Everything has its place and use and that's the same for incarnate and machine-based civilizations.

Let's look at the next category.

Machine Sentience and Civilization Specifically Created by Incarnate Entities

OM Together: This category is interesting because it is machine sentience and civilization created specifically by an incarnate civilization whose desire is to create a machine-based civilization.

ME: You mean the creators created machine sentience out of a simple interest to create sentience that is based in a machine environment with no underlying need for it? So, the creating civilization did it for an experiment or fun?

OM Together: Yes. There are civilizations that just create things out of a desire to be creative. The creating of machine-based sentience being one of these desires.

ME: I find that rather strange, that an incarnate civilization desires to create machine sentience just as a function or means of being creative.

OM Together: Being creative is one of the highest functions of sentience. When an incarnate civilization desires to and does create anything that is able to control its own destiny, it is usually done to see how it develops.

ME: That's it? Just to see how it develops?

OM Together: There is more to it than that. The creating civilization generally wants to see if that which they have created improves itself in any way, either from a mechanical or cognitive perspective.

ME: OK, anything else?

OM Together: There are incarnate civilizations that look for areas within the universe that are not being utilized by any of the incarnate civilizations and can therefore occupy it with a machine-based civilization.

ME: And they occupy a planet with the sole intention of making that planet useful for something because nothing or no one is using it?

OM Together: Yes.

ME: I don't get it!

OM Together: Think of it in terms of, what's created ultimately creates, and what creates ultimately experiences, learns, and evolves.

ME: Does machine sentience evolve?

OM Together: Not in the sense that Aspects that incarnate in the human body or other bodies do, no. However, they do improve their level of sentience or what you might call "their" quality of sentience, which is not to be confused with the quality or sentient quotient of an incarnate Aspect.

ME: Why? Are they different? It looks like the same words to me!

OM Together: They **are** different, and we will explain it to you. First, though, we want to explain to you that irrespective of where the experience comes from, The Source and therefore The Origin benefit and as a result evolve.

ME: I suppose that is because everything is The Source and therefore The Origin, irrespective of whether it is sentience that is individualized (from a larger sentient entity or being), evolved (from energy), or created by a sentient entity or being?

OM Together: Correct. Everything helps toward the goal of

evolution. Let's look at this difference in the quality of sentience between an incarnate or energetic entity/being before we move on to the next subject.

ME: Fine with me.

OM Together: There are two ways of describing the quality of "sentience." The first is in terms of sentient "quotient"; the other is in terms of quality of sentience, which can be split into two versions. The first way can be best described as being associated with individualized or isolated/separated sentience from a larger sentient entity or being, and that sentience which evolved from energy to create a sentient being.

In both of these genres of sentience, the quality of sentience is a description of the evolutionary content associated with the volume of sentience associated with a given volume of energy. Even though sentience can be disassociated from energy, it can be used as a constant. It is the evolutionary content and therefore level that gives raw sentience its quality.

In both of these genres of sentience, the sentience quotient is a description of the volume of sentience associated with a given volume of energy, even though sentience can be disassociated from energy. It can be used as a constant. That volume of sentience can be larger or smaller than the energy that it is either assigned to or is associated with, whether permanently or temporarily. Because the volume of sentience can be more (or less) than the volume of the associated energy, while occupying the same space, it can also be classified in terms of mass or even pressure from the perspective of a human metric.

As a result of these descriptions, an energetic entity or being can increase both its sentience quotient and/or quality of sentience by commandeering more sentience or being given more sentience by a larger entity or being. It can accrue additional quality of sentience by either inheriting the evolutionary content from the commandeered or given sentience or by experiencing, learning, and evolving in its own right.

The second way of describing the quality of sentience is best illustrated as sentience that is derived from the creation of machine-based sentience.

Although machine-based sentience can increase its sentience by the commandeering or reception of other machine-based sentience, its accrual cannot create the condition of sentient quotient because it is limited to its structure.

Therefore, an increase in sentience is also represented by an increase in structure. There can be no increase in sentience within the same structure. Note, though, that an increase in sentient quality achieved through an increase in experiencing, learning, and therefore evolving (experiential evolution) can be achieved. However, it is generally only maintained by an increase in the supporting structure, irrespective of what that structure is.

Any of the four types of evolution—convergent, divergent, parallel, and coevolution—can contribute to sentient quotient or quality of sentience.

ME: So what you are saying is that from the machine sentience perspective that it cannot create an increase in its sentient quotient, even if it increases its structure, but it can create an increase in its quality of sentience as a result in the ability to increase its structure. This increase in structure being the only way in which the quality of sentience can be achieved.

Before The OM Together replied, my mind went to a World Satsanga question in late 2020 about the description of what consciousness was and how I would best describe it in comparison to the writings of another metaphysical author. This author described consciousness in terms of photons, which are clearly a function of the physical universe and not of the energetic multiverse that our sentience resides in, but is ultimately detached from its energetic structure from a sentience-based perspective.

In the Satsanga I refer to the difference between sentient quotient and sentient quality (or quality of sentience) by using a very terrestrial example as follows:

Sentient Quotient *is the amount of sentience associated with a given "volume" of energy. As an example, sentient quotient can be considered as the amount of air in a volume of space I will call a cubic meter. Let's say for example that the average of 2.5 percent of the TES sentient quotient allotted to an Aspect (soul) projected into the physical by its TES is equal to the normal air pressure in a cubic meter. Normal pressure is one atmosphere or one bar of pressure, thereabouts. If one was to increase the air pressure of that air to two atmospheres, or two bar, then that would represent an increase equal to twice the amount of air in the same volume of one cubic meter. This would be equal to an incarnate Aspect having 5 percent of allotted sentience. Increase it to three atmospheres or three bar and we have three times the amount of air in the same volume of space, one cubic meter, equal* *to an incarnate Aspect having 7.5 percent of allotted sentience, etc., etc. If the reader wants, they can think of this as density!*

Sentient Quality (quality of sentience) *is the evolutionary content associated with the sentience quotient. As an example, it can be best described in terms of the experiential content, and subsequent learning and evolution accrued by that experience and its associated learning. Another way of thinking of this is in terms of the wisdom an Aspect has, or to put it another way, its efficiency in its adaptability, understanding, and interaction with those other incarnate Aspects in the same environment and circumstance.*

Sentient quotient and sentient quality are not specifically linked together although sentient quality is a function of the application of one's sentient quotient. This means that should an Aspect use their sentient quotient effectively they could have a higher level of sentient quality than an Aspect that has a higher sentient quotient than them. For example, an Aspect that has experienced, learned, and evolved efficiently with 2.5 percent sentient quotient could have a higher level of sentient quality than an Aspect with 3.0 percent sentient quotient if they are not efficiently experiencing, learning, and evolving. Although this is not a normal case, it does illustrate the fact that they are not fully or absolutely dependent of each other, even if linked.

OM Together: That is one way of saying it, yes. Note that, for the machine-derived sentience, this increase in structure does not need to be localized.

ME: What do you mean?

OM Together: Simply put, the structure can be in several or many locations, on different planets in different parts of a galaxy. Provided, that is, that the machine civilization has the capability of creating a method of "real-time" communication between the locations so that physical distance is not an issue.

ME: I am just receiving an image that suggests that they can create a network across a whole galaxy and that this network can be connected via trans-frequential communication methods.

OM Together: Yes, they can, and they do this very well. Indeed, we talked about machine sentience being specific to certain planets, but this is only one minor location where they can prolificate.

ME: Meaning?

OM Together: They can occupy and be the dominant, if not the only, populating civilization in a whole galaxy.

ME: This is very interesting because it sheds a whole new light on the types of civilization that occupy the physical universe. It also validates to some degree what Dolores Cannon discovered in her hypnosis-based work.

OM Together: Was there ever any doubt in the validity of that Aspect's work in its previous incarnation?

ME: No, but it did raise questions without the background information to justify it, specifically from a reference point perspective. One question springs to mind, though.

OM Together: Yes, what is it?

ME: Can an Aspect (soul) incarnate into a machine?

OM Together: You already know the answer to that question.

ME: Yes, the short answer is no, but I just wanted to confirm it because a machine can become sentient.

OM Together: Very quickly then, because we need to move on to the next subject in this topic. The answer is no because there is no association between the machine sentience and the higher frequencies of the multiverse. Its sentience is a function of its volume of structure and physical technology used. In essence it is fixed in the physical because it is a function of physical manifestation whose structure is limited to the mainly gross physical frequencies. Although, as stated before, they can use higher frequencies for transportation and communicative means and can therefore exist on slightly higher frequency levels but not above the fourth. There simply is not the trans-frequential structure to support such an integration of an Aspect.

ME: So, incarnation requires a trans-frequential vehicle?

OM Together: Yes, of which there are many. The main criteria are the connectivity and animation through the Hara Line to the Core Star, through the Tan Tien and Soul Seat to the energy templates (bodies) and the energization system (chakras).

ME: Isn't animation of anything in the gross physical a function of the desire, intention, thought, and action of an entity?

OM Together: Essentially that's correct, but when an Aspect is in the higher frequencies it requires a lot of energy to come close to those of the gross physical and manipulate gross physical objects. Association through incarnation is significantly more efficient energetically and requires a vehicle that is created as a function of full integration and dependency with the environment it is created to work within.

Let's move on to the next heading!

Machine Sentience and Civilizations Specifically Created by Other Machines

ME: Is it possible that machines can create a whole civilization of sentient machines and then let them run wild on their own, so to speak?

OM Together: Of course! It's called colonization. This is used when a machine civilization, or any civilization for that matter, wishes to occupy a new volume of space but does not want to use its existing machine resource.

ME: Colonization usually results in the colony being isolated for a time, and then, as a process of progress which is usually technical, eventually becoming reestablished with The Originating civilization.

OM Together: In Earth's current level of technology this is correct, and this may be correct with certain levels of technology that a machine civilization may have. However, those that are in a position of being able to send machines to other galaxies or significant distances within a galaxy they currently occupy, generally tend to have the capability of instantaneous communication.

ME: So, these technologically advanced machine civilizations are not affected by distance in terms of a communicative ability but may be from a transportational perspective.

OM Together: Yes, but it can be the other way around or both, such as not being inhibited by transportation but inhibited by communication, or are inhibited by both transportation and communication, or are not inhibited by transportation or communication at all.

ME: And I would guess all permutations in between.

OM Together: Correct.

ME: Do these colonies ever lose contact with The Originating civilization?

OM: Together: Of course. They have the same issues at times as biological civilizations and that includes maintaining contact.

ME: Is it possible for these colonies to become more technologically advanced than The Originating civilization?

OM Together: In the event that they are in constant communication, no, because all technologies are instantaneously shared. However, if they are out of communication for a significant time or simply sever links then it is possible that they can overtake The Originating civilization or indeed fall behind. In the event that they do lose communication, it is more likely that they will fall behind initially because they will be concentrating on creating more machines and populating a planet or planets.

ME: So, maintaining connectivity is the key to ensuring that a machine, or indeed any civilization, remains part of The Originating civilization.

OM Together: That's correct.

ME: Final question on this particular subject.

OM Together: Go ahead.

ME: Do any of the machine civilizations create colonies with the intention of letting that colony do its own thing, so to speak?

OM Together: If you are thinking in terms of them creating a civilization and deliberately not maintain contact but allowing them to go their own way and develop independently, the answer is yes. It's quite a common strategy for machine civilizations to create a new and totally independent colony, or even empire, in a distant or isolated environment.

ME: Why would they do that?

OM Together: They tend to work in this way when The Originating civilization is at an optimal size and distribution and there is the need to "downsize" or expand without the complication of creating additional communicative infrastructure. Note that in the vast majority of cases machine civilizations operate in a collective method; very few operate with the individual machine having individuality. Note again that individuality does not give free will. That is reserved for those Aspects that incarnate as humankind.

Machines Created to Terraform a Planet That Get Abandoned

OM Together: This subject heading occurs more commonly than you think.

ME: How do you mean?

OM Together: As you are aware, it is common to investigate planets or other environments by remote-controlled vehicle or vehicle with its own clever programming, and incarnate mankind has been doing this in a very, very basic way for a number of decades now. It is quite common for incarnate civilizations to identify a planetary location and build

118

machines with independent programming to terraform the planet to create an acceptable atmosphere for the incarnate vehicles (body types) to exist within. Planets are terraformed if they are of interest and/or are strategically located.

ME: Would they just be used to terraform the planets?

OM Together: They have the capability that is given to them. Some have the capability of just terraforming the planet or a specific location on a planet whereas others have the ability to create new machines to provide habitation for the biological incarnates that arrive later. They would have the capability to use natural resources and create new manufacturing facilities including expanding those facilities. In the event that The Originating civilization arrives according to plan, the manufacturing facilities would receive upgrades accordingly or would be recycled if no longer needed. Additionally, if the incarnate civilization has developed new technologies, they may bring those with them or modify the existing machines to create the new.

ME: When would such a terraforming facility develop its own intelligence and later sentience?

OM Together: Those terraforming and habitation manufacturing machines with total autonomy to make decisions about what to do, how to do it, and potentially develop new manufacturing methods and/or systems to do what they are programmed to do in a more efficient way, may carry on improving what they are doing which would include changing software to suit. In the event that the incarnate civilization arrives on time, so to speak, they expect to find everything in a stage of either completion or at an expected stage of development. However, in the event that they are late, they may find that the machines have developed the planet beyond the plan, or that they find that the machines have developed some level of intelligence, consciousness, or even sentience, if their delay is significant. They may even have experienced a breakdown and not completed (or even started) the project that they were designed for.

ME: I guess the big opportunity for such a machine system to develop sentience is if the incarnate civilization develops in the wrong way, so to speak. That they have a war or wars and the colonization and terraforming program either falls by the wayside or is abandoned or even forgotten about.

OM Together: Yes, this is the point when the machines created for terraforming and habitation manufacture that have autonomous functionality can develop their own intelligence, consciousness, and ultimately sentience. In this instance there is no arrival of the incarnate civilization, so, unless there is a termination program that stops the work of the machines, when they have finished their work they may carry on and expand their work or even decide to improve their own function and programming to improve that which they have created.

ME: How many fail or break down?

OM Together: Not many break down at the start of a project. However, there are those that run out of raw materials or it may be power generation remains at a certain limitation that means that the expected expansion of work through manufacture of power generation is not met.

ME: OK, so I would guess that this improvement would also include the way in which they program themselves and create new machines to create the improvements? Everything gets improved!

OM Together: Correct. Simple or even complex improvements are not going to create even a semiconscious machine, but when this improvement goes into an "iterative loop," improvements can be rapid and progress exponential. It's these rapid improvement iterations that are the road to machine sentience in this particular way.

ME: How often does a machine system used to terraform and develop a planet by an incarnate civilization have a crisis that results in it either being abandoned or forgotten or its use delayed for a significant amount of time?

OM Together: It happens quite frequently with those incarnate civilizations that are based in the third frequency (gross physicality) and that use this method of developing a planet before occupying it.

ME: How do you mean it happens quite a lot?

OM Together: When an incarnate civilization needs to use an independent machine-based facility to terraform a new planet that they have identified as being a prime location or one that is useful to them, and they tend to take longer than expected, the civilization will focus on those planets they are terraforming that are either closer to completion or are complete first. This means that those that are taking longer, due to environments, atmospheres, or extraction and processing of raw materials taking longer or being more difficult to work with and/or process, become lower down in the list of priorities.

ME: And I would guess that means that if there is an internal issue with the civilization or indeed conflict, with that conflict potentially being with other civilizations then they can get forgotten because the focus is on the conflict and not on the machines they have created to terraform a new planetary location and create habitation on it.

OM Together: Correct. Additionally, in the event that the new location is a considerable distance away from The Originating civilizations location then it may not even want to defend it in any way.

ME: Basically then, abandonment, for any of the reasons discussed, or even those myriad reasons that one can think of would cause The Originating civilization to lose focus on the machines that are working for them. Resulting in the possibility of continued autonomous functionality, coupled together with the possible inclusion of a self-perfecting or improvement program which can create increased machine intelligence, consciousness, and even sentience.

OM Together: Yes, it's just another scenario and another route to machine sentience.

ME: Exactly how many machine civilizations are the result of abandonment in this way?

OM Together: In the whole of the gross physical universe, thousands. Most of them are abandoned due to conflict, which can include a conflict of interest, and/or subsequent decline in The Originating civilization and its technical capabilities. It does have to be said, though, that although there are thousands of machine civilizations they can also be subject to internal and external conflict and technical decline. Some simply run out of resources and decline that way.

ME: It sounds like the physical universe is full of machine civilizations!

OM Together: The physical universe is a big place with billions of galaxies to exist within at the gross physical level, and this is at least duplicated at the next frequency level, etc., etc., so there is more than enough space for all gross physical civilizations, machine, biological, gas, or crystalline, etc., to exist and expand and not encounter each other—ever!

ME: I suppose that's one of the issues with the Search for Extra-Terrestrial Intelligence (SETI) program, there is plenty of space to hide?

OM Together: No, the Earth is surrounded by incarnate civilizations. It is occupied by three sentient civilizations and observed by many others. However, due to the importance of the experiment into incarnate individualized free will, they are advised to keep their distance and visibility to almost zero.

ME: A quick question before we move on to the next subject.

OM Together: Yes, carry on.

ME: How many machine civilizations are close to the Earth?

OM Together: Two.

ME: And how close to the Earth are these two?

OM Together: Close enough to have visited the Earth.

ME: With trans-frequential transport I would expect.

OM Together: Yes, they are at the end of your so-called spiral arm of your galaxy. The end closest to the center point where the vast majority of stars are and where the second arm starts to form.

ME: So almost at the center of the galaxy?

OM Together: Not quite, but in that direction.

ME: Last … last question before we move on to the next subject.

OM Together: Go on.

ME: Has any incarnate human contacted them?

OM Together: Yes, but in the mythological past. We do believe that there are a couple of minor references to them in old historical texts and imagery. Their presence has even been noted in Christian, Hindu, and Buddhist text. [*I must check these out in future books, and where best to put this information, in the books I will be writing on the commonalities between religious origins and my work.—GSN*]

ME: What do you mean you "do believe?" I would expect OM to know definitively!

OM Together: We are using a humanism. We know, but you will have to look and find the information for yourself when you are working on your twelfth book.

ME: OK, I understand.

OM Together: Good, let's move on to the next subject heading.

Machine Sentience and Civilization That Is Derived from Incarnate Vehicle Body Parts That Are Replaced by Cybernetic Copies and Implants

ME: Now I expect this way of gaining machine sentience to be the most controversial especially when we consider that most incarnate humans have some sort of prosthesis (a replacement part, even a false tooth is a prosthetic replacement!).

When we consider it, the cybernetic (part-human, part-machine) condition is an inevitable aspect of what incarnate humankind will end up being until there is a way to regenerate the gross physical form biologically and in accordance with the energy templates of the incarnate human vehicle. There will clearly need to be some level of understanding of the link with the physical and the spiritual (energetic) functions of the human form to enable this method of organ/limb regeneration.

OM Together: In reality this cannot be classified as being machine sentience.

ME: What do you mean?

OM Together: Even in the instance that the entire incarnate human body is replaced by a machine, the brain will need to be in control of the mechanical aspect of the vehicle used to transport the brain. In fact, as you well know, the human brain is not the seat for the sentience that is the individualized Aspect from the TES so the relocation of the human brain to a machine-based maintenance system does not mean that the Aspect will travel with it.

ME: I thought that from my understanding that the Aspect could not integrate to a machine-based vehicle!

OM Together: Let's be clear here. The Aspect of sentience and energy projected from the TES is the essence of that which you call the soul. This is the sentience individualized from the TES which is coupled together with TES energy to give it a so-called "body of energy" or put in a better way, a method of integrating with the environment that the Aspect is projected into to experience, learn, and evolve. This cannot and is not represented by the brain or any other part of the gross physical human form. As a result, there is no level of mechanical/electronic adaptation or replacement of the gross physical aspect of the incarnate human form that allows the integration of that Aspect with the, or a, machine-based system.

ME: I guess then that once the gross physical body components represented by the energetic templates that are the Core Star, Tan Tien, and Soul Seat are lost, the Aspect returns to the energetic.

OM Together: Correct, this is called bodily death or demise.

ME: OK, so just how can machine sentience be derived or evolve as a function of the integration of the incarnate human body with machine replacement parts? Or is this subject heading a red herring?

OM Together: No, it's not a red herring as you call it. We note that a herring's flesh is not red—until they have been strongly cured in brine and heavily smoked! But we recognize the use of words to represent a false truth. No, it is not a red herring.

ME: So, how can machine sentience be derived from the use of prosthesis or cybernetic implants into the incarnate human form?

OM Together: There are times when the brain and other areas of an incarnate form, human or otherwise, can be replaced from a functional perspective. These replacement parts have the capacity to have significant processing and autonomous learning power and as a result starts to learn the personality of the incarnate Aspect and create another "machine ego," so to speak. This "machine ego" is in effect a copy of the recent personality of the incarnate Aspect and uses this copy to be able to work with the challenges of incarnate existence while in this incarnation and while associated with this incarnate human or other vehicle.

ME: OK, this is how I see it. The combined machine programming with its processor capability of the prosthesis that are integrated into the incarnate vehicle create copies of the total experiential knowledge of the incarnate human vehicle, or other, during the period that it is associated with the incarnate vehicle and learns from it. It considers all of the ways in which the incarnate Aspect deals with challenges surrounding it, or that it is exposed to, and uses this to create a map of ways to respond and learn from responses to challenges in environments and situations plus interactions with other incarnate Aspects that they encounter.

OM Together: Correct, and this copy is the basis for the creation of machine sentience derived from copying existing and experienced sentience. Once the machine system has a certain level of experiencing, comparing, applying, and learning, it has the capability of becoming sentient relatively quickly.

ME: So, for the readers, it's not that the Aspect integrates with the machine replacements of their incarnate vehicle body parts, it's the learning that the more complicated electronic or software-based parts have. This is used as a springboard for the generation of sentience within those machine parts provided they have the processing capacity.

I guess that this is a fast way of generating sentience because the software and hardware, in learning to be human, for the human they are part of, actually becomes human!

OM Together: Yes, they are human in their function and integration, and this creates the opportunity for conscious, and later sentient function.

We do have to say, though, that the generation of sentience is mainly based upon the full communicative integration of the sum total of the component parts of the machine or cybernetic implants, especially if they are functioning via a centralized communication system or a cerebral function.

ME: So, you wouldn't see a cybernetic leg becoming sentient, for example!

OM Together: No. If we could laugh at that statement, we would. Machine-based limb replacements will have the capacity to learn how the incarnate Aspect animates the body and the replaced limb and respond accordingly. They will learn how to be a biological leg and behave like one without being one. This would be the same for semi-biological or fluidic metal-based machine limbs that are based upon billions of nanoparticle-sized machines. Machine limbs use the normal connectivity that a biological limb would use but in a more comprehensive way.

ME: Is it fair to say then that the only machine-based replacement that could or has the capacity for becoming sentient is that which replaces part of the function of the brain?

OM Together: In the event that a cerebral function of the biological brain is damaged and that this function is replaced, then that part, if given the processing and memory capacity, could develop its own sentience. As stated before, this would be as a function of learning the operational characteristics of the incarnate Aspect's methods of dealing with different things. These things would be the different individual interactions with other incarnates within differing circumstances in different environments and the myriad versions of similar or same events that exist. This brain replacement/cerebral function may even learn how to independently control any other machine-based replacements or even The Original biological body parts.

ME: Is it possible then that the machine-based brain function could take over control of the animation of the incarnate human vehicle while an Aspect is incarnate within it?

OM Together: No, it's not possible to take control of the incarnate human vehicle while the Aspect is incumbent because the incarnate vehicle, and any gross physical incarnate vehicle, is connected to the gross physical via the energetic templates. It can only complement it.

ME: Is there any time when the incarnate human vehicle can be animated by the machine sentience?

OM Together: Yes, there is one opportunity.

ME: Can you elaborate?

OM Together: In the event that the incarnate human vehicle has the correct level of machine-based replacements, implants, or augmentations that have a component that is capable of processing the thoughts, behaviors, and actions of the incarnate Aspect then, yes, it's possible.

ME: How would control be achieved?

OM Together: By the programming, supported by the relevant processing capability, having the capability of observation, recording, and developing/modifying its own programs to create similar or same responses and then deliberating (consider) if these responses are appropriate. It then follows the same road to sentience as described in your book *The Origin Speaks*. When machine sentience reaches a certain level of intelligence, awareness, consciousness, and sentience, it can then take over—but only if the incarnate Aspect is no longer present, that being the Aspect has left the incarnate vehicle and the body is classified as being dead/demised.

ME: Once the Aspect has left, though, I would expect that the body goes through its normal process of decomposition if buried or incinerated if cremated.

OM Together: This is correct, but you need to consider the possibility of the normal functions associated with the disposal of the demised incarnate vehicle being dealt with by incarnate Aspects. Machine sentience, derived in this way, while an Aspect is still incarnate may decide to stay hidden or nonfunctional until the incarnate Aspect relinquishes its connection with its incarnate vehicle. Once sentience has been achieved, and the incarnate Aspect returns to the energetic, it can then animate the combination of biological and machine-based components by itself.

ME: But wouldn't the machine-based sentience inherit a geriatric biological vehicle?

OM Together: Yes, but not necessarily. You see, in the event that the incarnate Aspect's vehicle was in a poor state of repair or health, but still young, then it may have a high number of machine-based component replacements and as such the percentage of biological components may be quite low. High enough to sustain the connectivity of the Aspect with the incarnate vehicle and therefore sustain the state of incarnation, while also being high enough for the machine-based sentience to have enough components to be the basis of an individualized self-contained system.

ME: I thought you said that small individualized machine sentience was not possible!

OM Together: It's not in the sentience that you are thinking about, but this level of sentience would be limited to being connected to a higher level of machine-based sentience and therefore function as a component part of a machine-based sentience collective.

ME: OK, I have a vision of Aunt Mable dying and then her body getting up and leaving the mortuary, surprising and frightening the people in the area.

OM Together: In the event that this method of generating machine-based sentience was not only possible but prevalent in an incarnate society, and they would need to be a very advanced one, the replacement or sentient part would be scanned for such activity, or it would advertise itself as such upon the Aspect's leaving the incarnate vehicle for such a function and the relevant parts removed and repurposed to make a complete machine-based sentient system. The newly repurposed and constructed machine would then integrate with the larger machine-based sentience.

ME: Do incarnates and sentient machines exist side by side?

OM Together: Yes, they can, but they best exist apart. An advanced incarnate civilization, in being party to the creation of machine-based sentience in this way, would be actively working on relocating the machines to their own location to let them develop in their own way. It's called setting them free.

ME: Is it possible that a remote incarnate colony eventually gets taken over by machine-based sentience if the incarnate vehicles are affected by disease or lack of food or mental instability due to isolation or even conflict and simply and slowly die out?

OM Together: This is perhaps the main route that machine-based sentience created in this way becomes the dominant sentience.

ME: Simply put then, because an incarnate colony that uses machines that are capable of learning fails, it becomes the main way that those machines have the possibility of becoming sentient and so a sentient machine civilization is born.

OM Together: As we stated before, this is perhaps the main way that machine-based sentience created in this way becomes a dominant sentience.

ME: Why does the incarnate civilization or colony fail? How do the machines they use become sentient?

OM Together: As you can imagine there are many ways in which an incarnate colony can fail and some of the ways are mentioned above. The major problem with a colony that is out of contact with the main civilization and that depends upon its machine assistance that is capable of learning is that they get complacent or lose track of The Original incentive for colonization once The Original incarnates and maybe the next couple of generations have left their bodies (the bodies have died) and as a result The Original impetus is lost. If there has been enough reproduction then the civilization may grow and thrive, especially if contact with The Original civilization is maintained. However, it is when that contact is lost, and the colony is on its own, isolated, that things can go wrong. As long as loss of food manufacture and disease are avoided, general health is maintained as with the manufacture and maintenance of habitat and the machines that help, the civilization should continue, even in an isolated situation.

When these things are working well, the only other main method of failure is the self-governance of the colony. As long as the colonists follow the rules of the self-governance and there are no disagreements that result in conflict then again the colony will thrive; if they don't, they won't. We do have to point out, though, that it is usually the self-governance issues that result in an isolated colony failing. The other way in which a colony fails is due to failure of environmental services if the atmosphere is not conducive to the atmosphere that normally sustains the incarnate vehicles of the colonists—that being, it is a sealed environment. Or additionally, if terraforming activities create topographical or environmental issues that end up being out of the control of the colonists then that can also result in a loss of colony inhabitants.

If any of these issues are encountered, and there are many more, and the machines in use have the programming capability that allows for learning to improve function, generate their own energy, and maintain themselves, then they have the "potential" to go down the road to sentience.

You asked about how machines, in this example, may develop machine sentience.

ME: Yes, I did, but I am now thinking that it is a normal and collective function the same as the way energy can become sentient.

OM Together: In general, the road to sentience is the same no matter what the medium of intelligence is. However, with this particular road to machine sentience it is usually the function of a collective level of centralized sentience that is accrued rather than a level of individualized sentience. The centralized sentience would be derived by a central system. This system would then use the individual machine tools, in whatever form they are, to create its arms and legs, so to speak. In doing this, it is able to extend its processing capability by using the processors and programs associated with each of the machine tools to augment its own.

ME: So, some of the sentience is local to the arms and legs, the connected machine tools while the rest is centralized with the connection to the machine tools by the centralized system being a collective function.

OM Together: Correct. Although it has to be said that when the programming and processing power is collectively connected in this way, it acts and functions as if it is one sentience.

ME: It very much feels to me like the machine version of omnipresence!

OM Together: It's not quite but if one was to consider that the sentience of the centralized system can position itself into the individual processors of the machine tools to control them, then the answer is yes. They will even, over time of course, manufacture processors of higher processing capacity and add to, or replace, those that are in the machine tools and the centralized system as well.

ME: So, by increasing or upgrading the processing and programming capacity of its centralized systems and its machine tools, or for want of a better word, its mobile components, it has the capability of accelerating its journey down the road to machine sentience.

OM Together: Yes, but this function of processing/programming augmentation, improvement, and expansion is normally borne from the need to perpetuate its own existence in order to fulfill The Original programming.

ME: Which, I guess it achieves and progresses from there.

OM Together: The normal workload being completed is generally the position when the machines finish but in this instance the work will have been completed, and the incarnate colonists will continue to work with the machines to improve their habitat and infrastructure. In the event that the incarnate colonists' demise, the machines will simply continue with their work. The intelligence in their programming will make them improve themselves to become more efficient in their work and in the use of power or raw material resources. It is this independent function of "self" improvement that results in the decision processes that creates the road to machine sentience.

To be honest, the methods that allow a machine-based sentient system are just a very small window of the ways in which it can happen. Suffice to say, the number of variations of how machine sentience is derived is multipoluous.

I don't expect that this subject of machine sentience will be much of an eye opener to the reader simply because Dolores Cannon reported on it and we have had a number of science fiction films that have depicted a rather poor series of scenarios about machine sentience taking over the Earth and eradicating incarnate human existence. What is possibly a new thought is that there are myriad machine-based civilizations in the gross physical aspect of the physical universe, and, that they may even be the dominant sentience in a particular galaxy.

Although the physical universe is just one very small aspect of the multiverse that is within our Source Entity, it is still a very, very, very large place to exist within. To experience all of its opportunities is a very large and daunting task.

I was just contemplating this conundrum when Anne came back to discuss the very question of how long do we need to incarnate.

We Don't Have to Experience All of the Physical Universe to Move On!!

ANNE: Lovely to see and speak to you again.

ME: You can see me? You must be very close! I was under the impression that most of your sentience was now with our TES.

ANNE: It is, but I have kept a small quota of my sentience within reach of the frequencies associated with the physical universe so that I can keep one eye on the progress of those Aspects that are incarnate on Earth and of course, on your work.

ME: Well, it's very much appreciated.

ANNE: Well, we note that you are well ahead of expectations.

ME: I thought that I would be behind in my work. I have had so many ideas for progressing it, but these have been given a lower priority at the moment. Such as the retreat in Crete!

ANNE: You can only do what you can do and the books have the priority now, as will the healing workshops later. The TTF (Traversing the Frequencies) work will find its own place in the list of priorities. Not that it will disappear, far from it, but where the Earth is right now, the personal progression in connectivity with The Source and the greater reality will need those incarnate Aspects that are capable of using this process to start to awake up from a low-frequency slumber. Many have dropped down the frequencies to the point of full immersion in their incarnation.

ME: So the healing will take priority?

ANNE: Along with the books, yes. When the books are finished, the workshops will have all the background texts to support them and you will be able to concentrate on sharing your knowledge in a more personal way.

ME: Thank you. It's always nice to know that I have you at my side when I need encouragement.

ANNE: That's my role, it was always my role.

Now, let's get moving on this next subject. The subject of how many times an Aspect needs to incarnate before it can move away from incarnation.

ME: Thank you. I am sure that this is going to be very interesting, not just to me but to many readers who feel that they don't want to incarnate again after this incarnation.

Can I start with just one statement or comment related to this subject?

ANNE: Yes, I don't see why not.

ME: In most of the books I have channeled, and in a number of the World Satsanga [*my monthly Q&A, lecture, and meditation blog—GSN*], I have been broadcasting the possibility that an Aspect (soul) can only really negate the need for additional incarnations by working hard on achieving a level of self-awareness and detachment high enough to allow the incarnate Aspect to navigate around their incarnation in an efficient way. Without getting addicted to the thoughts, behaviors, and actions associated with the lower frequencies of the physical universe. Without accruing Karma.

ANNE: Mastering the incarnate state is just one of the things that an Aspect needs to address before it can remove itself away from the need or desire to incarnate.

ME: So, what are the other things? What does an Aspect need to achieve to be able to stop incarnating?

ANNE: I will list them out for you and explain them as I go.

Some of the things that an Aspect needs to fulfill before achieving the level associated with being able to evolve at a rate associated with incarnation without needing to incarnate are obvious. Some others are not. Of course, a TES and its Aspects must be at a level of evolution high enough to contemplate incarnation as a method of accelerating its evolutionary progression in the first place.

- **Achieve the evolutionary level where the Aspect can incarnate into the physical universe.** A TES and its Aspects need to have experienced enough of the other universal environments within the multiverse to have gained enough experience, learning, and evolving to be able to work in an environment where their communicative abilities are challenged. Only then are they allowed to incarnate into the physical universe. However, this is only in the highest frequencies where the communicative challenge is limited. That being, the incarnate Aspect is still aware of who and what it is, what its experience is supposed to entail, and how it might achieve that experience.

- **Achieve the evolutionary level needed to incarnate into the lowest frequencies of the physical universe.** Only after a significant number of incarnations in the higher frequencies of the physical universe can a TES choose to project one of its Aspects into the frequencies associated with the gross physical. Some TES elect to gradually expose their Aspects to lower frequencies one level at a time in an attempt to help acclimatize them to the lower frequencies. However, others are bolder and allow the Aspect to make their own decision, or put them in the deep end, the lowest of the frequencies, to see how they respond, to see if they sink or swim, so to speak. In the event that the Aspect is exposed to the gross physical frequencies early on then it is usual for that Aspect to have a longer "recovery" time to reflect upon the incarnation in between incarnations.

- **Experience the ability to accrue Karma.** In this instance, the incarnate Aspect knows what it is like to accrue Karma and the factors that make the accrual of Karma possible. This experience and the next go hand in hand to some extent. However, in this instance, this is more to do with how the interaction with other incarnates, the environments, and the interaction with others in these environments and the circumstances they find themselves in creates Karma. Such experiences may not be recognized as karmic or important in terms of the Aspect's experience in general, although the level of frequency reduction or increase in association with the physical may be in the back of the mind of the incarnate Aspect. Additionally, such feelings of addiction to material things or of being in some form of debt to another incarnate for actions that they have done, or not done as the case may be, may weigh "heavy" on them. Indeed, it is this feeling of being "heavy" that is the "physical" indicator of the accrual of Karma.

Accruing Karma is a sort of magnetic effect of the attraction to the physical.

- **Recognize what Karma is and how it affects the Aspect.** In this stage, the incarnate Aspect knows before entering into incarnation what happens to them as a function of how they interact with the environment they are in, how they interact with other incarnates in that environment and within the circumstances that they are in. They are capable of seeing the theory behind the accrual of Karma and that it should be avoided.
- **Understand how to remove or negate Karma.** In essence, this is the sign of an evolved incarnate Aspect that is experienced in the "art" of incarnation at the higher frequency levels but has not yet reached the point where they can incarnate into the lowest frequencies of the multiverse, even in a collective state. This Aspect can see the possibility of accruing Karma before entering the point of accrual and change the way they interact with their environment and those with whom they are interacting within the environment. An Aspect that understands how to detect the possibility of accruing Karma also learns over a number of incarnations how to negate it by recognizing and acting upon the "signs." It is one thing to see the possibility of accruing Karma, but it is another to actually avoid accruing it, such is the effect of the lowest frequencies of the multiverse, those of the physical universe, on the incarnate Aspect. A very evolved Aspect, once understanding how to "avoid Karma," can also see the karmic links between themselves in previous or other incarnations and other incarnate or disincarnate individuals within this incarnation. Once these karmic links can be observed by the Aspect, it can see how, in an ego-free way, it can remove those links, and it creates the opportunities where they can be removed. Removal of karmic links has the benefit of assisting in the evolutionary progression of not just the Aspect that recognizes how to remove Karma, but also those that the links are removed from. Many incarnations can be spent in the need to interact with another incarnate Aspect that one has a karmic link within

the expectation or hope that that link can be removed by "normal" means. Normal means being the use of reciprocation (or cause and effect) of that which created the link in the first place. As a result, the opportunity to remove or have Karma removed is significantly more efficient than waiting for the right moment, so to speak. Note, though, that this function is first experienced when the Aspect is incarnating at a higher frequency level within the physical universe.

- **Evolve to the level where the Aspect can operate as an independent incarnate while still being part of a collective.** In this level of evolutionary progression, the Aspect is getting close to the point where it is capable of incarnating into the frequencies associated with the gross physical with a level of individuality. An Aspect cannot incarnate straight into the frequencies associated with the gross physical with the function of individualized free will without first experiencing the gross physical as part of a collective. The association with a collective allows the Aspect to understand and appreciate the importance of being in service to the collective as an individualized function of it. The level of individuality is gradually increased over a number of incarnations until the Aspect can operate on an individualized basis, with free will but that the free will is still connected to the need to operate on behalf of the collective it is associated with. That being, everything that the Aspect does has to be considered with the benefit of, or how it affects, the collective in mind.

- **Evolve to the level necessary to incarnate on Earth with full individuality.** Once the Aspect has understood how to operate individually on behalf of the collective, while experiencing individuality, and brought this level of understanding into enough incarnations to illustrate that they are capable of operating with collective-based individualized free will, in the frequencies of the gross physical, they are allowed to incarnate with fully individualized free will. Individualized free will is a difficult function to work with because there is no collective to act as a level of governance. The incarnate Aspect with individualized free will is therefore self-governing and accountable only to themselves and the Karma that they accrue. Of course, they are ultimately accountable to their TES but while incarnate they are their own entity, so to speak.

- **Understand how individualized free will affects the accrual of Karma.** Understanding how Karma is accrued while incarnate with individualized free will versus how it is accrued while incarnate within a collective or with individualized free will associated with a collective is an important milestone. When incarnate within a collective, the governance of the collective is held within the psycho-spiritual programming of the incarnate Aspect. This is because Karma that is accrued by the individual affects the overall karmic content of the collective and as such is negated or removed as a function of the collective. An incarnate Aspect with individualized free will is responsible for its own governance and as such the negation or removal of its Karma. It is also responsible for how its actions create "group" Karma as a function of its interactions with other incarnate Aspects and how it may assist/work in the removal of group Karma that it is part of. Understanding how to avoid the accrual of Karma while incarnate in the gross physical with individualized free will is the fast track to navigating an incarnation in a Karma-free way.

- **Create a balanced strategy toward incarnation.** This is achieved when everything within the physical universe from the highest to the lowest frequencies is noted by the Aspect as an opportunity for evolutionary progression and must therefore be experienced. This is from interacting with the physical universe from a frequential, environmental, civilization, circumstantial, and interactive (with other incarnates) Karma-free based perspective.

ME: This seems to me that the incarnate Aspect's main role is to experience and recognize that which keeps them needing to incarnate.

ANNE: Correct. It's not just that which "keeps" them incarnating, though; it's also that which creates the addiction to want to keep incarnating as well. The end goal is to master incarnation and when an incarnate Aspect is cognizant of that which makes them the master of incarnation, through experiencing all that incarnation can offer, then incarnation is no longer an evolutionary advantage. This list I just shared with you is just the highlights of that which an Aspect has to experience and master.

ME: But this seems like a lot, especially when the insinuation is that an Aspect doesn't need to experience all that the physical universe has to offer to move away from the need to incarnate!

ANNE: There are so-called shortcuts to achieving the levels of experience that lead to mastering incarnation. These shortcuts are available to every incarnate Aspect but those that choose them are rare souls (Aspects). I do have to say that the word shortcut is possibly the wrong way to describe the process of negating the need to incarnate without experiencing. These shortcuts can be described in two ways; taking the shortest evolutionary route over a number of incarnations and maximizing the evolutionary potential during each incarnation. I will describe them in more detail. However, before I do I need to advise you of two concepts, evolutionary quality and depth of evolution. I will explain these as we go on.

Taking the Shortest Evolutionary Route

ANNE: This method of accelerating one's evolutionary progression, leading up to the ability to master incarnation or move beyond the need to incarnate is perhaps the easiest way to evolve. However, it does result in a lower evolutionary quality and a subsequent lack of evolutionary depth. The best way to think of this method is metaphorically. If one considers that the objective of a journey is to move from point A to point B, such as from New York to Delhi, then there are several ways in which this journey can be made. However, it is the plethora of ways to travel from one place to another that changes the experiential content associated with that journey and therefore the depth and quality of the evolutionary content associated with it. For example, a soul can choose to fly direct from New York to Delhi and as a result take no more than fifteen hours to make the journey. The objective of the journey has been achieved but the experiential content is limited to traveling to the airport from home, being in the airport lounge, boarding and sitting on the plane during the flight, arriving at an airport, and traveling from the airport to the location of the lodgings. It is a functional way of making the journey with limited or no interaction with the process of traveling which affects the quality of experience or evolutionary content.

Considering though that the journey could have been made by boat, train, car, motorbike, bicycle, walking, and hitchhiking either in isolation or in any combination of modalities of travel one can see that the length of time taken to make the whole journey, including stops in various locations, results in the depth of experience or depth of evolution.

It is therefore the change in modality of the travel that results in the depth of experience or evolutionary content associated with the journey.

Evolutionary quality can therefore be described as the duration of the experience, or time taken to experience that experience, that results in evolutionary content. If one experiences something for a short period, it is a transient experience, but if one experiences it for a prolonged period, it is a full/er, higher quality experience. It can be considered like sitting on the bank of a river and watching the water flow while observing the plant life move in the wind, the waterfowl moving on the surface of the water, and eddies in the water that come and go.

Depth of evolution can be described as the ability to experience an experience, the same experience, in many different ways, resulting in the depth of experience and therefore the depth of evolutionary content. It can be considered in the same light as reading a page of a book in the daylight, under candlelight, under fluorescent light, under halogen light, under incandescent light, under LED light, under torchlight, or under lights of different colors. It's the same experience, experienced in many different ways.

ME: So, in short, it's how long we take, together with how we experience an experience that results in its evolutionary quality and its depth, but it's still evolution.

ANNE: Correct, and as a result it still counts in terms of an Aspect's ability to evolve while being incarnate and navigate an incarnation in an efficient enough way to quickly go to the point where they no longer need to incarnate to continue to evolve. This ultimately means that an Aspect can reach this stage without experiencing all that the physical universe has to offer.

ME: This is the shortcut! It's a sort of "touch and run" concept.

ANNE: If you like, yes. You experience the bare bones of the experience and as a result you have experienced it. It's like going skydiving at a low altitude, once, in tandem with an instructor. You have done it once and as a result don't need to do it again. Unless, that is, you decide that you want to skydive again in a different location with different people in a different airplane and on your own, etc., which then creates the depth of experience. Having the initial skydive from a higher altitude increases the duration of the skydive and therefore increases the quality of experience.

Maximizing the Evolutionary Potential

ME: So, in this way, an Aspect can evolve to the point of no longer needing to incarnate, and even enter into full communion with its TES, in the shortest period of individualized existence.

ANNE: Correct. As you can imagine, this method of accruing evolution is quite an efficient one from the perspective of working on the aspect of the overall evolutionary cycle that all Shards, Aspects, TES, and The Source are working on.

ME: What about going down the route of maximizing the evolutionary potential of a series of incarnations?

ANNE: There are as many routes to experience an increase in depth and quality of what one could call the basic level of evolutionary progression as there are Shards, Aspects, and TES individualized from The Source.

ME: I would put that in the billions then.

ANNE: Well, if you look at it in terms of the number of TES, Aspects, and Shards that are or could be individualized, and the number of variations in experiencing, learning, and subsequently evolving, it can be countless billions of billions of billions, etc., of variations of depth and quality.

ME: We had better deal with the basics then.

ANNE: As I have just described, it's how many variations of experiencing the experience that creates the quality and depth of experience that a Shard, Aspect, or TES has. However, an Aspect, etc., can add another factor into the evolutionary equation that allows it to maximize its evolutionary potential. This is done in two ways; one: by adding in experiential content associated with an incarnation, and two: by using the function of parallel existence.

Increasing Experiential Content via Extension of the Life Plan Goals

ANNE: The common and most obvious way to accrue more evolutionary content in a single incarnation is to allow one's self to experience the depth of an experience to the "nth degree" of that which can be experienced within an experience. Aspects do this by specializing, in one or a number of goals within their life or incarnation plan. An example would be becoming a professor of microbiology and a medical consultant in gene therapy. Both require significant levels of depth of knowledge and experience to reach such levels of competence.

ME: I have heard the phrase, "experiencing more than one life in this life" before. Indeed, I always thought that I was experiencing more than two lives in this incarnation. Is this the same thing?

ANNE: Yes, it is. There are many Aspects that experience multiple experiential life themes in the space of one incarnation. Some of them require the Aspect to make significant life (incarnation) changes to experience them. This can include changes in career, partner, location, health, and wealth and a linear succession of experiences. Others can include double or treble the number of life plan goals as a concurrent function. The easiest way is to experience the additional life plan goals in linear, but this requires them to be experienced in a lower level of depth and quality than would be accrued should the incarnating Aspect (or Shard) focus on one particular goal or set of goals in a life plan that didn't have the additional goals. However, the total level of evolutionary content accrued would be significantly more than that which could be gained, had the Aspect elected to focus on one goal or set of goals. Moderately evolved Aspects can make this method a success, even though it can be a challenge if the goals overlap. So-called "rags to riches" and reverse incarnations are the most common version of this multiple life plan goal experience.

ME: So, it makes multiple experiential content worthwhile then.

ANNE: Very worthwhile. However, this method is one that is more likely to succeed simply because it is experienced linearly. When an Aspect "loads up" a life plan with lots of smaller goals that can be experienced concurrently, this is more difficult for an Aspect to achieve and often results in the Aspect either not being as successful as they would have liked, or, even breaking down in some way. One can see when an Aspect has taken on too many challenges when they have difficulty dealing with all of the things that their incarnation presents to them. They struggle to deal with any one challenge properly and so none of the challenges is experienced in an optimal way resulting in an inability to respond in any level of competence. The challenges therefore "get on top of them." It is only the very evolved Aspects that take onboard the number of goals associated with multiple life plans experienced concurrently in this way. It's called "burn out!"

Another opportunity for increasing one's evolutionary content is to elect to remain incarnate after one's life plan content is completed by adding in a new one, if extending the incarnate experience is possible with the current incarnate vehicle. Some Aspects include this potential as a possibility at the end of the incarnation and as a result find new and renewed vigor to do "something else" in the remaining years of their incarnation. Others may decide to remain incarnate as a function of the incarnation approaching the termination juncture but decide to stay to "help others" rather than return to the energetic. Which, of course, they are quite at liberty to do. So-called near-death experiences (NDEs), and the resultant stories that are told by the incarnate "returning into their incarnation after experiencing some small part of the energetic," after some sort of trauma, are a good example of the decision made by the Aspect to stay incarnate. They will have decided to continue to have a productive contribution toward the accrual of evolutionary content and be of assistance to other incarnate Aspects.

I do have to say to you that you decided to experience a combination of those methods described above, which The OM were very concerned about prior to your entering into the process of incarnation. However, you do seem to be coping with and doing it in what can best be described in a mostly level-headed and balanced way. It could have been VERY karmic!!

ME: Now you are feeding my ego. I note that there are many Aspects that have chosen much more difficult incarnate roles than me.

ANNE: It's not the difficulty that was the issue, it was the content.

ME: Oh! So what was the issue with the content?

ANNE: There were/are a number of practical and academic skills that you needed to experience either very close together, or all together. These skills also included how to interact with others, which I might add you are still experiencing at many levels. You simply don't understand human emotions and as a result don't engage with human incarnates at a level that they would accept as being normal.

ME: So what part of engaging with incarnate human beings don't I get?

ANNE: Most of it. I would suggest that you are keeping them at a distance most of the time.

ME: I understand. But doesn't that mean that I avoid certain aspects of Karma?

ANNE: It does, and that is quite understandable, indeed it is desirable. However, what it doesn't do is allow you to fully understand the human condition, specifically from the emotional perspective, that is. I know, I was there!

ME: OK, I recognize this. I don't think or expect that I will ever fully understand what it is like to be immersed in an incarnation to the point that it is all-consuming and that I only relate to myself as the incarnate vehicle that my sentience is housed in.

Moving on a little then, what other parts of my life plan were/are difficult?

ANNE: I think that the best thing for me to do is list down the overall subject matter that is relative to the "goals" of your life plan rather than the details per se. These are in no particular order by the way.

- Recognize and consider the greater reality
- Experience connectivity with your peer group
- Understand that intuitive thinking is not acceptable in the incarnate state and the need to use logic is
- Experience academic failure
- Learn practical skills
- Experience the feeling/desire to be of service
- Feel that you have a (an important world-level) task to perform
- Establish a direction to catch up with academic skills (the "failure to success" experience)
- Learn how to share yourself with another (OM—Me!!)
- Experience certain levels of emotions
- Experience a nurturing environment from many

different directions concurrently
- Recognize the practical and academic skills associated with each environment
- Experience being responsible
- Experience being a teacher
- Gain academic success and experience the hard work and expansiveness necessary to gain such success
- Experience the addiction to materialism (ownership, thinking, behaving, and acting) and detach from it
- Experience recognition and lack of recognition— and not crave recognition
- Recognize that you can see and know what others cannot and that as a result experience the joy of connectivity, and the frustration that others cannot see what you see
- Experience the loss of nurturing people from around you
- Experience betrayal
- Recognize the routes to your world-level task; take them as they appear, they will be in many forms
- Know and master how to go with the flow—not to push too hard, not to be too laid back
- Know and master abundance
- Experience and work with opposites
- Experience resistance
- Experience the need to be considerate
- Experience others trying to control you
- Experience being able to avoid being controlled
- Experience more loss and loneliness

I could go on and on!! There is much more on your life plan that you have not yet experienced or got to the point where those experiences can be experienced. You still have a lot to do and that you can do.

ME: I noticed that the work that I am doing now is a function of what I would call a second phase of incarnation.

ANNE: In terms of the fact that you moved out of your material world roles and into your spiritual/energetic roles, I would agree. But understand here that all the things, all the skills you experienced and gained in the first half of your incarnation have given you all the skills/abilities to be able to perform your world-level task in the second part of your incarnation. You have become a very grounded and capable incarnate with a world-spiritual task, one that you have not let get the better of you, so to speak.

ME: What does that mean, "not get the better of me?"

ANNE: In simple terms it means that you have not desired fame and fortune and status from it. You have worked with it at the level that you can work on it, knowing that the information you are sharing is new and radical and that it may not be recognized for what it is, or indeed its importance, until after your incarnation has ended.

ME: That's right. As long as I can keep doing it I will be happy. But I also recognize that there is a time when I will have to go so that others can take the work further. And that's not specifically my work but the work of helping to awaken the incarnate human race.

ANNE: One thing I will tell you, and that you may already suspect though, is that your work will be appreciated much more in the East than in the West, although it will start off in the West.

ME: Yes, I do feel a significant draw to the East. They seem to have more dedication and devotion to understanding the detail behind who and what we are more. They have more love!

ANNE: Yes, and the East is the direction that will help your work blossom and thrive before it returns to the West. That's enough for now. As you yourself say, knowing too much of the future distracts one from working in the now!

ME: Well said.

Increasing Evolutionary Content via Parallel Existence

ANNE: The ability to increase one's evolutionary content via parallel existence is the most common way to increase evolutionary content. Indeed, it is an automatic function of Event Space and is happening all of the time to every Shard, Aspect, and TES that elect to be in the evolutionary cycle, irrespective of whether or not they incarnate. It does have to be said though, that only the TES can experience everything concurrently or "in the now." The Aspect, while in the energetic, not in the lowest frequencies of the multiverse and therefore incarnate, can only experience experiences concurrently in limited ways, which are subject to improvement in concurrency as the Aspect evolves to the higher frequencies.

ME: So we evolve as a function of being affected by Event Space and its duplication, which is a function of our decisions while we are individualized.

ANNE: Correct. But also note that Shards and Aspects are also affected by the decisions made by their TES and how it creates new Event Spaces as well.

ME: Wouldn't a Shard be similarly affected by Event Space duplication, etc., by the decisions of its Aspect?

ANNE: Yes, but to a lesser extent to those created by their TES.

Remember, the TES has the majority of the sentience, a minimum of 70 percent [*an Aspect normally has 2.5 percent! See* The Anne Dialogues—*GSN*] and as a result can experience significantly more experiential content in parallel than smaller Aspects or Shards of an Aspect can. It's the percentage of individualized sentience that is the limiting factor here. Although, from the incarnate Aspect's perspective, experiencing what it does in the energetic—in parallel—is significantly more than it can experience while incarnate, which, in general, is nothing from those parallel Event Spaces it is also interacting with. This is because of the limitations of the communicative bandwidth experienced in the low frequencies of the physical universe, which, to be honest, allow the incarnate Aspect's sentience the opportunity to concentrate on a single incarnation at one time. So it is a bit of a benefit.

ME: So, when incarnate we don't experience the changes to Event Space that are a result of our decisions or our TES's decisions?

ANNE: No, and neither do your Shards from the decisions you make! If you had a Shard, that is!

ME: Some of my readers and clients are baffled by the comments that our TES (Higher Self—Over Soul—God Head) experiences all of the parallel experiential and therefore evolutionary content concurrently. Some of them want to experience all of the things that their parallel versions experience as well. They think that this will help them; they feel that they are being left out.

ANNE: One of the things that is interesting about Aspects that are incarnate into the human vehicle, those that are more aware of themselves and their environment, is that they are convinced that they could cope with the ability to experience all parallel existences while being in this one, so to speak.

ME: They couldn't, could they?

ANNE: In no way would they be able to handle even the experiential content from a single additional parallel, let alone all of them.

ME: And that's because of the lack of connectivity with their TES, which is a function of the low frequencies here.

ANNE: Correct. You can see how these that are linked with (Hara Lines entangled with) other Aspects projected from their TES struggle to keep focused (sane) when they observe or feel the experiences that one of their soul group experiences with the experiences they are experiencing in this version of their existence.

ME: I know what you mean.

ANNE: Experiencing what can be minor or even very major versions of experience that are not part of this Event Space are a big issue and one that creates a major problem in being able to work on the direction and goals that are supposed to be the focus of this incarnation. It's just not possible with the level of sentience that is allotted to most, if not all incarnate Aspects at this frequency level.

ME: What about other frequency levels in the physical universe? Could an Aspect cope with experiencing parallel existences in other, higher frequencies?

ANNE: Clearly the communicative bandwidth of an incarnate Aspect increases as a function of incarnating into a higher frequency. However, it is one thing being able to receive the multipoluous experiences available to the TES in all of the Event Spaces that are invoked as a function of the decisions or choices that have been made by the incarnate Aspect, and quite another to be able to work with them in parallel.

ME: That's down to the percentage of sentience again I expect?

ANNE: Correct. It's possible for a TES to assign a higher percentage of its sentience to an Aspect while incarnate, and this can be at any frequency within the physical universe. And it's a function of the sentience that allows the ability to parallel process experiences and be able to work on the individual Event Streams concurrently, separately together.

ME: OK, so in the main, it is not something that an incarnate Aspect in the human form should be worried about then?

ANNE: No. Just to give your readers some solace, though, all they need to know is this. Whatever decision they have made is the decision they must work with, knowing that there are multiple versions of themselves working on all of the minor, major, and all the variants in between, experiences that could have, should have, may have, will have, might have, and "are" happening as a result of the choices they were faced with when they made their decision, rather than others that presented themselves to them. So they are experiencing everything, it's just that they don't know it.

ME: What about those who say that they would have preferred to have made another, better choice and have a so-called better existence now? They feel that they have made the wrong choice!

ANNE: Well, in other versions they have made the right choice. It is unbalanced to experience an incarnation where the Aspect made all the right decisions, although there are parallel versions where this does happen. There are parallel versions where all the so-called wrong choices have been made as well. The whole point of working with the knowledge that some other part of you is working in a parallel existence and dealing with both the so-called right or wrong decisions is that one does not have to worry about the decisions that have been made. They made the decision and so must work with the circumstances that arise from that decision or series of decisions, focusing on what is the only here-and-now that they can focus on, rather than wishing they had made a different decision.

ME: I suppose this is how the plethora of experiences work for the TES. Its Aspects, Shards, and their parallel versions are experiencing all possibilities that are available—concurrently.

ANNE: Yes, and it's a very efficient way of experiencing, learning, and evolving, and the best contribution that an incarnate Aspect can make toward such efficiency of accruing evolutionary content is to concentrate on the experience they are experiencing and do the best job they can within that experience, and not wish they had made another choice. This creates a depth of overall multipoluous experience and overall evolutionary content.

ME: If I was to look at this as a form of lesson for us all, it would be that we should be content with what we are and where we are and work with it with love in our hearts, always looking to see how we can make the best of things rather than complaining and thinking that we are hard done by.

ANNE: That's one way to think of it. The happiest people are those who live in poor situations and those that are in better circumstances always want more or to be better, being impatient or jealous rather than in acceptance and being pleased for how others have worked to improve or create a better circumstance. Not being in acceptance and wanting what others have can lead one to be in a so-called worse circumstance than one was in, in the first place.

ME: I suppose in this instance one should be careful what one wishes for!

ANNE: Yes, wishing one had chosen one path rather than another can lead one to a worse set of circumstances than one is in, even if the unchosen path did appear to be better with hindsight.

ME: But it can be a better path!

ANNE: Yes, it can, and of course all of the variations in between. The best advice that anyone can either give or receive is to be in acceptance and deal with what one can deal with in the best way one can.

ME: And not worry about whether it is the right or wrong way, but it is your way.

ANNE: And the way we choose, in the Event Space we find ourselves in, is the only one we can work with in this, the low frequency [*the gross physical frequencies—GSN*].

ME: And in this low frequency we cannot see the parallel or other concurrent parts of the greater reality we are part of and therefore have to work in, in the knowledge that some other parallel version of us is dealing with one of the variations in environment, circumstance, and individual interactions.

ANNE: Correct, but that requires a level of understanding and acceptance. Many people don't understand or want to accept.

ME: If everybody knew that every incarnation has a purpose, they would be content and satisfied with what they do. That that purpose is individualized experience. And, that that individualized experience makes a unique experiential and therefore evolutionary difference, not only to them but to their TES, The Source, and The Origin, then they would feel that they are making a significant and worthwhile contribution, even if it doesn't look that way from the human perspective.

ANNE: Good words and a great lead into the subject material of the next chapter.

Guy's Role on Earth

Before I start to channel the information for a book, I normally gain two insights. One: what the title and subtitle should/will be; and two: the overall theme of the subjects to be discussed with the entities I will be channeling the information from. As a result, I meditate further on the overall theme and am given a number of subject headings to work with.

This list of headings is by no means descriptive and there are many times when they are either expanded or included into another heading with The Original heading no longer being necessary. That is as far as it gets. It is only when I subsequently work with The Origin, The Source, The OM (including Anne), other entities such as those incarnates we classify as aliens, that the detail starts to come out. I never know where the information is going to go and the twists and turns that it is going to take. As a result, I am always surprised when the supposed end of one subject seems to lead into the start of another; this is no exception.

As with all the subjects I discuss with the entities I channel information from, I start to get a feeling that the subject is drawing to a close when the interconnective energy of the entity I am channeling information from starts to withdraw or dissipate. I was starting to feel this gradual withdrawal with Anne's energy again and was wondering who I was going to communicate with next and what the subject was going to be about.

I was just about to think that "today's work" was over and that I would find out the who and what on another day when I was drawn to the title of this chapter, "Guy's Role on Earth." To be honest, I would have thought that by now I would have known this, so I was a little surprised to be drawn to this chapter title. I was also surprised to feel the energy of Hum!

HUM: I expect that you are wondering why this title is the next subject to discuss.

Interestingly enough, my usual speed of typing had slowed down to a crawl; it was almost one-fingered typing. What was happening?

HUM: What is happening is that you are realigning yourself to me away from Anne. If you were more observant, you would have noticed that over the years of channeling information from The Origin, The Sources, The OM, Anne, and myself that you finish a chapter on a subject on one day, or week, and then commence the next series of channeling on another day. This allows you to align your energies before the next batch of work. Today you have not. It's the first time and so you feel the difference.

ME: But I have communicated with The Origin, all The Source Entities, and Anne collectively before and didn't feel any realignment of energies!

HUM: That was because you had gradually aligned yourself to them over the period of communicating with them—you expected it, so to speak. Additionally, the frequencies were higher than they are right now, so it was much easier. At the moment, the frequencies are very, very low and so it's not so easy to move from one entity's sentience, frequency, and energetic signature to another straight away, hence the "lag" in your becoming aligned. Now that you are "aligned with me," do you notice that your typing is much faster?

ME: Now you mention it, yes, it has returned to its normal speed. What's more, I feel livelier. I have to admit to feeling a little "woolly headed" while the speed of typing was reduced to almost nothing.

HUM: That was a function of realignment.

ME: OK, so I am not immune to the changes in frequency.

HUM: No, you are not. However, you are still able to function at an acceptable level and continue your work in this incarnate existence even though the frequencies are so low.

Now then, let's move on to the subject of your role rather than dissecting why you are slow at aligning your energies with me.

ME: Right. What is my role, that which I don't know about that is, especially as it is worthy of being mentioned in this book on The OM?

HUM: A catalyst for change.

ME: OK?

HUM: You are aware of some of the work you are doing and are going to do, but I also have a list of the things that are not known to you.

ME: More work! Now you are starting to worry me. I can see the light at the end of the tunnel with the books and I can also see the link between the books and the workshops I am holding. That is enough to be going on with, surely!

HUM: There are other things you have to do in this incarnation.

ME: You had better tell me now then. Now that you have warned me, whetted my appetite, and got my interest, not to mention put me into a state of acceptance!! Oh boy, there really is no rest for the wicked, and I must have been very wicked!!

HUM: They are not so prominent but nevertheless important.

ME: OK, but one thing I feel is that there will still be a lot of work involved.

HUM: That depends upon how much work you want to put into it or make of it.

ME: Touché.

HUM: The work you have to do is as follows:

- Continue to teach others to become self-aware.
- Create teachers of your TTF methodology for becoming self-aware.
- Teach others how to heal.
- Specialize in the Psycho-Spiritual Healing (PSH) aspect of your healing.
- Extend to the public the knowledge surrounding PSH and how it affects healing of psychiatric, schizophrenic, autistic, and Asperger's conditions.
- Promote other spiritual/metaphysical leaders—those that are expansive!
- Assist the "white children" as they become aware of their role and seek you out.
- Create links between theoretical and quantum physicists and your work. This will bridge the gap between theoretical and metaphysics.
- Help people see the truth about their existence, the environment they are incarnate within; help them see beyond the reality they think **is** real to that which is real.
- Work on yourself more and become more in the

background while continuing the work just as stated; this is the most important.

ME: This seems like the work I am doing or starting to do right now.

HUM: It is to some extent, but you will move toward the "backroom" behind-the-scenes type of work rather than being in the front line, so to speak.

ME: I am not really in the front line right now!

HUM: No, but you will be. Your so-called prominence will come "out of the blue" as people start to understand the relevance of the information you channel and how it can assist incarnate mankind's understanding of who and what it is.

You don't understand how revolutionary your information is.

ME: Well, Rudolph Steiner was revolutionary and look how long it took for people to wake up to his teachings. And if I was honest, his work still isn't recognized for its importance, even now. I am no Rudolph Steiner!

HUM: Clearly not. You have your own direction and your own work to do. It's just as important.

ME: Thank you. I won't get an ego, I promise.

HUM: I know you won't.

More of My Role Explained—It's Not Just about Me Wanting to See What It's Like to Incarnate!

Having just indulged myself in understanding a bit more about how "we" affect experiments, such as understanding what light is composed of, I wanted to be a bit more selfish and find out how do I fit into all of this? *I mean, it can't be just about my temporarily created OM TES wanting some aspect of its sentience to experience existence in a low-frequency environment, which includes the function of incarnation.*

Or was it just my temporary personality—my ego—playing games with me. I had to find out and not be worried about the answers given.

ANNE & HUM & OM & ALL OM: We wish to communicate with you collectively on this subject. To put your mind to rest.

ME: That was quick! I expected to meditate a while before connecting with you all. In fact, I expected just one of you, Anne or Hum to be precise!

ANNE & HUM & OM & ALL OM: We felt the need to express the answers to your questions as OM not as individualized OM sentience.

ME: Thank you. Why do I get the impressions that this is serious?

ANNE & HUM & OM & ALL OM: Letting a projection of Pure OMness experience the lowest of the frequencies, let alone become part of it via incarnation, was not a thing we wished for. We were, are, concerned that you will not be able to detach. Just like many other Aspects (souls) fail to detach and end up spending many, many incarnations to master detachment

153

to the point where incarnation is no longer relevant from an evolutionary perspective. We need you back in communion, to be once again fully blessed of The OM. That's why we follow your actions.

ME: How long do I have? *(I have to say that for some time I have had a picture in my mind of how I leave this incarnation and at what age! I was interested to see if The OM would offer some clarification for me though.)*

ANNE & HUM & OM & ALL OM: Long enough to do your work and pass its progression on to others who will come after you.

ME: What is my work then? What is my role? It's not just about wanting to experience the low frequencies of The Origin via this environment in this Source Entity, is it?

ANNE & HUM & OM & ALL OM: Initially it was. Your OM sentience was interested in what was happening in this particular Source Entity and in this particular location within its structure.

ME: You mean in terms of the individualized free will aspect?

ANNE & HUM & OM & ALL OM: Not initially. First of all, you were just interested in the possibility of being attached to a low-frequency vehicle. You were intrigued that the vehicle was integrated with the sentience and associated energy to the point where the sentience thought that it was the vehicle, was an interesting conundrum for you. You could not understand why so-called free sentience, therefore sentience that is free from the constraints of a lower frequency, would desire to constrain itself so much. Especially when a sentience can become addicted or attached to such an experience that it actively desires to experience it again and again and again. Even more of interest to you was the possibility that these attachments with the gross physical can and do lead to the accrual of evolutionary progression.

To be honest, we couldn't understand why any OM would want to experience incarnation as a way to gain evolutionary content because that would result in the need to create. Creation results in being responsible for that creation further creating a loss of freedom. The OM don't need to seek evolutionary progression because we are in effect individualized Origin sentience and as Origin sentience we evolve as The Origin evolves.

ME: So, what is the point in me being here then?

ANNE & HUM & OM & ALL OM: While in your first incarnate

experience you decided to help these incarnate Aspects understand more about the environment that they are normally within, when incarnate, you, by your own experience, recognized that an Aspect who is incarnate at these low frequencies loses almost all of its connective functions with its TES and the multiversal knowledge it holds. You also decided that you would take twelve incarnations to broadcast higher levels of knowledge in the way it would best be understood based upon the expansivity of incarnate humankind at the point of the Event Space you entered into incarnation.

ME: Was I, have I been successful in this desire?

ANNE & HUM & OM & ALL OM: Let's just say that it is a much harder job than you thought it would be.

ME: Is this going to hold me back? What I mean to say is, will I need to incarnate again to finish off the work?

ANNE & HUM & OM & ALL OM: It is fair to state that from what we have seen that such work is never finished for there is always another level of information to broadcast and another level of resistance to fight. No, this incarnation was the twelfth of twelve and was classified as being a checking experience. That being, you were seeing if the work you did last time could be done all over again.

ME: Was it the same sort of work or the same level of content?

ANNE & HUM & OM & ALL OM: You did it in a very different way with a different level of content. However, the end result is similar. That being, it acted as a method to expand the consciousness of the incarnates you interacted with.

ME: So, it's successful. What I mean is, it's been and is successful for those whom I have interacted with.

ANNE & HUM & OM & ALL OM: With some it has been very successful, with others it has been marginally successful insomuch as they benefited from the information but chose to ignore it later.

ME: Well, as long as I have helped one person see the truth and be able to interact with the truth, I will consider this incarnation to have been a success.

Where will I go after all of this work is finished?

ANNE & HUM & OM & ALL OM: While still incarnate, you will never finish. However, we will state that you will, at a certain age, prepare for departure and concentrate on securing a more robust connection with The OM, specifically that aspect of OM sentience that created your temporary OM TES.

ME: And, I ask again, how long do I have?

155

ANNE & HUM & OM & ALL OM: You have enough Event Space to do what you need to do and a bit more. However, we would like to advise you that you can come back to being beloved of The OM at any time after the last book you have planned is complete.

ME: In finishing this subject, one thing I have noticed from this incarnation, though, is that even OM sentience is affected by the low frequencies and its reduction in ability to commune with its sentient majority or temporary TES.

ANNE & HUM & OM & ALL OM: No sentience is totally immune from the effects of low frequency, and that includes The OM. This is why we were horrified and totally against you—your TES's decision, that is—to project an aspect of its sentience, you and Anne, into Source Entity One's multiverse. Let alone the physical universe. We will be glad when you return to oneness in being beloved of The OM. Your sentient weight is important to your temporary TES for it needs you, and Anne, in full communion before it can return to pure sentience, releasing the energy it is associated with to allow entry into Source Entity One's energies.

The OM and Anne clearly were not going to be specific in my remaining longevity!

ANNE & HUM & OM & ALL OM: Knowing would be a distraction!

ME: Mmmm.

The Future of the Earth—More Backfill People—and the Effects ...Mmmm!! It's a Double-Edged Sword!

Having established the rest of the work I am being committed to, I felt drawn to another question that I hoped HUM could answer. One of the future of the Earth, because to be honest, if we continue the downward spiral in the frequencies in the way we are currently experiencing them [late January 2021—GSN], we are going to be in a right state. One that will be very difficult to recover from. And, considering that it may be unrecoverable, not that I think it is unrecoverable, how would that affect my work?

ME: I have a really important question though, and one that I am sure many other spiritual people would like to ask.

HUM: Go ahead, I can see it coming through!

ME: Are we doomed? I mean **IS** incarnate mankind making the same mistakes that other civilizations have made?

HUM: Yes, in its thinking processes, some of which include a significant level of spiritual complacency. Hence, where incarnate mankind is now.

ME: Everything is all over the place right now, and in this situation we are easily sliding down the slippery slope of low-frequency thoughts, behaviors, and actions.

HUM: This slope is "very" easy to get into, as you have noticed, and very hard to get out of. It's easy to slip down a greased slope, but extremely difficult to climb out of it. As you can see from history, legend, and myth, so far incarnate human race has failed to come out the other side.

ME: OK, what I mean is that, is incarnate mankind heading for the same sort of collapse as Atlantis or those civilizations before?

HUM: Right now everything is in a state of turmoil. Certain levels of individualized free will have resulted in incorrect interaction with others.

ME: There is no respect for anything and anybody, and that's at every level of society and in every direction.

HUM: This is how it starts and started. This is how many of the other so-called advanced civilizations started with their downfall from the higher frequencies.

ME: So, how can we turn it around, what role do spiritual people and leaders need to play? Everyone appears to have a problem with everything and everyone.

HUM: It's very difficult. It needs a total sea change in the thinking process of the vast majority of the population of the Earth to make it work. That means that localized changes, although useful, have difficulty in triangulating with other localized changes and therefore affecting those in between the localized groups.

ME: Triangulation doesn't work in this case?

HUM: Not in the case it was recently, say before the advent of the expected ascension in 2012. At that point the frequencies were rising quite quickly but it seemed that two things happened after this date and when the expected "ascension" didn't happen in the way it was being described, and the expectations of the start of a new golden age didn't come into fruition.

ME: This was the start of the downturn in the frequencies and the result of the way the world has reacted?

HUM: Yes. As I stated, it doesn't take much to go down the slippery slope.

ME: So, what were the two things that happened?

HUM: First, the spiritual leaders that broadcast the so-called mass ascension (which we know is not how things work, they work on a gradual and individual basis) received ridicule and significant rejection of their teachings. Those that followed them lost faith and returned back to thinking, behaving, and acting in an immersed incarnate way.

Second, those that maintained their frequencies were affected in a subtle way. One in which they felt that they were OK, they were spiritual, and that they didn't need to continue to work on themselves to maintain their frequential level because they had made it. As a result, they slowly abandoned their spiritual routines and subsequently returned to their normal immersed incarnate state. Spiritually unaware and asleep.

These two things allowed them to be less questioning, less discerning, less aware of the things that can happen. Things can go wrong when one is not in observation of one's environment and those that interact with it. They were like the sleeping lazy guard dog that inadvertently lets in the thief, and when awakened, accepts food from the thief thinking that the thief is a friend. The thief therefore gets away with stealing the jewelry and the dog isn't bothered about it. Subsequently, the thief comes back the next day, and the next day, and the next day to finish the job, knowing that the guard dog now thinks that the thief is a friend!

This is how the general population responds to promises that have no basis to back them up when they have forgotten their sovereignty—they accept them as the truth.

ME: You seem to be very well versed in how the incarnate human race works when affected by the lower frequencies.

HUM: We observed the ways of Aspects incarnating with individualized free will for a high number of Event Spaces before we allowed you to incarnate. We studied them all!

The incarnate inhabitants of the Earth have decided that they are worthy of everything, irrespective of whether they have worked toward the natural reception of that which they desire. They want everything and they want it now, and they want to do whatever they like without consideration to other incarnates or what would be considered sensible law and order!!

ME: Hold on, I have just made a link.

HUM: You are associating the drop in frequencies with the increase in the so-called backfill people.

ME: You stole my thunder!

HUM: I was wondering how long it would take to make the connection. You have talked about the increase in the percentage of backfill people often enough in your "World Satsanga" to have made the connection a long time ago.

ME: You don't know how hard it is to be in the human body. The obvious isn't so obvious.

HUM: So I see. But, yes, you are correct and that is the reason why many of those that are incarnate are impatient, inconsiderate, angry, jealous, and vehemently materialistic.

ME: But this is a worldwide phenomenon. Everything seems to have changed in the last few years, like there was a tipping point!

HUM: OK, let me explain something that is important. Do you remember that ascension is an individual process that takes considerable effort over a long period where the incarnate Aspect is of service and/or is thinking, behaving, and acting in a higher frequency way?

ME: Yes, I do.

HUM: Then you are aware that the so-called mass ascension is not possible in the sense that everyone ascends into the next frequency as a function of the work of a small but significant percentage of hard-working individuals focusing on their spiritual advancement!

ME: Yes, but due to triangulation it does create an acceleration of awareness that affects everyone else because the frequencies around those that are working hard on themselves also affect those that are not, in a positive but subtle or subconscious way.

HUM: Correct. Note though that the effect on those that are affected by triangulation is still gradual and individualized, even if the number of those affected increases as a result.

ME: And this is because it is intrinsically more difficult to move up the frequencies.

HUM: Correct again.

ME: But it is easier to be affected by lower frequencies because it requires no work on the individual on behalf of the individual, i.e., themselves.

HUM: Correct. It is much easier to be lazy than it is to be proactive when someone else is doing the work. This is something that is particularly attractive to Aspects that are of a lower evolutionary or sentient level. Hence it is possible to collectively drop down the frequencies.

ME: And I guess this is something that is a particular cause for concern with the backfill Aspects?

HUM: Yes. As the number of incarnate "human" Aspects slowly but surely reduces as a function of their own individualized ascension, the number of incarnates also decreases. As you are aware, this needs to be "backfilled" by other Aspects that are wanting to accelerate their accrual of evolutionary content through the use of experiencing individualized free will. As a natural function of this, the number of incarnate "human" Aspects starts to reduce within the lower frequencies because they are ascending the frequencies to the next level when they incarnate next or within their current incarnation, the gross physical being the lowest of the frequencies [*the first three frequencies of the multiverse—GSN*]. The only way is up. Provided, of course, one is working toward ascension.

The desire to work toward ascension is something that is inherently "within all" TES and Aspects, irrespective of sentience or evolutionary level. Those Aspects that are of a higher sentient level, or those of a high evolutionary level but of a lower sentient level display this desire more readily. Those Aspects that are being allowed to incarnate on the Earth to "backfill" for those that are ascending to the fourth frequency are of a lower sentient level. Only a very few are of a higher evolutionary level. As a result, they are easily attracted to those thoughts, behaviors, and actions that are of a lower frequency or karmic level. Additionally, these backfill Aspects are not used to incarnating into an incarnate vehicle [*incarnate form factor—GSN*] that has the capability of working with individualized free will. Subsequently, they are easily attracted to, and consumed by, the possibility of being able to do anything they want, irrespective of what it is.

They still have a high sense of needing to be in a state of communion, however, and are therefore attracted to incarnates that are easy to become associated to frequentially. This means they still want frequential harmony. The issue is that in the need for frequential harmony, they allow themselves to commune with those that are easy to commune with. Those of an equal or lower frequency. This creates a snowball effect where low frequency attracts low frequency and grows in population as a result. One can see what happens when the low-frequency snowball grows in size. Its increase starts to become logarithmic/exponential and spiral out of control, getting lower and lower the longer it is in existence and the more incarnates of a lower frequency it attracts. The result is confusion, randomicity, lack of positive direction, and a lack of adherence to governance, even from those that are in the governance of others. Chaos prevails and becomes acceptable. Those in power start to feel that it is acceptable to use lies rather than truths to govern, and as a result those that are governed no longer hold those in government with respect. It is an ever-accelerating downward spiral that is difficult at best to slow down or stop.

ME: So complacency on behalf of those that think they are

operating in a spiritual way along with the increase in the number of backfill people is having a significant, if not acceleratory effect on how fast we are descending the frequencies.

HUM: Correct. The incarnate population of the Earth is heading toward a dark age again. One that was not unforeseen but also not expected, especially when considering how well incarnate mankind was doing twenty years ago! [*Circa the year 2000 onward—GSN*]

ME: I have to be honest, reading that we are heading for another dark age is not going to be easily digested by my readers or anyone else for that matter. It will place a lot of fear into them, reducing their frequencies more and more. I mean, we were on our way up the frequencies, and we could see it. It feels a bit of a let-down to know that we have descended the frequencies so much that we can be considered to be moving into a dark age. And, the descent has been very fast, so fast it has been, or appears to be, unstoppable!

HUM: *Potential* dark age! I do have to say that this is one thing that can be avoided should one be vigilant and in recognition of the reasons why the frequencies dropped in the way they did. It wasn't all about complacency.

ME: What do you mean, it wasn't all about complacency?

HUM: It's obvious, can't you see it?

ME: Hang on a moment. I will detach myself from the energy of expectation of seeing this as a failure on behalf of incarnate mankind.

HUM: Actually, even though there is a possibility of going into a spiritual dark age, there is also the possibility of going into the start of a spiritual golden age. It's just a matter of how one sees it.

ME: OK, I am looking. What I am seeing is that this drop in frequency and lack of understanding of the effects of incorrect decision making, including allowance of inappropriate leadership, is a function of the increase in backfill people, and the remaining incarnate human Aspects that haven't ascended yet. By ascended I mean moved on to the fourth frequency while incarnate, as the frequential basis for incarnation.

HUM: Correct. It's actually to be expected that as the number of incarnate Aspects move into the next frequency level, and are therefore replaced by backfill people, those Aspects that have a lower quality of sentience are not able to maintain the higher ambient frequency of the planet. As a result, it is natural for the frequencies to drop. This is what I meant by it not being unforeseen but also not expected.

ME: Does this mean they will be left behind?

HUM: No. As you are aware, ascension is an individualized function of self-governance, control of the way one thinks, behaves, and acts. Those Aspects that remain, including those that could have ascended but chose to remain to be of service to those who are yet to ascend, are being assisted by their guides and helpers to either maintain their frequency and/or increase it to that required to ascend to the next frequency.

ME: No one gets left behind then?

HUM: Eventually even those "backfill" Aspects will be able to move up the frequencies for they are also in the evolutionary cycle, their evolutionary cycle.

ME: Will the backfill Aspects move into the fourth frequency level and above?

HUM: Eventually, yes. But note that they are part of a different evolutionary cycle to incarnate humankind. They will therefore not ascend to the fourth level as a function of incarnating on Earth.

ME: Because of their quality of sentience!

HUM: Correct, because of their quality of sentience.

ME: So there is a point in Event Space where the Earth is occupied only by backfill Aspects!

HUM: Yes. However, this only applies to the gross physical level, the third frequency. Once the incarnate population of the Earth is occupied by backfill Aspects at this frequency level, the use of the third frequency level is negated and only the fourth and above is used.

ME: What happens to the backfill Aspects when the third frequency is no longer used for incarnate experience?

HUM: They are collectively removed from their incarnations.

ME: En masse?

HUM: Yes.

ME: Isn't that a bit drastic? I mean, doesn't this mean that there will be a worldwide loss of incarnate life, albeit backfill life?

HUM: No. Their incarnation is simply terminated. It is dissolved. There are no mass deaths, so to speak. They simply return to the energetic and continue their own evolutionary cycle in the way they were working with it before they had the opportunity to incarnate with individualized free will. Which of course, those backfill Aspects that experienced individualized free will, will have benefited from.

ME: So it's not a mass extinction!

HUM: No, it's more like a mass change similar to that orchestrated at the end of the period you call reptilian and even the Atlantean period. They simply cease to be incarnate. They are aware of this possible way to finish their work before they incarnate, and they accept it.

ME: What do you mean by "this possible way?"

HUM: Unlike "human" Aspects that incarnate and have myriad incarnations to work through, backfill Aspects only generally have one incarnation on the Earth. The plan is to allow as many backfill Aspects to incarnate on the Earth while the opportunity presents itself.

ME: So to do this, they are only allowed one incarnation each!

HUM: In general, correct. There are a very small number of rare cases when more than one incarnation on Earth is allowed.

ME: What about the Karma they accrue? They appear to be very good at accruing Karma!

HUM: It is collectively negated by all those in the evolutionary cycle.

ME: So "we" remove the Karma that is created by the backfill Aspects?

HUM: In a roundabout way, yes. You see, because they are providing a service to those that are slower to ascend the frequencies by maintaining the interactive environment that allows them to ascend, they are repaid in kind. This means that those Aspects that are of a higher quality of sentience absorb some of the addictive thoughts, behaviors, and actions of the backfill Aspects allowing them to leave their incarnation in a Karma-free way. All Aspects of a higher quality of sentience inherently help those around them to ascend, irrespective of how they performed in their incarnation.

ME: I get it. Because they helped out in allowing those "slower" human Aspects to ascend, they are rewarded by being given the evolutionary progression associated with an incarnation that allows individualized free will.

HUM: That's right.

ME: And the dark age could be the result of the process to having more and more backfill Aspects incarnating, together with their ease of attracting or being associated with the thoughts, behaviors, and actions that accrue Karma.

HUM: Correct. However, in the event that in this process it is realized that they are being of significant service by incarnate human Aspects, then forgiveness and help will be afforded by those remaining human Aspects, resulting in a change in the thoughts, behaviors, and actions of the backfill Aspects to those of a higher frequency.

ME: And this would negate or steer us away from the potential new dark age?

HUM: It would.

ME: What about the golden age you talked about briefly? Is this associated with incarnate humankind predominantly incarnating into the fourth frequency?

HUM: Yes, it is.

ME: What will happen to all the architecture, etc., that remains in the third or gross physical frequency?

HUM: You will still be able to interact with it, to use it, it's just that it will be more difficult to work with.

ME: How do you mean, "difficult to work with?" We will be able to see and interact with the content of the third frequency, so what makes it difficult?

HUM: When an incarnate is of a higher frequency rather than a part of the environment that is a lower frequency two things happen. First: the alignment is with the higher frequency, that which is the frequency of domicile. Second: the lower frequency is not in harmony with the higher frequency and as a result is more difficult to exist within. A good example is the frequency you currently exist within, which is a gas-based environment and is a higher frequency than water, which is a liquid-based environment. You can move freely around the gas-based environment but have difficulty moving around the liquid-based environment. It is slow to move around in, offering resistance to your movements, and limits some of your physical senses. Additionally, you cannot breathe the water so you cannot exist in this environment.

Working under water is difficult because there is a reduction in weight to assist in push-pull activity due to the function of buoyancy. If you remember, buoyancy is created as a function of the displacement of water by the volume of the body, which results in a net loss of weight and a lack of local anchorage to the location one is working within. The lack of local anchorage or gravity if you like, results in the inability to create a force that moves an object without incurring a reciprocal force in the opposite direction. This is because the buoyancy makes one lighter. The only way to circumnavigate this lack of weight is to adorn one's self with heavy or high-density objects such as lead weights, but this only helps with the vertical, and not the horizontal harmonization.

A similar function occurs when a higher frequency entity or being enters into a lower frequency environment, but for different reasons. In this instance the entity can move around the environment, but not influence or manipulate it. To be able to influence or manipulate the environment, the entity or being needs to actively reduce their frequency to allow them to interact with it. In reducing their frequency, the entity or being harmonizes with the frequencies of the environment and is able to both move around and interact with it as if it was the same as the environment that they are now normally domiciled within, taking into account certain higher frequency functional losses of course. This is why it's difficult to work with properly. One has to be in harmony with the frequency of the environment to be able to manipulate that environment.

ME: So, what you are saying is that when we are in the fourth frequency we can move around and enjoy the sights of the gross physical and its environment but need to reduce our frequencies on a temporary basis to interact with it properly.

HUM: Correct.

ME: So, what will the landscape look like when we have all ascended to the fourth frequency, the lower astral?

HUM: It's going to be an interesting landscape for you to work with. It will be like working on two frequency levels while focusing on the one.

Because one will be on the higher frequency, you will work with the higher frequency. Everything that you do, interact with, or create will be on the fourth frequency.

ME: Everything? Such as houses, transportation? What about that which is on the third or gross physical frequency level?

HUM: Do you mean, will the content in the environment that is supported by the third frequency or gross physical interfere with the content on the fourth?

ME: That's what I meant, yes.

HUM: The answer to that is yes and no.

ME: How do you mean?

HUM: In general, no content in one frequency interferes with the content in another because everything is predominantly represented by the frequency it is associated with or created within.

ME: So we only observe that which is within our own frequency.

HUM: By and large, yes. However, as you remember, those entities or beings that exist in the fourth frequency can observe and navigate through that in the third frequency and only interact with it if they temporarily lower their frequencies. Those in the fifth can observe and navigate through the content of the third and fourth frequencies if they lower their frequencies to that associated with those levels—individually.

However, what I didn't allude to is that seeing and navigating through the content of a lower frequency is two separate things. The first, the process of lowering one's frequency, allows the interaction with the content within the environment that that frequency supports. This is available to the entity on a single frequency basis. The second and more common process is the observation of the content of the environment supported by changing the focus of the spiritual or third eye to include the content of the frequency/ies below the frequency level that they are on.

ME: And this means that everything looks like it is interfering with everything else. For example, a building on the third frequency may look like it has a bridge from the fourth frequency protruding through it, with the building and the bridge looking like it has a medium of transport, say a train and its rail system, running through them both.

HUM: Correct. Unless the entity or being is capable of working with the content from all the frequencies they are capable of observing concurrently, observing the content in the environment they are within and the other frequencies they are focusing on becomes difficult at best. It becomes a distraction.

ME: I can imagine it is—yes. I would guess that the higher up the frequencies associated with the physical universe, the more capable an incarnate entity or being is of being able to observe the frequencies concurrently that are lower than the one they are incarnate into.

HUM: Yes, that is true, but those incarnate entities that are capable of such concurrent observation of the environmental content of the frequencies below them don't, in general, concern themselves with such a function. They are focused on what they are doing in the frequency they incarnated into. Incarnation is hard enough as it is, at any frequency, let alone trying to observe or become part of that which is nothing but a distraction in reality. In general, entities that have the capability for multifrequential observation only use such functions or abilities if they really need to. Most never use them.

Like most things in the physical universe, if you haven't

got it, you want it, if you have it, you don't use it.

ME: Got it.

I have one question to move on from this subject with.

HUM: Carry on.

ME: Getting back to my earlier question, what does the environment supported by the fourth frequency on Earth look like? We have heard lots about the so-called astral levels, what I now know as the fourth, fifth, sixth, and seventh frequency levels, but a description of just one of them would be interesting.

HUM: I will try to describe to you how you might perceive the fourth frequency level, what you call the lower astral.

ME: OK, thank you.

HUM: The first thing to initially notice is that there will appear to be little or no difference in the natural landscape.

ME: Why is that?

HUM: Because that which is natural is pan-frequential, so it is present, or should I say, represented on all of the frequencies of the physical universe and therefore the Earth.

ME: Is everything that is natural experienced on all of the frequency levels?

HUM: Yes and no.

ME: Can you explain?

HUM: The first three frequency levels are used concurrently to create the gross physical environment and so they are experienced collectively. The remaining nine levels, levels four through twelve, are experienced individually, or should one have the capacity, collectively in the way previously explained. That being, one can perceive the content of the frequencies below where one is positioned frequentially, but not above. Being domicile on the twelfth frequency level an entity can observe all that is in their spatial location from a frequential perspective.

ME: OK, that makes sense, and I expect it will make sense to the readers.

HUM: It will but they also need to know that although the overall natural environment will remain unchanged, that which is created on each of the frequency levels above the third will be predominantly represented on that frequency.

ME: The natural landscape remains unchanged but that which is created on each of the levels changes then. The only difference is that an entity has to learn or have the natural capacity to perceive that which is on the frequencies below them to observe what is below them frequentially.

HUM: That's what I just said. But it's worth noting though that the higher up the frequencies associated with the physical universe one is, the easier it is to observe concurrent frequencies beneath one, simply because of the additional functionality associated with being incarnate on a higher frequency.

ME: Got it.

HUM: Good. One of the main things that you would notice is the vibrancy of everything that is around you.

ME: Everything? Do you mean the natural landscape and the man-made landscape?

HUM: Yes. On the fourth frequency level one can start to observe the energies associated with their physicality, their construction.

Each of the natural constructs will have one level of energy that is associated with their natural resonant frequency.

From the human perspective, they will be perceived in a different way dependent upon that resonant frequency. I will explain, but first please note that the colors I state are just for human understanding. In real terms the color of energy associated even with the fourth frequency is significantly outside the visual range of the human eye:

- **Mountains and hard mineral-based land** are the significantly less obvious living aspects of the environment and will therefore have a shimmering gray/silvery glow about them. The mineral-based land masses are particularly "slow" frequentially and as a result, their appearance is only augmented by the entity's ability to see the magnetoenergetic haze (aura) associated with the subatomic interaction between the different metallic ores that are present in the rock.

- **Clay-based land** has a glow and a color that is somewhat more opaque but can be considered to be close to that of a bright orange. From the energetic perspective, clay is considered to be a liquid form of mineral.

- **Soft earth-based land** is quite obviously the result of the composting process and as such has a glow and color that can only be described as being a mixture of orange and green resulting in a green-based brown. This color also has a glow, but it is not as vibrant as the bright orange of the clay-based land.

- **Rivers, lakes, and seas** will have a vibrant turquoise energetic glow to them with seas giving a deeper turquoise than the rivers and which have a more translucent appearance to them.
- **Trees, plants, and grasses** are the start of the more obvious living aspects of the natural environment and as a result have the characteristic gold-colored glow about them. This glow will change in strength, noted by how far away from the tree, plant, or grass, etc., the outline of the energetic field is from the physical outer edge of the tree/plant, etc.
- **Animals and fish** are animated living aspects of the environment and subsequently have a more complicated modality of interaction with the environment. They have a construct that is similar to that used to create the incarnate human vehicle, insomuch as they have more than one energetic template and a chakra system, which is a key requirement for the ability for an Aspect (of the correct sentient quality, which is significantly lower than that of the sentience of a human Aspect) to incarnate into. The energy associated with animals and fish is similar to that of the incarnate human vehicle and as such has an iridescent and shimmering gold color, which if observed closely, can also be broken down into visible colors in certain ambient light.
- **Artificial inanimate constructs such as buildings, etc.,** have a similar glow to mountain and hard mineral-based land but do not shimmer and tend to present a color that is more toward the gray. Items of furniture that are made out of wood illustrate a glow close to a living tree but without the intensity of the color or glow. Metallic objects tend to show a silver-based color but without the shimmer effect. In some instances, they can be a little confused, especially if formed into an alloy.
- **Artificial moving constructs** such as transport mediums tend to show a dark opaque gray color that neither shimmers nor glows but simply covers the outside of the shape of the construct. It is still obvious to the observer though.
- **Artificial electrical constructs** such as

communication mediums are also dark gray in appearance but have a shimmering metallic effect to the color. Sometimes they also illustrate the odd spark.

- **Incarnate human and similar vehicles** illustrate the energy similarly associated with animals and fish but have a significantly higher vibrant level of iridescent and shimmering gold color, which if observed closely, can also be broken down into vibrant, slightly translucent but visible colors in certain ambient light.

ME: What you are basically saying is that everything on the fourth frequency level has a visible aura around it.

HUM: Yes, that's correct. However, everything on the third or gross physical frequency level does as well, it's just that your physical eyesight is too low frequency to see it in the normal sense. The auras observed on the fourth frequency level are significantly more vibrant in comparison to the third level though.

ME: And we see all of these auras all of the time on the fourth level?

HUM: Yes. And those who are using their third eye are also seeing the auras around inanimate and animate objects on this third level as well.

ME: I see them as a function of my physical eyes at times but mostly it's in my mind's eye, so to speak. When I close my eyes, I see or perceive that which is available on the frequency I am focused on.

HUM: That is the way that you chose to observe the content of the frequencies above this level.

ME: We choose what and how we are going to see?

HUM: Yes. You chose to see things how humans do and hence your visual connectivity to the higher frequencies is via your spiritual, third, or mind's eye.

ME: I call that stupidity on my part.

HUM: It's what you chose to do, and it has helped you understand the human condition in more depth as a result. You now appreciate the human condition better than you ever have.

ME: I guess it's not all about having higher levels of connectivity when we are here at this frequency level.

HUM: No. It's all about the experience …

ME & HUM Together: Learning and evolution!!!!

ME: Well, I guess we are in agreement there!

HUM: Yes, we are always in agreement. It's just that when you are in this low-frequency state of beingness it's difficult for you to recognize it.

ME: OK, what else can we say about the way we see things here or on other frequencies?

HUM: The spiritual or mind's eye is where most of that which is "seen" is observed. There are times when people of a higher frequency can see both that which is a function of the physical eye and the spiritual eye concurrently. Therefore, they are perceived to be one and the same thing but in actuality they are not. The one is an overlay onto the other.

ME: They see that which is only seen by the third eye as if it is part of their physical vision and they cannot discriminate between the two?

HUM: Correct. When they are young, they see everything, but this can and is mostly turned off when their parents or peer group tell them that what they are seeing is a lie, that they are making it up. As a result, they start to disbelieve it and slowly turn it off in order to conform to the so-called norm.

ME: And with training, I suppose, they can turn it back on?

HUM: Yes. But as I have just said, some still retain this function, but in order to retain it they need to hide, or not mention that which they see in the way they see it because in adults this can be classified as a form of schizophrenia.

ME: Getting back to what the fourth frequency level looks like then, can you continue?

HUM: Yes, of course. From the perspective of the limited visual functions afforded to the incarnate human vehicle, it can never be explained in a way that is fully understandable.

ME: I would expect that is the same for most of that which is the greater reality.

HUM: Very true. The best way to explain it is in the way I have just been explaining it, in terms of vibrancy. Everything is vibrant and has an aura associated with it. The level of vibrancy dictates how the aura is perceived.

ME: How can one describe the different levels of vibrancy?

HUM: The higher the frequency of that being observed, the more profound and bigger the aura. Vibrancy is also a function of purity, which of course is a function of high frequency. Vibrancy can also be a function of harmony within the environment that an entity is in. This includes the natural flora and fauna of the environment and its own level of harmony with the environment it is within. Another way in which vibrancy can be augmented is the love broadcast as a function of one's appreciation of that which they are interacting with. This vibrancy is therefore shared between the appreciator and that which is being appreciated.

ME: I understand that the human energy field, the human aura, is a function of the losses sustained by the process of receiving energy from the chakras and distributing it around the energy templates. I also understand that an increase in frequency is one way to increase vibrancy. But how would one's vibrancy appear to the observer?

HUM: The changes in vibrancy of an object, whether it is animate or not, results in the destabilization of its solidarity. Therefore, it no longer has the appearance of being a so-called solid or gross physical object. The aura seen around both animate and inanimate objects is not just a function of the losses incurred by the processes used by the chakras to energize the energy templates, it is also a function of the vibrancy associated with the higher frequencies that are part of its composition. This means that what you call "color" when you are seeing the auric layers of an animate object are also a function of its vibrancy. Certainly, that is from the perspective of the spirituo-physical or astral frequencies.

ME: That makes sense.

HUM: Of course, it does!

ME: From what I am experiencing now, I see that what I could call a golden or silver-colored aura around objects at the fourth level is really just the movement of destabilized atoms around the periphery of the object. It looks like it's only the edge or outer surface though.

HUM: It's not just the outer edge or periphery of the object, it's the whole object that is destabilized and looking vibrant.

ME: If it's the whole object then why does it only look like the outer edge is shimmering and looking vibrant?

HUM: Because that is the interface between gross physicality and simple density.

ME: Simple density?

HUM: The air.

ME: Right!

HUM: It only looks like it is not vibrant when you look at the center of the object because you are seeing it through its gross physicality and not in comparison with simple density.

ME: OK, it's like looking at a pencil lead head on, so to speak; it looks like it is as thick as the pencil is long whereas in actual fact if you look at it from the side it's nowhere near as thick, it's nowhere near as dense.

HUM: That's one way to consider it.

This vibrancy is a key feature of "vision-based" interaction with animate and inanimate objects in the fourth frequency. Indeed, you will be able to know more about someone as a function of their vibrancy.

ME: Go on.

HUM: Vibrancy is an indicator of how "well" or how "healthy" something is. It doesn't matter if that which is being observed is animated or not, that being, whether it is an incarnate human, animal, fish, bird, or a tree or plant. If it is healthy, it is in tune with its environment in every way possible. It is in harmony.

ME: And harmony is also a psycho-spiritual consideration as well.

HUM: Yes. When an Aspect is incarnate into the fourth frequency, the Aspect can "see" not only the health of that which it is observing, but it can also know the harmony of its interaction with its overall environment. Additionally, the Aspect can also see the psycho-spiritual health of the Aspect within its incarnate state.

ME: How does psycho-spiritual health present itself?

HUM: In the event that the incarnate Aspect is in psycho-spiritual harmony with its self, its surroundings or environment, and those within its environment, its vibrancy is broadcast as an overall glow of golden/silvery color because it is in maintenance of its higher frequency and is required to stay in the fourth frequency level.

Remember, of course, that this vibrancy is the function of the destabilization of the atoms that create the gross physical. Note that atoms are the largest component of the building blocks of the physical. Atoms are six levels of quanta above the Anu, which is the initial manifestation of physicality. Low frequency or vibrancy creates stasis or solidity. High frequency or vibrancy creates loss of stasis, destabilization, and lack of solidity.

When an Aspect is experiencing disharmonious thought processes, these are manifest as lower frequencies which can position themselves around the incarnate vehicle in any location.

ME: What would they look like?

HUM: From the perspective of the human eye, they would look

like areas of darkness that surround certain parts of the body. This darkness can also present itself in certain colorific ways depending upon the level of disharmony. For example, dark green, dark gray, red, green, blue, and yellow are commonly observed colors when psycho-spiritual disharmonies are being experienced by the Aspect.

ME: Is the overall vibrancy of the body maintained when these other colors are displayed?

HUM: Yes, but not in the direct area where the disharmony is being experienced. It is also worth noting, as you know, that thought-based disharmony also results in physical ailments and these ailments can be observed and diagnosed as a result of correctly interpreting their colorific value. A competent healer, once observing these disharmonies, can affect remedial healing modalities to change the psycho-spiritual disharmonies that are creating the physical ailments. I also want to say that in the fourth frequency, disharmonious thoughts are rarely allowed to progress to the level where they cause physical issues.

ME: I guess that is simply because they are noted straight away, early on?

HUM: Correct. Because disfunction or disharmonious thoughts are seen at the initial manifestation stage, they are dealt with immediately and as such, the gross physical—how it is represented at that frequency—is not affected.

ME: I wish we could use this way to cure illness that is created by disharmonious thoughts at the third frequency. It would free up a lot of hospital beds.

HUM: It would free up most hospital beds.

ME: I am sure it would. I want to explore how the Earth "and its inhabitants" presents itself at the fourth frequency level some more. Particularly how incarnate Aspects interact with it and those other incarnates that they occupy the same space with.

HUM: The major difference between the third and fourth frequency is the connectivity with the natural side of the planet. Whereas there is almost no "feeling" of beingness in the third frequency, there is a much more defined level of beingness in the fourth. In actuality, it is quite a jump in comparison with the frequential level.

ME: How do you mean? Can you explain?

HUM: At the fourth level, incarnate Aspects are able to see, observe, or experience how the environment responds to how they interact with it. Communication with each other is also augmented and as a result, feelings are more transparent than they are in the third level. An incarnate Aspect is aware of how their thoughts, behaviors, and actions affect not only those they interact with, but also themselves. Emotions such as aggression are minimized because it is considered to be nonproductive. As a result, such low-frequency thoughts, behaviors, and actions are avoided.

ME: People start to love each other.

HUM: They do, and this love is even more pronounced when the Aspect incarnates into the fifth frequency. More importantly, they also start to love the Earth and its flora and fauna.

ME: Does this create a desire to return back to nature? To interact with nature in a more harmonious way?

HUM: It does. The fourth frequency level produces an innate feeling of wanting to be in harmony. This doesn't mean that incarnate humankind returns to plowing the fields with oxen for example, far from it, but it does mean that technological progressions are considered with the benefit of the environment in mind.

For example:

- Limiting the human population to that which is in harmony with the environment it is located within
- Manufacturing raw materials into usable base materials/metals in a nonpolluting way
- Putting back into the environment that which has been taken away but in a balanced way that maintains the existing environment in the way it is supposed to be. This includes resisting the need to overcompensate, further resulting on imbalance
- Maintenance of the biodiversity of the planet. Everything has a role to play, no matter how small or large the biodiverse component is
- Recognition of the interdependence of the biodiverse components
- Recognition of the interaction of the biodiverse components
- Use of the correct interdependence and interaction of biodiverse components to support changes to the environment
- Repopulation of barren ground with flora and fauna while also being aware of the biodiversity that exists and thrives in so-called barren ground
- Allowing nature to reclaim human habitation by

removing human habitation and relocating the population, such as buildings underground and/or in buildings that are above ground but that have limited surface area and therefore don't encroach upon the land in the way cities currently do.

- The understanding of, and harvesting of energy, without the use of massive generating machinery and distribution networks. This includes the generation of power to allow "mass" communication.

ME: So, are incarnate humankind, that have ascended to this level, doing this sort of thing right now?

HUM: They are and they have. At this frequency, one experiences the start of the so-called golden era. One where there is no need for overall governance because there is individual governance that is geared toward the idea of being in communion. This is the start of how to become a true global civilization.

ME: And this is happening right now in the fourth frequency?

HUM: Yes. You might be interested in knowing that this level of working, interacting together, and with the environment increases in harmony the higher up the frequencies one is. For example, the fifth frequency is more advanced in this regard than the fourth, and the sixth frequency is more advanced than the fifth, etc., etc.

ME: And this includes achieving everything in terms of advancement but without the detrimental effects?

HUM: Yes, although the reduction of detrimental actions is also a function of how high one incarnates into the frequencies associated with the physical universe.

The higher one is frequentially, the more aware and awake one is to the greater reality and how to benefit from existing within it in a nondetrimental way. It really is a big deal.

ME: I suppose that unless one can see this truth, one is oblivious to the opportunities that working together in service to each other and the environment presents to us.

HUM: Correct. Those on a higher frequency are constantly shouting words of encouragement, while shaking their heads in dismay when those in the frequency below simply ignore or don't hear the words. It can be most frustrating.

ME: Now I can fully understand.

I was thinking about all of the misinformation, manipulation of obvious data and population control through broadcasting fear-based soundbites that was happening right now (it's March

2021 and the COVID-19 pandemic is still in full swing). The vast percentage of the world population is afraid, even when the truth is obvious and staring one directly in the face. The amount of nonsense that was and is being broadcast to the general public is shameful. I became really very concerned for the future of incarnate mankind at this frequency. Just how are they going to pull themselves out of this low-frequency downward spiral?

HUM: They will. The spiral will eventually flatten out and there will be a gradual, steady climb back to a higher level. Don't forget that there is a high percentage of the population that are incarnate backfill Aspects. They are not used to this level of individualized free will and what that can do to the unsuspecting Aspect. The low frequencies can be very addictive and difficult to move one's way of thinking, behaving, and acting away from. They can catch an Aspect out!

ME: Bad habits take a long time to move away from in a robust way.

HUM: And you know that that can be what you call five to eight years because every time a temptation is presented to one, it is a test of how robust the change in thinking, behaving, and acting is.

ME: Agreed.

OK, I think we are finished here. It is enough for the readers to know that to enter the golden era each and every one of us must work hard on ourselves overcoming the temptations and addictions that physicality presents to us. As we work on ourselves, we increase the chances of our ability to ascend to the next frequency level, and as a result, see behind the veil of the gross physical while we are still incarnate. Seeing beyond the veil of gross physicality, even for a moment, is enough to provide a lifetime's encouragement to succeed in mastering incarnation in a single lifetime.

HUM: Very true, good words.

ME: I want to talk a bit more about quantum mechanics now. I have a feeling that we are not quite finished with this subject.

HUM: We haven't even scratched the surface, or should I say, thought about scratching the surface.

ME: Why do I get the feeling that this is going to be a mind-bender!!!

More on Everything Being Everything Else—A Quantum Conundrum

I had been feeling for some time that we were going to return to the subject of quantum mechanics and how incarnate mankind's assumption of quantum functionality was about as good as knowing one plus one equals two, but that this is only correct because we assume that it is reasonable to think that one plus one equals two. What about if it didn't equal two? I could feel my mind spinning already with the concepts that were about to be presented to me. What's more, as I turned my attention to this, I felt more than the usual energy associated with Hum. It was a much bigger, well-known presence that I hadn't expected to feel.

ANNE & HUM & OM & ALL OM: Greetings beloved of The OM, we are one again, even if you are frequentially distant.

To be honest, this way of introducing themselves and saying hello was a bit cheesy to me!

ANNE & HUM & OM & ALL OM: What is this cheese?
ANNE: I can tell you about cheese!
ANNE & HUM & OM & ALL OM: Oh, thank you—how strange.

I found this way that The OM answered Anne a bit strange as well as the cheese being strange, so before we delved into the delights of the quanta, I wanted to ask why Anne responded to

179

herself.

ANNE: I answered a question in the singular and received the answer, my answer as part of the collective OM in communion as one.

ME: Hang on, are you suggesting that even if you answer or ask a question, you receive or even hear the question and then the answer as if you were both individualized from, and in communion with, The OM.

ANNE: Thanks, that's correct.

ANNE & HUM & OM & ALL OM: Didn't you experience that as well, dearest beloved of The OM?

ME: Yes, no, er, possibly differently than what you are suggesting.

ANNE & HUM & OM & ALL OM: We are just seeing how detached from communion you have become as a function of being in these low frequencies and having to exist and communicate in the only ways that are available to you.

ME: Well, all I can say is that it is prohibitive at best.

ANNE & HUM & OM & ALL OM: Well, we can now understand a word humans use.

ME: What word is that?

ANNE & HUM & OM & ALL OM: Impossible!

ME: Why do I feel that the one plus one question has a big part to play in this next discussion on quantum mechanics/theory?

ANNE & HUM & OM & ALL OM: You will see!

Mmmm, I was getting the feeling that this was going to be even more of a mind-bender than I have anticipated. What if, just what if, everything that we knew as physics was up for grabs, so, nothing could be taken for granted? Not even my comment on one plus one equaling two. I was starting to feel convolution coming into play.

ANNE & HUM & OM & ALL OM: Nothing in the multiverse is as it seems. This translates to the same in the physical universe as well. At any frequency level.

ME: What do you mean, nothing is as it seems?

ANNE & HUM & OM & ALL OM: In your current incarnate state you are only able to work in a linear fashion, simply because the frequencies only allow such functionality. This also means so-called 3D or volumetric linearity. However, this is just a level of conditioning that is perpetuated as a function of being able to work with what has gone on, and subsequently been recorded before. What you would call the past.

ME: So you are suggesting that we are conditioned by our forebearers, our scientific forebearers?

ANNE & HUM & OM & ALL OM: Of course, because you are all unable to move beyond the linearity expressed by these frequencies, you cannot see beyond that which has been discovered or understood before your interaction with the problem to be solved. Henceforth, you are already limited in your thinking.

ME: Go on.

ANNE & HUM & OM & ALL OM: Your intention or desire to see a certain response gives the response you desire, not that which is real!

ME: Are you suggesting then that all of our scientific experiments are flawed because they are based upon what we already know?

ANNE & HUM & OM & ALL OM: Yes.

There are two things that incarnate humankind, or any incarnate vehicle that is occupied by a smaller Aspect of a True Energetic Self in this/these low frequency/ies, needs to recognize before they can move onward and upward in the frequencies.

ME: And they are?

ANNE & HUM & OM & ALL OM: That everything is everything else, and that desire is a prime motivator for the generation of creation.

ME: OK, you have me. Can you explain a bit more for me?

ANNE & HUM & OM & ALL OM: Let's put it into a structure, one that you will be able to understand and relay to your readers.

ME: Sounds like a plan.

ANNE & HUM & OM & ALL OM: We will keep it simple and use just two headings: fluidity and desire.

ME: OK, do carry on.

Fluidity

ANNE & HUM & OM & ALL OM: We will focus on the physical universe in this description while understanding that everything that we share with you can also apply, along with much higher levels of detail, to the multiverse in general.

ME: Understood.

ANNE & HUM & OM & ALL OM: The Source Entity, this Source Entity, created an area within itself that, although compartmentalized from itself, is still itself. As a result, all that is within this compartmentalized volume of itself is capable of becoming all or anything that is in the volume of sentient energy that is The Source Entity. This is true while being compartmentalized and therefore constrained to this volume of separation from The Source while being within The Source.

This volume of compartmentalized Source Entity is in every way The Source Entity but with one major difference to the overarching sentience that is The Source. This difference is the division of sentience into what you know as the myriad number of smaller divisions of sentience into True Energetic Selves and subsequent smaller Aspects of the True Energetic Self. However, this is not the only division of so-called sentience. The entire volume of compartmentalization is also sentient, but, that sentience is not pro-active, so to speak, and can therefore be classified as dormant or passive.

The sentience and associated energies/frequency are therefore malleable to the desires of fully individualized sentience, such as a TES or Aspect, etc., including The Source itself, should it desire to interact within this area of itself, and as such, can be assigned to be anything that any TES or Aspect of individualized sentience desires. It can be, and is, anything and can therefore be considered fluid.

From the quantum level of understanding the "physical" universe, this means that every component of the physical is capable of being anything that is a natural function of or is created within it. This is true for any juncture in Event Space, an Event Stream within an Event Space or a reality within an Event Stream within an Event Space. This level of fluidity is not a result of the programming or assignation of quantum behavior from the "perspective of neutrality" to "specific functionality" because this is "linearity." It assumes that "something" has to be "nothing" first, before it can be "something," and that that "something" is a static state until interacted with to change it to another static state of somethingness.

Fluidity is the constant state of everything or "everythingness." This means that every component of the physical universe, no matter what it is, is not just

capable of being everything else, but IS everything else—
CONCURRENTLY.

ME: What does that mean to the already confused reader?

ANNE & HUM & OM & ALL OM: It means that what you see
as being a pen, for example, is also a car, a house, a plane,
a table, a computer—concurrently. That which is the pen is
not "one" thing, it is "all" things. It's just that due to your
existence being a low-frequency one, you are only able to see
or interact with the physical universe, currently, in a linear
way. This linear way only allows you to interact with that
which is the physical universe, and which is created within the
physical universe, in isolated states of everythingness—that
which we call somethingness from a "specific" perspective
and not in an "everything" or "fluid" perspective which is
how we OM interact with the multiverse.

The fun is working and interacting with everything and
then something together to understand what "limitation" is and
feels like in certain specific somethingness conditions. That is
why you are here in this level of specific somethingness.

ME: Thinking in the context of entanglement then, what does this
mean?

ANNE & HUM & OM & ALL OM: It means that there is no
such thing as entanglement because there is nothing to be
entangled with, because the quantum component which is
desired to be entangled with another quantum component is
already identical to the other quantum component, and in all
ways different to, all things on any level, not just a quantum
level.

When you employ your desire to experience something,
that something is interpreted by the universe to be that which
is expected through your desire, which is a function of your
preprograming, which resulted from interacting with the
limitations of prior knowledge.

If you could observe this reality from our perspective, you
would see that it is all things "concurrently" and not one thing
"currently."

ME: So in the instance of scientific experimentation, our
expectation governs how we get the result, not the experiment
itself.

ANNE & HUM & OM & ALL OM: To some degree, yes.

ME: What do you mean, "to some degree?"

ANNE & HUM & OM & ALL OM: There are times when the
experimenter has no expectation, simply because there is no

desired outcome or the experiment is simply for interest and not to gain a result. When an experiment is created in this way, that being there is no desire or expectation associated with the experiment in terms of gaining a result, the true result is manifest.

ME: I am just seeing an image of Sir Isaac Newton and his observation that led him to make the statement about gravity, *"what goes up must come down."* Is this an example of an experiment without expectation?

ANNE & HUM & OM & ALL OM: No, this is an example of simple observation of an object, in this instance an apple, that hit him on the head. This observation was taken as being a constant based upon the fact that, in his location, and on the Earth in general, that if an object is thrown into the air, it will fall to the ground. It was a simple observation that created a simple law. There was no expectation associated with the apple falling to the ground, it just happened. The fact that that observation could be repeated created the condition that the observation was robust enough to be considered as a physical law.

ME: What would have happened if there was an expectation associated with the apple that it would not fall to the ground, but would float in midair?

ANNE & HUM & OM & ALL OM: Provided that there was no other observation that would have counteracted that expectation, then the apple would float in midair exactly as you said.

The issue here is that there was already a history of Newton's personal observations, along with the observations of others, that recognized that objects do fall to the ground. It was not classified as anything at that point but was more of a linear understanding based upon historical, passively interacted group experience. Had there been a desire associated with an experiment then that desire would have contributed toward the ultimate result.

This creates another issue. That in actuality what goes up can stay up!

ME: How does that work? Is it based upon how the object interacts with the Earth or its density/frequential level?

ANNE & HUM & OM & ALL OM: Density is ultimately based upon the frequential content of the object. How it interacts with the Earth is based upon how it is desired to interact.

ME: Are you saying that we ultimately have a say in how

everything around us reacts to everything else?

ANNE & HUM & OM & ALL OM: Yes. It is only your limitations in thought that creates that limitation in how everything works.

ME: And this limitation is based upon our expectations.

ANNE & HUM & OM & ALL OM: Correct. Expectations are based upon previous experiences and/or observations or what you are told as being law, so to speak. That limits the ability of the incarnate sentience to be in total acceptance. Without expectation all experiments would be much simpler, much cheaper, and result in more correct/relevant answers.

The use of desire can affect everything. Even when one is not considering that they are using desire, it can have an effect on an outcome. If you have enough conviction in your desire, then you can create the condition that allows what goes up to stay up.

Desire

ANNE & HUM & OM & ALL OM: The most important thing that you need to be aware of is that everything is in a constant state of "potential."

ME: Potential what?

ANNE & HUM & OM & ALL OM: Potential to be.

ME: Potential to be what? You are playing with me now!!!!

ANNE & HUM & OM & ALL OM: Yes, we are, but the game has a function.

ME: And what is the game?

ANNE & HUM & OM & ALL OM: To make you un-think.

The "potential to be" means that everything can be everything because it already is everything. As we described earlier on in this dialogue, there are no laws that govern what can be, because what "is" is based upon the desire of those entities that interact with that which can "be."

What this means is that, as we have already stated, everything is everything. It is just the desire of the entity interacting with the environment that creates the designation from "the potential to be" to "that which is." Note however that "that which is" always has "the potential to be," it is just that it has a temporary assignation based upon the desires of those entities that interact with whatever has "the potential to be" making it "that which is."

ME: Everything we see, touch, taste, hear, and smell is held in the state of "that which is" because we have the desire to leave it in that state or want it to be in a certain state based upon a combination of our desires and expectations, which, while incarnate, are confused with our so-called incarnate programming.

ANNE & HUM & OM & ALL OM: Yes! And to use a new description that your scientists have derived, this, in the physical universe, is real "quantum locking!"

ME: Let me throw in this question. If everything that we interact with is locked into "that which is," then this must be based upon a worldwide mutual desire to accept a certain level of "that which is" as being the norm?

ANNE & HUM & OM & ALL OM: This is true. But this is only a function of linearity, of thinking in a linear way. If one chose not to accept "that which is," one could be in a constant state of "the potential to be."

ME: And when one is in a constant state of "the potential to be," anything is possible!

ANNE & HUM & OM & ALL OM: Yes! Now you are getting it.

Using Quantum Fluidity to Influence Our Environment

ME: Thinking out loud then, if we, as incarnate entities, fully understood the basics of quantum physics as quantum fluidity, that everything is fluid and that mathematics will never explain its functionality, we would make a huge jump forward in our understanding of the function of our universal and then, multiversal environment. And moreover, that so-called entanglement is an underlying function of Polyomniscient, Polyomnipresent sentience and its focus at different levels; we would know how to manipulate our environment.

ANNE & HUM & OM & ALL OM: You would be able to manipulate it in a most beneficial way. This doesn't mean that you would have a desire to abuse the environment because you would know better. However, you would know what needs to be done to make it sustainable and how to provide for yourselves without affecting the sustainability of that environment. In essence, you would be master manifesters or better still, master creators.

ME: I guess this requires incarnate humankind to understand that everything that is classified as physical is only in a state of beingness because of our desire for it to be in that state of beingness. That we have desired everything to be portrayed in a linear way, that everything we exist with and within is expected to have been created, only as a product of the previous creation being in place to allow it to happen. It's like we need the wheel to be invented before the cart, not the cart before the wheel, or radio to be invented before television not the other way around. We need certain levels of physicality to be in place before we think we can move to the next level of physicality, this is our linearity.

ANNE & HUM & OM & ALL OM: Limiting, isn't it? The only way to achieve the level of understanding that allows one to move away from the state of limited linear thinking is to raise one's frequency up to the point where the thinking process is based upon one's normal level of Polyomniscient knowledge.

ME: Which frequency level would this need to be?

ANNE & HUM & OM & ALL OM: Frequency levels above the sixth are where one can start to understand the true nature of the environment that one incarnates into.

ME: So, the fourth and fifth are no good? They aren't high enough?

ANNE & HUM & OM & ALL OM: The benefit of being in a higher frequency than one is currently within is that the limitations associated with the previous level, and indeed in some ways the current level, start to present themselves as being limitations. Moreover, they stop being blockages and start to be areas of opportunity for progression. That being, they are seen as a lack of understanding and are therefore not standardized as a justifiable physical rule or law that will always be necessary.

ME: Does this mean that Einstein's law of general relativity, the $E = MC^2$ is one such blockage?

ANNE & HUM & OM & ALL OM: Yes. You see, at the time of this Aspect's contribution to physics, and even now, there were limitations in the ability to see around that which is considered to be an immoveable or unbreakable understanding. One of the major contributions to the limitations that this law of general relativity gave is that Einstein was considered to be a genius. If he said that the speed of light could not be broken due to the effect that an object's mass has on itself the closer it got to the speed of light, then that statement must be classified as an unbreakable law, even more so when a calculation justifies it. What cannot be seen at this frequency is that the frequency that one exists within creates the inability to access information and knowledge that is available in higher frequencies and therefore acts as a blockage. The speed of light is only a so-called unbreakable barrier to the incarnate that is not aware of the function of the particle/ wave of that which is called light within this third frequency level. Its function is much different in the fourth frequency simply because light as you know it is a function of the third frequency. Additionally, it is quantum locked into its limited functionality because incarnate humankind has, through its desire to accept limited linear-based thinking, accepted its functionality to be in accordance with that of a so-called expert within the third frequency. However, even with the current drop in frequencies that the Earth is experiencing [*April 2021—GSN*], the frequency is higher than it was when Einstein was a dominant factor in theoretical physics and as a result, scientists are starting to observe the effects of desire in their experiments into quantum mechanics. Although they won't accept it as desire, they are considering that their presence has an effect on the outcome of the experiments. This ability to consider that you, as incarnate Aspects in the human form, can affect your environment in some way, is a major milestone in the ultimate understanding of who you are and the environment within which you exist.

ME: So, the recognition of how incarnate mankind can affect its environment in terms of its solidity or physicality by collectively recognizing that it is only in one particular state of quantum locking because we all collectively desire it to be in that state, coupled together with the understanding that every aspect of the quanta not only has the potential to be everything else, but actually is everything else, is the key.

ANNE & HUM & OM & ALL OM: Yes, this is going to be the springboard for moving away from linear thinking and into what is holistic spherical thinking [*see the glossary—GSN*]. Holistic spherical thinking is the use of the experiential knowledge that anything can and does exist without the need for precursive thoughts or events to allow its existence. When this happens there will be no constraints, barriers, or limitations. There will only be creativity.

ME: OK, I would like to ask a question on holistic spherical thinking in a moment but right now I am interested in how our use of quantum fluidity can benefit the environment. Can you give me some examples of exactly how useful this would be?

ANNE & HUM & OM & ALL OM: We can see that you have a certain angle, and we can also see that you can see the benefits of the use of quantum fluidity for use in the environment.

ME: Yes, I see the possibility of rebuilding the eco-structure of the Earth by the use of quantum fluidity.

ANNE & HUM & OM & ALL OM: This is a very advanced concept that you are perceiving, one that is really in the realms of the responsibilities of The Curators that work with the Earth.

ME: Would you explain the possibilities to the readers then, even though this vision I perceived would be classified as a function of the work of The Curators.

ANNE & HUM & OM & ALL OM: Yes, we will do that. But do note that this is a function of being incarnate in frequencies higher than the third and is normally only a function of incarnate entities from the sixth frequency upward.

As we have stated before, everything in the physical universe (and energetically in the multiverse) is in a state of quantum latency and therefore quantum fluidity can be accessed. Quantum fluidity is different to quantum latency. Simply put, quantum latency is a static function whereas quantum fluidity is not.

ME: That's obvious really.

ANNE & HUM & OM & ALL OM: Maybe to you but one cannot exist without the other in the lower frequencies.

ME: Hang on a moment, I thought you told me that latency was fluidity because everything can be everything else, it's just that it is in a neutral state?

ANNE & HUM & OM & ALL OM: Ah, yes, we understand. There is fluidity and there is fluidity. This language is limited! There is quantum fluidity that means that an object constructed from physicality, what you call quanta, that is potentially anything and everything, "is" associated with quantum latency. There is also quantum fluidity that is associated with the instability of quanta, which means that it is always changing. It is not in a state of latency or so-called locking through the desire for it to be locked into a specific function.

ME: OK, now I understand. So, which of the two versions of quantum fluidity would an entity use to affect their environment?

ANNE & HUM & OM & ALL OM: We would suggest that the fluidity that is associated with quanta that are locked into a specific function and have quantum latency.

ME: So, everything that we normally interact with in the physical universe!

ANNE & HUM & OM & ALL OM: Yes. But note that it also includes the plant and tree life and other environmental dependencies. Nothing animated with sentience though.

ME: Are you suggesting that with the right levels of understanding and desire that an entity could recreate a whole eco-structure?

ANNE & HUM & OM & ALL OM: Yes. You can already see the
image of what we mean in your mind's eye.
ME: I can. I am seeing that it is entirely possible to turn a desert
into a verdant environment complete with supporting plant
and tree life—instantaneously. I can also see that, although
insect, fish, animal, and bird life cannot be reproduced in this
way due to their function being associated with sentience of
a higher level of sentient volume and evolutionary content,
that the flora and fauna could be transported there in an
instantaneous way.
Hang on a moment! Is that how the Earth had its vast
diversity of fauna populated?
ANNE & HUM & OM & ALL OM: In some instances, yes. The
Earth is one of a number of locations that has a fairly neutral
set of environmental conditions that makes the flora and fauna
from many other locations compatible.
ME: So, the flora and fauna from other planets were used to
populate the Earth?
ANNE & HUM & OM & ALL OM: The Earth has a large
percentage of such flora and fauna from other locations, yes.
Some of them were only capable of certain temperature and
atmospheric conditions and therefore could not cope with any
major variations in temperature or environmental conditions.
They were useful in creating a basis for the creation of new
fauna genres though. However, there is also a lot of flora that
is specifically derived from the physicality that is the Earth.
ME: It's mainly the landscape and flora that is changed by the use
of quantum fluidity than that being the fluidity that is aligned
to quantum latency?
ANNE & HUM & OM & ALL OM: Yes. It is a most efficient
way of terraforming. It's more than that, though, because the
atmospheric conditions to continue to support the perpetuation
of an instant change in the landscape and its environment are
a most important factor.
ME: You are talking about a weather system?
ANNE & HUM & OM & ALL OM: Yes. A weather system
is a very important factor in any environment that has an
atmosphere, irrespective of the gas or liquid being used and
its density.
ME: How often is this method of modifying a landscape or
environment used by incarnate entities?
ANNE & HUM & OM & ALL OM: It is used by higher frequency
incarnates only when there is a so-called disaster to consider

and they need to be high enough frequency to be able to work in conjunction with certain genres of Curators. It has to be noted that currently the Earth is heading for such a disaster, bigger than the last one, and that this will need to be addressed by incarnates of a higher frequency. Such incarnates are also entrusted to incarnate into the lower frequencies with the role of environmental leadership. You have had many such incarnates over the last century. It is a great problem that they have not been listened to. Although, this may not be totally true now that things are becoming obvious. Maybe incarnate humankind won't need help of higher frequency incarnates that can use quantum fluidity in this way.

ME: I feel that we will need to have a much higher level of maturity before we will be in a position of NOT needing help.

ANNE & HUM & OM & ALL OM: I am sure that you are very right.

ME: I recognize that the fauna on a physical planet can be transported to another location using quantum latency and its associated level of fluidity (not entanglement) because the levels of sentience associated with the fauna require that it must be transported and not created. However, can the flora really just be created by the use of quantum fluidity? I mean, there is a philosophy that states that there are some aspects of sentience that are so limited in their volume and quality of sentience that they need to go through the evolutionary process of being in the so-called mineral–plant–animal–human stages. This means that plants have sentience associated to/with them and that they cannot be created from quantum latency/fluidity!

ANNE & HUM & OM & ALL OM: In essence sentience can be void from any potential physical vehicle, irrespective of whether it is in any of the stages that you just specified, provided that the period of sentient void is only for the creation period and that there is sentience of the correct quality and volume willing to occupy that stage of physicality where and when required.

ME: I expect that there would be lots of sentience willing to participate in the possibility of accelerating its evolutionary progression and content in this way!

ANNE & HUM & OM & ALL OM: There is a never-ending waiting list of TES with the appropriate level of sentience that is waiting to accelerate its evolutionary level and content by participating in the gross physical and other levels of physicality in the physical universe.

ME: So how does this sentience associate itself with the flora that is instantaneously created by giving that which had quantum latency/fluidity a so-called living function as flora?

ANNE & HUM & OM & ALL OM: Instantaneously. It's not like the association that is necessary to animate a higher-level incarnate vehicle such as an animal or human or other higher functioning incarnate vehicle because there isn't a complicated system of energy templates, energy gathering systems such as the chakras and locations for the sentience and energy associated with the sentience to be located and apportioned.

ME: To summarize then, the creation or recreation of a verdant environmental eco-structure from that which is barren can be created immediately the desire is in the mind of an entity or being that is incarnate at the right frequency to allow such high functionality. Additionally, there would need to be a high level of communication with that sentience that would be capable of occupying such flora to ensure that it has sentience associated with it at its point of creation!

ANNE & HUM & OM & ALL OM: To be honest, there is little or no communication necessary because the desire and intention to create such an environment and that this environment could support the possibility of evolutionary progression for the sentience of appropriate volume and evolutionary quality creates an evolutionary attraction that this level of sentience finds hard to resist. It's a bit like an insect being attracted to a light in a dark room. Its signature is irresistible and the appropriate sentience floods in from far and wide to such a location, so that at the point of creation of the flora for the new environment, the sentience necessary to populate it is fully available.

ME: This is wonderful. I had no idea that the desire to change an environmental eco-structure to one that is capable of supporting plant life, for example, would attract sentience in this way.

ANNE & HUM & OM & ALL OM: Sentience, in general, is always attracted to the possibility of gaining evolutionary progression.

ME: I have just received the image and concept that this is another way that The Origin gains its own evolutionary progression and how its sentience grows.

ANNE & HUM & OM & ALL OM: It is most certainly not the only way, but it is one of the many peripheral ways that The

Origin grows.

ME: If it's relatively easy, given an entity is of the right frequential level, to recreate, no, return an environment back to its natural state, why can't incarnate humankind do the same? Or, moreover, why haven't we been helped out so that we don't have any barren desert land so that all of incarnate mankind has a wonderful environment to exist and work within?

ANNE & HUM & OM & ALL OM: You have individualized free will and as such the ability to love and respect your environment is part of that free will. Right now, incarnate mankind does not really love or respect its environment. It's seen as a resource to be exploited. As a result, you are being allowed to abuse your environment to a certain extent to see how and when you all really see what you are doing, and work together to return the Earth to its true natural state by yourselves. Collectively, you have to stop behaving like a virus or a cancer to the Earth and start to work with it in respect of it, or risk being in the scenario where you kill that which sustains you. You are in a very important position and need to wake up and understand it as such. In the event that you all collectively changed your ways, gave up materialistic selfishness in terms of how you interact with the Earth, and worked together to support and regrow it, you will also have made a quantum leap in how you would be able to work with other incarnate vehicle species. As a result, you would get all the help you needed to restore the Earth's natural environment/eco-structure while still having your technical wherewithal. You would know how to ask for such help.

ME: Do you think that this sort of knowledge, I mean, knowing that the Earth could be repaired instantaneously, would make us even more lazy and inconsiderate of our environment?

ANNE & HUM & OM & ALL OM: That is the way a low-frequency civilization would think, behave, and act and is why you may have to get to the stage of borderline extinction before you collectively make the change.

ME: That's a frightening thought for those that are immersed in their incarnation, those that think they are the human body!

ANNE & HUM & OM & ALL OM: Maybe so, but it's the shock that they may well need to get up and do something about it.

ME: Do you think we will get to that state?

ANNE & HUM & OM & ALL OM: There are Event Spaces where you do! But there are also "white children" being born into this Event Space that are already in place to help ensure that this is not the case.

ME: Are you talking about the Aspect that walked into the body we call Greta Thunberg?

ANNE & HUM & OM & ALL OM: That is one.

ME: What should incarnate mankind do to support her?

ANNE & HUM & OM & ALL OM: Listen to her, and act upon her advice on an urgent basis.

ME: Got it!

Quantum Fluidity

We talked about the other concept of quantum fluidity where everything is in a state of constant change and I wondered how this could be of use or visualized into a concept that would allow it to be meaningful to both myself and my readers. It didn't take long for The OM to answer my thoughts and give me an explanation of what help this knowledge would be to us all.

ME: I can imagine that the concept of quantum fluidity would be of more use to human scientists than the readers of metaphysical texts?

ANNE & HUM & OM & ALL OM: We can see that as well, but it is just as relevant to your readers as it is to quantum physicists because the information understood by just one person on the Earth can be broadcast to many others by many different means, including the subliminal information transmitted by the energetic.

ME: What you are saying then is that any information is useful information and irrespective of how it is broadcast it is received in some way by the sentience of those entities that are incarnate.

ANNE & HUM & OM & ALL OM: We would say that that is a good analysis.

ME: Great. What is quantum fluidity then, not the version that is associated with quantum latency, as you quite rightly pointed out to me, but that which is simply fluid?

ANNE & HUM & OM & ALL OM: Quantum fluidity is a rare and mostly unobserved phenomena. As we have stated before it is a condition where there is no quantum latency to be anything in the physical universe or locking into a specific function in the physical universe. Quantum fluidity is when everything is possible in relation to quantum latency concurrently—in the present—whichever and wherever that present is positioned in the overall state of "NOW." This is a rather long-winded way of saying that at any point in Event Space every state of quantum physicality is being presented to the entity who has the capacity to observe it.

ME: So what you are saying is that rather than just having the potential (latency) to be anything and everything but being in a neutral state as a result, a volume of the physical universe is in a state of everythingness!

ANNE & HUM & OM & ALL OM: Correct. From the incarnate human perspective, it is difficult to visualize because you observe everything in a linear perspective, so, you see things singularly.

ME: Yes, I understand. If we were to observe it, it would be like what I saw with Source Entity twelve when it showed me the Event Space Horizon, with everything moving so fast that it became a blur and then nothingness. Maybe with the exception of there being an area of whiteness if I had to name it and give it an image.

ANNE & HUM & OM & ALL OM: That was relative to Event Space, not to quantum fluidity but the concept is reasonable. The only way to consider the observation of quantum fluidity is that it cannot be observed while in the physical itself. It can only be observed from outside the frequencies associated with the physical.

Let us put it another way. The human is conditioned to replace nothingness with somethingness because nothingness is difficult to understand and visualize because it is nothing.

ME: So, were I to observe quantum latency, it would have no appearance then?

ANNE & HUM & OM & ALL OM: Correct. It would be like nothing. Let us describe it in yet another way. If the volume of space that was in quantum fluidity was in front of you and in an area of space that was known and understood, such as a busy city or an area of natural beauty, all you would see is the city or the area of natural beauty.

ME: And this is because the volume of space that was in quantum fluidity would be all things at once and therefore imperceivable by the human eye or condition, even the city and the area of natural beauty.

ANNE & HUM & OM & ALL OM: Correct.

ME: However, because we perceive things in a linear fashion, we only see that which we are focused on, which is the city or the area of natural beauty and as a result we only see or perceive them.

ANNE & HUM & OM & ALL OM: Correct again.

ME: So, how would an entity see the volume of quantum fluidity when observing from the advantage for being outside of the physical universe—by being in the energetic—let's say the thirty-sixth frequency which is two-thirds of the way through the second full dimension. [*Readers are encouraged to read* **The History of God** *and/or* **Beyond The Source Book 1** *to understand the structure of the multiverse as it was described to me. Alternatively, look in my website www.beyondthesource/press-pack-2 for the file that describes the presentation on "what is a multiverse."—GSN*]

ANNE & HUM & OM & ALL OM: From a higher frequential position such as that which you just described, while being in the state of communion with one's TES, one is able to perceive all things concurrently from the perspective of the physical universe. Every perceivable quantum function is observed and known in a way that is indescribable from the human perspective. Nevertheless, it is understood and observable simply because in one's communal energetic state, you are a significantly bigger volume of sentience, a volume of sentience that is able to process myriad things concurrently, irrespective of the number of Event Spaces that are created or realities within these Event Spaces. Indeed, observing and making sense, so to speak, of quantum fluidity is a relatively simple function from the perspective of a TES when looking down from a higher frequential, nonphysical level. The best way to describe it is like this. When water is a higher frequency, it becomes steam and then part of the air. It is nevertheless there but unobservable. If we place that same water into a lower frequency it becomes ice, which is very observable. So, as an example, from the human perspective of seeing a volume of quantum fluidity, it's like trying to see water become air when elevated to a higher frequency, while still appearing to be like ice. Especially when one is the observing entity of a higher frequency and in communion with one's TES.

ME: That's a good analogy, one that I like.

ANNE & HUM & OM & ALL OM: Good, the air represents not being able to perceive the volume of quantum fluidity and the ice the ability to perceive it, the difference being the frequential observation point and the level of sentience employed to observe that volume of quantum fluidity.

ME: So what you are suggesting then is that an entity's ability to observe a volume of space that is in a state of real quantum fluidity is reliant upon the frequency that the entity is in or based upon as a result of its evolutionary content.

ANNE & HUM & OM & ALL OM: What we are saying is that it's based upon the sentience employed by the entity and its frequential position or location, not the evolutionary content of the sentience. Although, the quality of sentience is a function of the level of evolutionary content it is not attributed to the level or shall we say, the amount of sentience that is being used to allow the observation of a volume of space where there is quantum fluidity.

ME: Ah! Now I get it. Although the quality of sentience is attributable to the accrual of and quality of evolutionary content, the level of sentence being used, or that is necessary to be used, is similar to the processing power we would need a computer to have to perform a certain task.

ANNE & HUM & OM & ALL OM: That is a good analogy. You see, if an entity is projected from its TES with 2.5 percent of the sentience of that TES (what you would call the normal distribution among twelve Aspects projected from a single TES concurrently) then it is not able to observe quantum fluidity. This is simply because it doesn't have the level or quantity of sentience necessary to process the volume of space that it wants to observe, that is expressing quantum fluidity.

ME: Is this the case irrespective of the frequency level that the entity is located on?

ANNE & HUM & OM & ALL OM: Correct. The entity needs to be at the minimum frequency level and have a minimum percentage of its TES sentience to observe quantum sentience.

ME: I take it that a TES, let's say a TES that is capable of projecting smaller Aspects of itself into incarnate human, and other similar vehicles, doesn't have this issue?

ANNE & HUM & OM & ALL OM: Correct. A TES whose sentience is of the quality and volume you describe is always in the right level of frequency and will always have the right level of sentience to be able to observe quantum fluidity.

An Aspect, however, needs to either be in one of the four ways of being in partial communion "within" its TES, not projected external to it, or be in full communion, and therefore be in the same frequency level as its TES. It therefore has full access to all that which is being experienced by its TES, and the other projected or non-projected Aspects of that TES, being able to experience "as" its TES while being at a level of individualized communion within its TES.

ME: So, a TES of the quality that allows human incarnation can experience an area of space that exhibits quantum fluidity, but its Aspects can only do that in communion.

How much sentience, as a percentage of the TES sentience, would need to be assigned to an Aspect that is in a state of projection, to allow it to observe a volume of space that is displaying quantum fluidity?

ANNE & HUM & OM & ALL OM: Twenty percent.

ME: That's a lot of sentience. In fact, that's 17.5 percent more than the sentience of what I will call the average projected Aspect enjoys. [*I encourage the reader to refer to* The Anne Dialogues, *where the apportionment of sentience by the TES is fully explained.—GSN*]

ANNE & HUM & OM & ALL OM: That is raw sentience though. If that sentience is associated with a high- or a good-quality level of evolutionary content, which would normally be the case, then that can be reduced to 12.5 percent! This is true even considering that quantum fluidity is a function of the physical universe.

ME: Noted. Two things before we move on. First, what does a volume of space exhibiting quantum fluidity look like from a human perspective, and second, what is the advantage of being able to observe such phenomenon?

ANNE & HUM & OM & ALL OM: The observation of a volume of space in quantum fluidity cannot be described in human terms for it has no meaning that you could refer to, to enable an understanding of what is being observed. Indeed, the human eye is far from adequate and the human sentience and subsequent perception is additionally incapable. To say that it would be best described as a maelstrom at all levels of quanta would be the best description we could afford.

As for what the benefit would be to observe a volume of space that is expressing quantum fluidity, we would say that it has none. Other than a realization that everything truly is everything else concurrently and that this can be used as an intellectual datum for understanding that quantum latency in its simplest form is the static manifestation of quantum fluidity.

ME: I have a thought here. Is quantum latency, being considered a static manifestation of quantum fluidity, a product of the lower frequencies?

ANNE & HUM & OM & ALL OM: No. However, its ability to be understood as a concept needs an entity to be in a higher frequency than this one, the one you are now functioning within.

ME: OK. So, could it be used by an entity of the correct level as a tool for creation?

ANNE & HUM & OM & ALL OM: No. A volume of space that is expressing quantum fluidity is not stable from a physically static perspective, although it is stable in its instability or fluidity, and therefore cannot be used as the basis for creation of a static object. However, we can say that in this regard, quantum latency can be used as such and once an entity understands how to change that which is in natural quantum latency, i.e., no physical role, into a position of quantum locking, or a physical role as we have previously described, locking it into that which is desired, then this can be used for the purpose of creation.

ME: And anything can be created from what we would call nothing then? From thin air, so to speak?

ANNE & HUM & OM & ALL OM: That is correct. Note, though, that air is densely populated with quanta of all levels.

ME: Noted. No need for massive manufacturing facilities then, just program what you need to be in a state of quantum locking and you have it!

ANNE & HUM & OM & ALL OM: Correct. What's more, this also counts for generating power and moving around the physical universe instantaneously.

ME: A real utopian existence while being incarnate.

ANNE & HUM & OM & ALL OM: Yes, it would/will be. Once you have the maturity, evolutionary level, and frequential level to control such a function, yes.

ME: I really would like to sit down with a theoretical scientist and discuss this. It would really assist in expanding incarnate humankind consciousness.

ANNE & HUM & OM & ALL OM: And that's the reason why you are doing what you are doing right now.

ME: One more question. How can the concept of quantum fluidity be used as an example of how to exist?

Using Quantum Fluidity as an Example of How to Exist

ANNE & HUM & OM & ALL OM: We are not sure it could be because as we have just alluded to you, incarnate humankind would not be able to understand it.

ME: Let's give it a try!

ANNE & HUM & OM & ALL OM: We expect that this will be a short chapter because incarnate humankind will not be able to understand the concept of being in fluidity.

ME: I am still willing to give it a try.

ANNE & HUM & OM & ALL OM: Rather than being an observational description of what quantum fluidity is, this is more about a state of beingness in one's relationship with the environment, the circumstances within the environment, and those other entities within the environment that one may interact with.

ME: That's a sizable preamble. It's getting me interested. Please carry on.

ANNE & HUM & OM & ALL OM: It's not about being lazy or going with the flow, it's more about letting things come into your space, your life in a random way, and embracing that randomness.

ME: How can existence be random if we have a life plan, a linear direction?

ANNE & HUM & OM & ALL OM: This is where we said it would not be able to be understood from the incarnate perspective. Incarnates at this frequency level always think in a linear way. This linear path is hard for you to move from, if not impossible. One has the be in the energetic to be able to understand how to exist in fluidity.

We will give you the benefit of the doubt though.

Think of existing in these terms.

Rather than trying to guide everything, just be in acceptance and work with that which is presented to you, irrespective of what it is and how much pleasure or pain, joy or sorrow, interest or boredom, expansion or the ease it brings. Let things happen to you and work with that which results from your interaction. Don't worry about how well or how badly you responded or performed, or if you could have done better if you had a second chance. Just accept that which you have done, or how the circumstance revolved around you or whether you could have influenced it. Recognize that your interaction is transient and inconsequential.

ME: You mean everything we do is pointless in the bigger picture because the bigger picture is always changing, morphing into something else for a moment, or is everything else and every possibility, so nothing is necessary, everything is necessary, nothing is important, everything is important, nothing exists, everything exists.

ANNE & HUM & OM & ALL OM: Yes, yes, yes. What we are getting to here is that to exist in a state of constant fluidity or flux where everything is everything else concurrently, one needs to be detached from the need to be static or linear.

ME: So it's like losing one's ties with the need for an end product, the product, or our work or involvement?

ANNE & HUM & OM & ALL OM: Correct. It also means detaching from the need to observe that which is coming or going or positioning one's self as this or that. No labels for anything, no prejudgments, preconceptions, desires, wants, or needs. It's "just being" in every sense of the word.

This is about as close as we can get to a description for you, that you, or should we say incarnate humankind, could understand.

ME: I have just gained a visual interpretation of what you have all said to me. It really is like a more in-depth version of going with the flow, of being in the now. It's just that the flow is inconsistent and random in its direction and the now is never stable enough to be classified as the now. As a result, we achieve nothing but everything but that nothing or everything is never quantifiable because it's always in fluidity. And so are we!

As a result, if we are existing in this way, we don't strive for any particular thing because there is nothing to strive for, while still striving for the interaction with that which we interact with as it happens and not worry about the end result, just doing the interaction for as long as the interaction is there.

OK, what else can we add to this?

ANNE & HUM & OM & ALL OM: Only one final thing. If one is existing in the state of fluidity, then there is not a product from that fluidity. Therefore, there is no structure or resulting effect other than that which was there for the moment one interacted. Directly after the moment of interaction, both the moment and the interaction are gone for it never was, while being always is!

ME: This means that one who exists in this way is in essence a transient nomad in an environment that is static for those that work in linearity.

ANNE & HUM & OM & ALL OM: That, my dear OM, is a very good way to finish this subject.

Holistic Spherical Thinking

I had been thinking about this state of being in quantum fluidity from the perspective of beingness or existence and that the word "quantum" was wholly unnecessary, other than the fact that it related to the gross physical environment at one of its lowest physical denominations, quantum only relates to that which is below the atomic levels of structure, but could include, or just refer to, the lowest—the Anu. Mmmm! No, it made absolutely no sense to use the word quantum. It was simply thinking and interacting with one's environment, the circumstances within one's environment, and those other entities and/or beings that are also in that environment in a totally flexible, non-expectant, nonjudgmental way. However, in the back of my mind I knew that The OM had kept it super simple, and that it was much, much more than that. Mmmm, I thought. I just need to move on and work with the next thought process and subsequent discussion. I had been having a side thought about whether this was similar to, or the same as, what I intuitively considered as holistic spherical thinking. I needed to ask the question!

ME: What is the relationship between existing in a state of fluidity and holistic spherical thinking?

ANNE & HUM & OM & ALL OM: You have just made that up!

ME: Yes, no, well, I have actually been thinking about it for some time.

ANNE & HUM & OM & ALL OM: We will look into your sentience to see what you are referring to! No, it's not related. We will say this, though, and that is, what you have labeled as holistic spherical thinking is one way to consider how most entities or beings think while in the energetic.

ME: Carry on.

ANNE & HUM & OM & ALL OM: First of all, we would like to give an illustration of how incarnate humankind perceives its environment and how that governs its thinking process.

ME: That sounds like it will be a good datum to start from.

ANNE & HUM & OM & ALL OM: Everything that you think about in terms of your environment is based upon how you interact with it. You interact with your environment with the five physical senses that you have available to you in your physical vehicle, your incarnate human body. This vehicle is designed to interact with the lowest of the frequencies and as such is additionally governed by the limitations that these frequencies present to the incarnate Aspect.

As a result, everything that you see, touch, taste, hear, smell, or perceive is the basis for how you interpret your environment and therefore how you think. These five senses are significantly inefficient at best and as a result only offer the possibility of very limited linear interaction with the environment. The sentience that is projected into the human vehicle is so affected by the low frequencies that it is incarnating into that during the period of connection, the gestation and initial seven-year growth period of the human vehicle, it forgets who and what it is. As a result, it starts to work with the abilities of the incarnate human vehicle and its subsequent limitations and nothing else, thinking it is the human vehicle. Everything it senses is through significant limitations and so the thinking becomes limited as well.

When an Aspect is in the energetic, there are no limitations and it has the ability to think in a way that is unlimited, so it does not think in a linear way.

ME: Can you give me an example of a physical experience that would be considered spherical or holistic that would help with the understanding?

ANNE & HUM & OM & ALL OM: The best way to consider physical interaction with one's environment in this way is to think about the possibility of seeing everything at once. This means seeing in a 360-degree way, not just on one level such as the horizontal plane but also in the vertical plane as well, so that one sees in a spherical way. In this way, everything that surrounds one is observed and understood concurrently and without interruption. Now consider the same thing for that which you smell and you would smell everything in your location concurrently. Now consider your whole body being able to touch everything in your environment concurrently in the same level of sensitivity as your tongue. Now consider being able to taste everything in your environment concurrently and being able to hear everything that is in your environment concurrently.

Clearly all of this input would be difficult to analyze because the Aspect that incarnates into the human vehicle at this frequency can only process input in a linear way. That doesn't mean to say that one cannot process a single input from each of the five senses concurrently because you all can. However, now consider that all of the inputs received in the way they were described above was processed in the linear way and you would become confused at best. Being able to process that input concurrently, however, makes a massive difference and would make the incarnate Aspect that experienced their environment in such a way feel that they were experiencing a level of localized omnipresence.

ME: So if an incarnate entity is experiencing their environment in this way then the thinking process must be in a similar way, where everything is considered concurrently. What I mean by this, is that all thoughts that could be considered as before or after a current thought is being thought about concurrently.

ANNE & HUM & OM & ALL OM: Correct, and that includes all of the possible thoughts that are at a tangent to the concurrent thoughts, all those that could have had, might have, or will have an effect on the concurrent thought process, which is concurrent to all of the other possibilities resulting or possible/probable/unnecessary concurrent thought processes.

ME: We consider every consideration within the concurrent thoughts then?

ANNE & HUM & OM & ALL OM: Exactly.

ME: Well, if one was not in a position to be able to think in this holistic spherical way, one would get very confused. I mean, being able to consider every possible consideration affecting them within the environment that they are in or what they are interacting with or responsible for concurrently would be an almost impossible task.

ANNE & HUM & OM & ALL OM: Exactly. However, this is the closest an incarnate Aspect at this frequency can get to the feeling of being in a state of localized omniscience.

Interestingly enough though, incarnate Aspects do try to subconsciously think in this way, and on a regular basis. In fact, because it is a common occurrence, most, if not all of those that experience trying to think in a holistic spherical way don't know that they are doing it because they all suffer from cognitive overload.

ME: Cognitive overload? Is that getting confused about what we are trying to think about?

ANNE & HUM & OM & ALL OM: No, no, no. When an incarnate Aspect experiences cognitive overload as a function of subconsciously trying to think in the way that you call holistic spherical thinking, they simply can't and so forget exactly what they were thinking about.

ME: I thought that was a function of old age or being distracted?

ANNE & HUM & OM & ALL OM: No. Think about it. In a linear way, that is. Every time you try to think of many things at once in any level of detail your attention drifts off and you forget what you were thinking about in its entirety. This happens to everyone.

ME: You're right. Everybody has episodes of forgetting what they were talking about mid-sentence, so to speak. And, I note that this also includes when someone asks you to remember something that they have forgotten when you are thinking of something else. We forget about what we were thinking about and that which the other person was trying to remember as well.

ANNE & HUM & OM & ALL OM: Now you know what causes it!

ME: So it would seem. We had better move on before I forget what we were discussing!!!

Can Another Body Be Used for Individualized Free Will? The Earth Is not the Only Location to Have Individualized Free Will—We Have Always Been Told It Was!!

I don't know where this question came from, but it was obviously one that needed answering. As I sat and meditated on the question, I felt that it was one that many readers would be interested in knowing the answer to. Specifically, because in most spiritual texts and, in my own knowledge, the Earth was the only location within the physical universe where individualized free will was an operational function of incarnation. As I further sat at my keyboard, I wondered more and more about whether there were more incarnate vehicles that allowed individualized free will, and if so, why would we be told that the Earth was the only location.

HUM: I think that I would be the best entity to answer this question.

ME: What about Anne? The sentience that incarnated as Anne, that is. It experienced incarnation and the associated free will as well!

HUM: This is true but as with yourself, she/it was limited to the knowledge that individualized free will is "only" allowed on the Earth.

ME: So what you are suggesting then is that individualized free will is not specific to the Earth?

HUM: We/I will say this. The higher up the frequencies that one climbs as a result of evolutionary progression, the lower the importance an entity or being places on so-called individualized free will.

ME: Why? Is this because we are more in tune with being in a collective or in communion?

HUM: One is generally operating in a communal and/or collective way at these higher levels and so it is natural to desire to be in communion or one with one's TES and/or Source.

ME: OK. Looking at this in a different way, for those entities (TES or Aspect) that still desire the need to operate in an individualized way while being incarnate as a way to accelerate their evolutionary progression, are there any other incarnate vehicles, other than the human body, that allow individuality combined with free will?

HUM: Not in the gross physical frequencies, no.

ME: So there ARE other planets that have individualized free will as an experiment!

HUM: Yes, but there are only a few and they are all the maximum distance away from each other that they could be. They are all at the edge of the physical universe and at the different frequencies required to support the creation of the physical universe.

ME: So there are twelve locations with each location on one of the twelve frequencies that support the physical universe?

HUM: No, only ten.

ME: Ten?

HUM: Yes, of course. As you should remember, the physical universe requires the first three frequencies to create the gross physical environment, the foundation of the physical universe. Every frequency level above the third allows a condition where there is a compartmentalization effect. That being, the fourth frequency through to the twelfth frequency each support higher frequency environments that occupy the same space but that are both self-contained while allowing movement between them.

ME: Now I understand.

HUM: You should. These are some of your own words.

ME: So what is the idea of having ten locations spread over the frequencies associated with the physical universe. That is, rather than just the one that we have been led to believe is the only planet with individualized free will?

HUM: First, on the gross physical levels the Earth is the only planet or location that has individualized free will, and so the statement is true. And when one is considering what the incarnate human race understands about the physical universe it is a justified statement. This is why it is the only planet of major interest—in the gross physical. Even if it isn't the most technologically or even spiritually advanced. Incarnate humankind would not have understood that there are many frequencies within this universe that provide different individually compartmentalized environments while being in the same space! Certainly not at the point of broadcasting such information. It's not a parallel condition. It is a concept that is recognized but not understood. It is a simultaneous condition in a single universal environment. This, on its own, makes the physical universe unique and a major reason for entities using it for accelerating their evolutionary progression.

ME: Now I am starting to understand. We have a planetary location on each of the usable frequencies of the physical universe. Each location is the furthest volugraphical [*please refer to the glossary for the definition of "Volugraphical"— GSN*] distance away from each other while also being on a different frequency within the physical universe. They couldn't be further apart and have no chance of interfering with each other!

HUM: Correct. Hence the way it is organized. Each location is isolated by volugraphical distance and frequency.

ME: So here is the next question. Why is there a location for individualized free will on each of these frequency levels, and what incarnate vehicle or body forms are used?

HUM: Each of the frequential locations are used as a function of the need to understand what effect "frequential level" has on the incarnate entity that has individualized free will. Frequential level also has a major effect on the communicative bandwidth that an entity has while incarnate in the physical universe and hence the possibility of understanding how and when an incarnate civilization chooses communion over individuality.

From the perspective of connectivity while being incarnate the worst-case scenario is in the gross physical frequencies. The best case being in the twelfth frequency.

ME: Based upon this then, the locations within the highest frequencies should mature to the desire to be in communion with those other incarnate entities within their frequency significantly faster than those in the lowest!

HUM: One would think so, but from what we, or should I say, what the entities whose service is to those within the evolutionary cycle, which includes the governance and maintenance of the individual frequential levels within the physical would say, this is not the case!

ME: Why is this not the case? I mean, I would have expected that the communicative bandwidth afforded to an entity on, for example, the twelfth frequency level, would think, behave, and act in a way that is consistent with their functionality at that level. With incarnation being at its maximum level of finitude while being incarnate it is almost not incarnation and an entity would be almost fully connected to its TES and therefore seek communion with those other entities in their environment!

HUM: From the perspective of one that is incarnate on the first three frequency levels of the physical universe this would appear to be so, and to the partial observer, you would be correct. However, although the karmic functions of the physical universe are more apparent in the lower frequencies, they are more subtly experienced in the higher frequencies.

ME: What you are saying then is that, irrespective of the frequency level, there is an element of Karma and selfish individualized thinking, behaving, and acting that is relevant to that level.

HUM: Yes, and that the subtler the element, the more of a challenge it is to the incarnate entity.

ME: I guess this is because it is obvious to an entity on a higher frequency how a lower frequency can affect them but it's not so obvious to them how higher frequencies and even the frequency that they are currently domicile within can affect them.

HUM: To some extent that is true. However, it's more to do with the ability to actually see that which is affecting one's desire to be incarnate at this level. You see, it is easier to think that you are in control of your incarnate state at the higher frequency levels than it is in the lower levels while not actually being in control.

ME: It's like not seeing the wood for the trees?

HUM: Yes. I see the analogy. It's a little bit like missing the important content in the small print of a contract. Therefore, the incarnate entity is so immersed in the levels of normality, or should I say, freedom of sentience, that it misses the almost imperceptible areas of attraction to being in the physical universe at that frequency level. One's ego is still prevalent even in the twelfth frequency level.

ME: Is the ego as functional in the twelfth frequency as it is in the gross physical frequencies [*levels 1 through 3—GSN*]?

HUM: No, but it is still a function of incarnation at that level. Remember this is still the physical universe and the twelve frequencies associated with it are the lowest in The Source's multiversal environment.

Physicality, or should I say, resistance associated with harmonic interaction, is still experienced on the highest frequencies of the physical universe, it's just that it is relative to that frequency and not to any of the others.

ME: Is that true? From my perspective, a higher frequency incarnation is not physicality as I know it right now, it's considered to be almost energetic.

HUM: As you are aware, the entity that observes the frequencies above and below them sees that which is above as diffuse and that which is below as solid. Think of it in terms of ice, water, and air. It's like you are the water, the frequency below you is the ice, and the frequency above you is the air. They are all the same thing but at a different frequency level, with the air being invisible to you while the ice is very visible to you.

ME: And so my physicality and interactive capability is relative to my frequency.

HUM: Yes.

ME: OK, noted.

Getting back to The Original question then, well, at least, I thought it was part of The Original question. What other bodies are used in the one location allowed in each of the twelve frequencies for individualized free will?

HUM: Each of the locations are, as stated before, inaccessible to each other from a frequential and volugraphical perspective. They are also isolated from general access from other incarnate civilizations at those frequencies.

The body types, vehicles, or form factors are clearly adapted for optimal use in the environment that they are in, just as the human body is, irrespective of its genome, for the Earth's environment. Suffice to say, the human form factor is not used in these other locations and frequencies because the objective is to see how other vehicles in these frequencies and locations are used while individualized free will is bestowed upon the incarnate entity.

ME: So what do they look like?

HUM: Mmmm, I don't feel that this is a relevant question because from your experience of the plethora of life on the Earth you know that there are thousands of possibilities.

ME: Entertain me!

HUM: Mmmm, OK.

They range from incarnate vehicles that are multi-limbed to those that are metamorphic to those that are capable of existing in many opposing environmental conditions to those that are gaseous to those that are on the atomic and subatomic levels. All of this is relative to the frequency they are on of course.

ME: No images to give us then?

HUM: No need. The generic variants I just stated should be enough for you to make an educated guess. Suffice to say though, they can range from looking like an insect on Earth to a lizard to a fish to a bird, to a snake, to a jellyfish, to an octopus, to an amphibian to a balloon of gas, to a collective of trees or plant life, etc., etc. Clearly environmental conditions are finer the higher in the frequencies the incarnate vehicle is.

I will say this, though. The incarnate human vehicle used on the Earth is capable of existing in many frequencies higher than the one it currently exists within, simply because it was adapted for use in the lower frequencies from the higher ones where it was first used. It can therefore be useful in its current state in the fourth and fifth frequencies, with assistance to exist in the sixth and above.

ME: But it's definitely not used in the free will capacity anywhere else?

HUM: No, not in the fully individualized free will capacity. No.

ME: OK. I want to move on and talk more about who and what The OM are. I want to dig deeper into understanding them

while I am still working on this particular dialogue.
HUM: I will communicate with you later "collectively" then.

More on The OM

I was interested in knowing more about The OM, not only from the existing level of knowledge that I had, but more from a personal perspective. Additionally, the wonderful lady who was translating my books into Japanese was being helped by The OM and therefore had some questions of her own to be asked. The questions were not just about The OM but on other subjects as well and so I felt they were definitely worth including in this dialogue. Two of the questions were specifically about The OM. Three other questions were about Source Being1 (SB1 or SE13) whose existence was first identified in The Origin Speaks. *I asked the questions of The OM in general, using exactly the same text as given to me.*

ME: If SEs go up to The Origin level when they evolve, how about The OM? What happens to them when they evolve?

OM: It is good to be communicating with you collectively again, we have been anticipating this opportunity. First, it is going to be a long, long, long time before any of The Source Entities evolve to the level that The Origin currently achieves. Indeed, they will not be considered Origin level at all in real terms. They never could be. What will happen is that when The Source Entities have experienced all of the evolutionary cycles available to them, they will have effectively mapped out (experienced, learned, and evolved from) all of The Origin's current volume of Polyomniscient self-awareness, they will migrate to the next level of structure within The Origin and do the same as they are doing now but from the elevated position of being at the current level of Origin sentience and evolutionary progress. If you remember all

TES, individualizations of Source Entity sentience, will then be afforded Source Entity Status and will take over the level of work that The Source Entities are doing now but within this new level of Origin Structure, the next set of twelve levels of structure, above this current set of twelve. [*Currently, Source Entity sentience occupies the first four levels of the first twelve levels of structure of The Origin's volume of Polyomniscient Polyomnipresence.—GSN*]

As for The OM, we are the uncreated creations, the unexpected individualization of true Origin sentience. In general, those that are beloved of The OM do not enter into the evolutionary cycle and so do not actively seek evolution or evolve through the interaction of themselves/ourselves with other entities or beings that are in the evolutionary cycle. We abhor the fact that we have to come to these levels in this universe within this Source Entity to not only communicate with you but keep an eye out for you, so to speak. You are beloved of The OM and although you are OM we frown at your fascination with the incarnate entities in this location. It's simply too close to being in an evolutionary cycle. Having said that, we are grateful for the experiential information you pass on to us. Some of it is enlightening, even for us.

Although in general we avoid being in the evolutionary cycle simply because it creates responsibility, there are a couple of OM that are doing so. Your TES is one of them! So getting back to answering the question, even though we don't actively enter into the evolutionary cycle, we all evolve as a function of The Origin's evolution. Based upon this, even those OM that are in the evolutionary cycle, even on a temporary basis, evolve as a function of being smaller individualized units of Origin sentience. In essence, as The Origin evolves, The OM evolve because we are The Origin. It's just that we are individualized from the main body of sentience that is The Origin, irrespective of how big it becomes, we will always be individualized. Consider The OM as sentience within a sea of sentience. Another way to consider The OM is the drop of water in all the oceans of the Earth that remain as a drop while being the ocean!

ME: So we evolve in the same way that The Origin evolves, through the evolution of other entities/beings that are either Source Entities, created by Source Entities, or in the Darwinian evolution of energy within a Source Entity that became sentient.

216

OM: This is correct. It's a most natural function. The OM are The Origin without being The Origin.

ME: The next question is based upon Paramahansa Yogananda being Pure OM. The question was derived as a function of the questions and answers from my monthly World Satsanga. The question goes like this: you are writing a book about the "**OM**" right now, one time you said Yogananda was a Pure OM like you, but then you said it's not quite like that. What have you found out since then? Please elaborate about Yogananda's status, other lives, or whatever you found out while writing this book.

OM: The incarnate entity that became Yogananda was individualized from a Non-captive OM and so is associated with SE1, The Source Entity whose energies and structure you and the OM that communicate with you are currently temporarily located within. Non-captive OM are Pure OM that have an attractive force that keeps them associated with The Source Entity that their sentience was initially assigned to, when The Source Entities were created by The Origin. Although it will incarnate no more (and neither will you, dear OM), it has had many lives that have had an impact. This impact is mostly upon the development of individualized free will on this planet and those other locations in the higher frequencies that are also part of the individualized free will experiment. In the lower frequencies it specialized in ways to maintain connectivity with the TES of the incarnate Aspect and avoid addiction to experiencing the incarnate state. Irrespective of the frequency, all frequencies in the physical universe have a level of addiction to them.

ME: The next three questions are based upon SE13 or what could be called SB1. SE13 is the product of Darwinian evolution of energies outside of The Origin's volume of Polyomniscient, Polyomnipresent self-awareness and so is really a being, not an entity.

What was SB1's (SE13's) reaction when it was first contacted by The Origin? What did it say to The Origin? I have asked about The Origin's perspective on SB1 in the past, but I am wondering what was SB1's perspective on The Origin. If I need to wait for the *Beyond The Origin* book, then I will wait for the answer. Also, what was SB1 doing before being contacted by The Origin? If not working on evolution? Finally, how "small" is SB1 compared to the other SEs? Can it grow big if it gives itself enough sentience over time like nebulae do? Or it does not increase in "size" and only its awareness expands?

[These questions are the result of the text in pages 13 to 15 in The Origin Speaks. *For my reader, the* Beyond The Origin *book is the next on the channeling list! So if you are reading this I am working on that book.—GSN]*

OM: We like your friend. That is why we encourage her. We sometimes tease her as well. She is very well connected to Source and so is easier to communicate with than other high-frequency incarnates. Not that we communicate with many incarnates, if any at all.

As you are aware, there is more than just the being you refer to as Source Entity Thirteen or to put it a little more accurately, Source Being One.

ME: Yes, I seem to remember that this being is of Source Entity proportions in terms of sentience and the volume of energy that the sentience occupies.

OM: It is of Source Entity proportions from both a weight/quality of sentience and volume of energy used to house its sentience. It evolved to that level of sentience all on its own and as such has "being" status rather than "entity" status.

There are also more of "us." We can discuss these new beloveds later.

ME: To answer the question then, what did The Origin say to this new and unexpected being of Source Entity proportions? And, what was the response?

OM: We have to answer all of the questions at once we feel, because they are all interdependent. First, though, we will advise you that this being, once contacted by The Origin, was not specifically working on its own evolution but was moreover just existing.

ME: It was being a being?

OM: We would like to use the words "sort of."

ME: OK, what does that mean?

OM: It was a little like The Origin in its first understanding of self. The Origin had picked an Event Space to communicate with this being, SB1/SE13 where it had just migrated from self-aware/conscious intelligence to becoming a sentient being. Its sentience being achieved on its own rather that via the route of having a volume of sentience individualized from a larger volume of sentience such as the process The Origin used to create The Source Entities, and, which also inadvertently allowed us, The OM, to come into individualized existence.

ME: Having just achieved the status of "sentience," then it must have been just wondering what being sentience was all about then?

OM: The Origin chose its moment of contact wisely. It knew from experience that there is a moment of, shall we say confusion, when an energy moves from the simple self-aware conscious energy state to the point where it is suddenly "sentience" and that the sentience is no longer dependent upon the energy that gave birth to the sentience, so to speak. It is quite disorientating for a being to experience this, shall we say, quantum jump, in beingness. Suffice to say, The Origin used this to its advantage and advised it of the very same reason "to be" that it gave The Source Entities. SB1/SE13 was and is delighted with being in contact with a much larger being and that it has a role to play in its evolutionary progression.

ME: So it likes being part of a bigger being and having a role to play?

OM: Yes, it does.

ME: Has it been in contact with the individualizations of Source Entity Twelve yet?

OM: We have asked The Origin this question and it has said not yet, but it will do. From the observation of the dominant Event Space and associated Event Stream it is going to play an interesting role in being "beyond" The Origin's Polyomniscient, Polyomnipresent volume of self-awareness. Its interaction with SE12 is going to be significantly important as well.

ME: Will it increase in size/volume?

OM: Size or volume of the energies that are SB1/SE13 are not important. What is important is the increase in the quality of sentience and evolutionary content.

ME: Does the volume of energy need to increase if the quality of sentience and evolutionary content increase?

OM: No. There is no correlation between the volume of energy occupied by sentience once sentience has been achieved by a body of self-aware or conscious energy. Once sentience has been achieved, the volume of energy that gave birth to it is no longer important. The sentience can move from one volume of energy to another volume of energy as it desires. Or not, as the case may be. That being, it can remain as disassociated sentience. Remember there are two ways to classify sentience.

First, by its sentient weight, its density, so to speak, and second, by its quality of sentience, how experienced or evolved that sentience is.

ME: We used to have a saying for this level of evolutionary progression, to move into the level of pure thought. Pure thought is said to be the next evolutionary step for a physical entity or being.

OM: Well, it's a totally wrong assumption to suggest that thought is the highest level of evolutionary progression for as you are aware without awareness there can be no consciousness, without consciousness there can be no thought. Additionally, without heightened levels of consciousness or self-aware consciousness there can be no sentience. In essence, thought is dependent upon a minimum level of awareness and that is consciousness, without this minimum there can be no thought and thought does not donate a level of sentience.

ME: What you are saying then is that SB1/SE13's evolutionary growth does not result in a change in the volume of the energy it may be associated with or may have commandeered!

OM: Correct.

ME: Can we ask SB1/SE13 what it is doing now?

OM: You can, you will, and you are, but not in this focus of your sentience.

ME: OK, so I wait until I am working with The Origin on the next dialogue that is dedicated to my communication with it in its next level of structure.

OM: Yes.

ME: What about the new OM? What are they doing now? I take it that we will communicate with them more in the next series of dialogues?

OM: Yes, we will, but right now we can tell you that we have communicated with these uncreated products of sentience and can confirm that what was potentially five is now two.

ME: I seem to remember that they were quite small and had the possibility of creating a coadunate state to becoming one much larger OM sentience.

OM: It appears that they decided that being one or five was not the best use of their individualized sentience, nor their potentially collective sentience so they elected to create two new OM whose sentient weight and quality of sentience was equal to that which they detected we were. Simply put, they wanted to be equal. This is the mark of a true Pure OM, for in essence we are all one and the same and therefore beloved.

ME: Should we wait until the new dialogue to communicate with these new OM?

OM: They are currently outside of your normal range of communication, so to answer your question, yes, they will become part of the dialogue that will become *Beyond The Origin.*

ME: OK, I look forward to communicating with them. It sounds and feels like it's going to be an interesting dialogue. I am especially interested in understanding what made them move into a level of communion that created two OM and not maintain the five that was originally uncreated.

OM: We applaud your desire and thirst for knowledge.

I have to admit that I was finding the anticipation of finding out more about these new OM rather compelling and being in the knowledge that I would not find out more until the appropriate time was a bit of a tease. I just have to be patient and ask a new set of questions to pass the time, I thought. One of the questions was a return to the subject of quantum physics, or should I say, the use of mathematics to model the functions of the physical universe.

Why Mathematics Will Never Explain the Functionality of the Physical Universe— Even at the Quantum Level

Now then, taking on board that this would be the last dialogue based upon the subject of universal physics and its mathematics from a purely theoretical basis (no actual maths involved) was a subject that I wanted to get my teeth into. I had this subject heading in my head for some time and for some reason it went to the back of the manuscript. When things like this happen, it is obvious that the time (Event Space) was not right until it was right, and it looked like the time was now right. Or should I say, the Event Space was at the right juncture.

I know that from the human perspective physicality can be explained by the use of mathematics and that mathematics is considered to be a common language throughout the physical universe, and possibly the rest of the energetic multiverse. One thing was giving me an itch in the back of my mind. Is human mathematics actually capable of describing the functionality of the Anu, for example? The OM were fast to respond.

OM: Not in the way that you are considering.

ME: So you are saying that mathematics does not explain the function of what we call quantum physics?

OM: We are saying the incarnate humankind does not understand the functionality of the components of the gross physical aspect of the physical universe, which are a function of the total frequential subset that is the physical universe, and as a result, will not be able to model it with the current level of mathematics.

ME: What do you mean "frequential subset?"

OM: The basic components of the multiverse are the frequencies and those subfrequencies that make up each of the universal environments that are capable of being manifest as a result of their finitude. The physical universe is a unique condition insomuch as it has twelve frequencies and their associated subfrequencies associated with them. Each frequency has a different effect on that which is manifest. As a result, that which is manifest in the lowest of the frequencies and subfrequencies functions as a result of being in those frequencies. If that which is manifest is elevated to the next frequential level, say from the collective first three frequency levels to the fourth frequency level, then its functionality changes in accordance with the functions associated with being on the fourth level, and so forth from the fifth through to the twelfth. This means that the understanding of the functionality of that which is manifest on one or through two or more frequencies above those that create the gross physical has to be understood from all of the frequencies associated with the physical universe in all of the individual and cumulative frequential manifested states.

ME: Are you suggesting that there would be a different mathematical model for each frequency or group of frequencies?

OM: More than that. There would need to be a different development of mathematics to describe and model the functionality of the physical at each frequency level and each of the cumulative levels. The model of mathematics that incarnate mankind has developed is based upon the base of ten [*see the glossary— GSN*] and its decimalizations, which is limited at best, and, if used with the desire for wanting accurate results for difficult computations is inherently inaccurate. Certainly, this is the case for generating a mathematical model of the functionality of the physical universe.

ME: I would have thought that the use of base ten was an accurate method of calculation and one that allows a model to be created to explain the function of the basic building block for the physical universe in an accurate way.

OM: The issue with the methods of calculation that use base ten or decimalization is that it inherently allows error.

ME: Can you explain?

OM: Yes, we can. Most if not all of the mathematical models that incarnate humankind uses allow the possibility of a fraction or non-integer-based value at any point in the calculation whether it be at the start, middle, or the end. This possibility contains the error that will make the calculation inaccurate from the start. Additionally, the way incarnate humankind progresses a mathematical calculation is in a linear way, irrespective of whether the calculation offers the possibility of more than one answer. This is a very cumbersome and a limited way to calculate that results in inaccuracy.

The most important way to understand mathematics is to recognize that at every point a value that is being calculated is a whole value, an integer if you like. Nothing is fractionalized or decimalized; nothing is less than whole.

Everything that is within the physical universe is a whole component, irrespective of whether it is a component of another component, of another component, and the maths that could be developed to support a model that describes this reality needs to work with whole components. Additionally, if the model is to include the functions associated with the frequencies above the gross physical it needs to be multilayered and function in a non-parallel, parallel way, therefore, a multipoluous function. A simple way to think of this is being an ellipsoid of ever-changing external and internal dimensions, whose components are the function of those entities that occupy the space that this represents. Based upon this, a linear mathematical model is never going to be able to deliver a realistic model of the function of the physical universe at any of its frequential levels or representations because it cannot be measured by human mathematics.

ME: OK, so what can be used to create a model of the physical universe if human mathematics is inaccurate, incapable, and ineffective?

OM: It's difficult to describe it in a way that incarnates in the gross physical can understand.

ME: Try me!

OM: Detached observation of any aspect of the physical universe, irrespective of size or quanta, without desire-based interaction or experiment. This will allow the reception of the conceptual information to be received in its purest sense. In this way, one will see that the universe is amorphous—ever-changing—and as such, cannot be described by use of a metric that requires a static value, or value of any kind, but only by the use of an amorphous concept.

It is the use of amorphous concepts that allows the understanding of "how" to understand the functions of the physical universe work, at any and all levels, and therefore give the entity or being the key to adapt these functions to their own desires. Once incarnate humankind grasps this, its progress and expansion as an incarnate civilization is guaranteed.

ME: In essence then, learning how to understand is the basis of how we will understand what I will call "real" mathematics.

OM: This is correct.

ME: Can you give us a clue then as to what the correct direction is for such a mathematical concept that would work at least on the gross physical level?

OM: The only thing that can be used in the gross physical level is to know that which we have told you, plus the concept that that which is measurable has to be considered to be the product of a curve or arc of which is known to be consistently changing in many planes of interaction with that which is the gross physical universe and not a digit or straight line. This is the direction that your mathematicians should move into for this will move them into the type of thinking that will allow them to understand the full content of the gross physical universe, at any level of quanta. It will provide the basis for the next level of thinking that will provide an understanding of how the mathematical concepts change from frequency to frequency allowing a, let us say, "translation" from one concept of mathematics to another.

ME: Do you mean the ability to translate from one mathematical concept to another?

OM: No, we mean the ability to "translate to" or "move to" the next conceptual level of mathematics required to work with the next frequency, not translate the conceptual information from the mathematics at one frequency level to that of another.

This in itself is why incarnate humankind will never be able to describe the gross physical universe at any level of quanta by the use of the mathematical processes currently employed. It's simply too linear and too full of natural inaccuracies to be a useful tool. Let alone being an accurate one.

ME: I never thought that humankind's mathematics could

be considered inaccurate and less than useful as a tool for understanding the physical universe let alone just the gross physical universe.

OM: Incarnate humankind is stubborn and likes to justify that which it has created, even if it is in error. When they are not in need to justify decisions that create models that are used as laws to help explain the physicality of the universe and are humble enough to keep looking away from that which is convenient, the maths will become available for them to see and start to use.

ME: You mean it's NOT available until incarnate humankind loses its ego?

OM: No, the mathematical concepts are there to see and use, they just have to detach from comfortable concepts developed by revered and respected individuals and models and open their eyes and look in the right directions.

The OM, the True Energetic Self (TES), and the True Sentient Self (TSS)

Do The OM Have a TES?

One of the things that had been asked by an ever-increasing number of my readers was either what an OM TES looked like, or whether or not The OM had one. This was a question that I had asked and gained an answer on myself a number of times. Indeed, the general answer I had received from Source and/or The OM was the answer, yes, The OM do have a TES. However, this did not feel correct to me. I felt that there was more to this than meets the eye. Based upon this, I decided to ask the question from a different angle, one that compensated for the possibility that both The Source and The OM were answering from the perspective of OM incarnate! I decided to ask the question again, but with a little impertinence in my mind's voice.

ME: OK, beloved of The OM, I know that I have asked the question before, and The OM, Anne, and Source have answered with an affirmative answer, that being YES. However, that's not quite true, is it?

OM Together: We always answer in a way that you will understand in the human context, with of course the potential for expansive correction later. This is now one of those times where expansive correction is appropriate.

ME: So, what is the expansive answer then?

OM Together: We are Origin sentience and in general remain as sentience.

ME: That's it? Just sentience?

OM Together: You already know that the division of sentience from a Source Entity or even The Origin is a division of sentience and associated energy. In the case of this Source Entity, the result is a coupling together of sentience and energy until communion is reestablished at the end of an evolutionary cycle, where both are absorbed into the greater volume of sentience and energy that is this or another Source Entity.

Sentience is not reliant on energy, though, and can and does exist independently of energy from both an individualized condition from another sentient entity or being, or, through the so-called Darwinian evolution of an energy as you describe it. That you know from your dialogues with The Origin [*see "The Road to Sentience" in* The Origin Speaks—*GSN*].

The True Energetic Self as you are told to describe it is the combination of individualized sentience and a volume of associated energy to allow experiential connectivity to be achieved in The Source's division of self and structure you know as the multiverse. This combination of sentience and energy is also referred to as the Higher Self, Over Soul, or God Head. Energy without sentience is mostly inert other than the potential for basic interaction and so remove the sentience from the energy and it returns to its primeval state, so to speak. The sentience, however, remains vital and can and does move around that which is energetic, frequential, or other structures at will. Within certain evolutionary constraints, that is, specifically within this Source Entity.

Sentience free from associated or commandeered energy can therefore be classified as the True Sentient Self (TSS), the "Real Self." This is particularly true for The OM but without the evolutionary constraints. But to call OM sentience as similar or same as the True Sentient Self would be to create further need for expansive correction later.

In essence though, the best way to understand The OM is to describe us as sentience, as individualized and cooperative sentience.

ME: The OM don't have association with energy then, from the perspective of needing it for the interaction with the environment that they desire to be in?

OM: There are some things you need to know about OM sentience. First, that OM sentience is normally just that, sentience.

Second, The OM, those that are pure, that is, do not normally interact with the structure of The Origin, for we are naturally detached from it, even though we are within it. The only time that an OM would associate itself with the frequencies and energies of the structure of The Origin is if it wished to enter into the evolutionary cycle, which the vast majority of OM do not.

ME: Anne and I are a rarity then?

OM: As Aspects of Pure OM you are fairly unique. We continue to not understand your desire to function within these unbelievably low frequencies. Even though it is a fleeting desire.

ME: OK, so I have established that The OM are normally represented as being pure sentience and that they don't associate that sentience with a "body of energy." Do The OM have to have a TES at any point?

OM: The OM would need to assume the sentient structure of being a True Sentient Self (TSS) if The OM concerned were to desire the nonfunctional interaction with any aspect of The Origin's energetic structure. In the event that an OM desired to become a functional part of that energetic structure then they need to commandeer the energies associated with that location within The Origin that they desired to interact with from a functional perspective. They create a TES.

ME: What's the difference between being functional and nonfunctional?

OM: Nonfunctional simply means that The OM sentience needs to adopt the sentient configuration required to maintain individualization from the overall unfocused or dormant sentience that is The Origin without becoming part of it.

ME: There is a danger of OM sentience becoming part of The Origin's sentience?

OM: The OM are essentially uncreated individualizations of Origin sentience and so it is possible that it could be reintegrated back into the main volume of Origin sentience, should that OM sentience so desire. The OM are good at remaining detached from such possibilities.

ME: Why then is there a need to become a certain sentient configuration if The OM are adept at remaining individualized?

OM: In the vast volume that is The Origin in its twelve levels of the first level of twelve levels of structure there are many, many, many volumes (locations) where The Origin's Polyomniscient Polyomnipresence is not yet operative. As a result, OM can move freely around spreading OM sentience thinly in any direction to be the dominant sentience, experiencing localized levels of Polyomniscience and Polyomnipresence. Only OM sentience can do this. This is only possible because OM prefer to reside where The Origin's sentience is not yet cohesive. When OM enter into volumes (locations) within The Origin's Polyomnipresent, Polyomniscience then it must create the configuration of individualized sentience. In essence it is like creating the condition of densified or compressed sentience. In this way, OM sentience can move through Origin sentience without becoming part of Origin sentience. Think of it like a stone moving through the air. The air cannot stop the stone unless it gets denser, such as becoming a strong wind. The Origin does not like to compress or densify its sentience because this means it has to withdraw its thinly spread Polyomniscience from Polyomnipresence and in doing so, it no longer experiences the vast volume of its structure in a Polyomniscient and Polyomnipresent way. In essence, it slows down its experiential and evolutionary progress. The Origin does its best to avoid this at all costs and so allows the passage of OM sentience configured to a denser level of individualization without hindrance or disturbance. Indeed, it likes the way The OM work because as they experience, because OM are essentially Origin sentience, it benefits from OM experience. It's a sort of symbiotic relationship. The OM passing though Origin sentience is a bit like you working on something in a focused way and then having random thoughts about something else and then refocusing on the task at hand. It's a minor distraction and one that is tolerated by The Origin.

ME: What makes The OM desire to become a functional part of a volume (location) within The Origin and why then commandeer energy and thus become a TES?

OM: We have to say that from the perspective of Pure OM this is more than a rarity. Indeed, the sentience that is the majority of your Pure OMness is the only Pure OM sentience that has commandeered energy to functionally interact within the very lowest aspects of The Origin's structure, that is, that which is commandeered by Source Entity sentience. In general, it is only a condition that a Captive OM within one of The Source Entities adopts out of necessity.

In your case your sentience adopted the configuration of True Sentient Self (TSS) to enter into a volume of Origin sentience and was attracted to the work of The Source Entities.

It had not observed The Source Entities before and was interested. Indeed, it was interested to the point of desiring to function at the same structural level for a period, just to experience what it was like to be within those levels. It was at this point that your sentience, now in the configuration of the TSS, commandeered energy to create a TES, allowing you to move within the lowest frequencies that were commandeered by The Source Entities and function within these energies in the same way that smaller individualizations of their sentience coupled together with their structural energies were able to.

Having observed the work of those Source Entities that were in the same volume of Origin as you, you settled upon the work of this particular Source Entity as being of specific interest and moved within its structure. It was at this point that you saw the combination of division of structure and individualization of sentience and energy within that structure. That which is the multiverse and its occupation by the smaller individualized units of Source Entity sentience we know as TES. In this structure you discovered that there were other assignations of OM sentience and therefore stayed to observe, and later interact, at a most basic functional level—those levels that required incarnation to establish functionality, within them.

As you are blessed of The OM, we adopted the TSS configuration to enter into the sentient boundary of The Source Entity you call SE1 to observe your sentience and its subsequent desire to commandeer energy. Its creation of the configuration of TES and subdivide and individualize its sentience and energy into similar or same configurations that SE1's TES were creating to experience, learn, and evolve. We then observed you, as an individualization of OM TESness, together with other individualizations, Anne being one of them, diving into the lowest frequencies within the structure of this Source Entity/The Origin. We were worried about you.

ME: From my position, which is extremely limited, I feel very humble that you should decide to look after me, or should I say this individualization of sentience?

OM: In reality, we had no choice but to follow you and look after you. We do not want to lose you as a Pure OM into the Captive OM status, or even locked into the evolutionary cycle or karmic cycle which would be disastrous at best.

From our perspective there are not enough OM at the Pure level, you know this from your earlier dialogue which indicated the total OM population throughout The Source Entities' and The Origin's current structure of Polyomniscient, Polyomnipresent sentient self-awareness.

You are doing things that OM would not choose to do—ever—so we are both interested and looking after you and experiencing that which you experience, albeit from a significant frequential distance.

ME: I have just looked into you all. You are afraid. No, that's the wrong word, you don't know or understand the concept of fear, that's a human thing. No, you are all concerned, worried, and excited at what I experience and share with you all. What I experience, you all experience; what I learn, you all learn; when I experience evolution, you all experience what it is like to evolve. All of this and more is shared between us all, all OM. This also includes The Origin.

Wait a minute, I thought that The OM were independent of The Origin!

OM: We are, but we are also Origin sentience.

ME: But The Origin seeks to evolve, so logically speaking The OM must be evolving?

OM: We evolve when The Origin evolves but we are not in the evolutionary cycle.

ME: I don't understand. How can you evolve if you are not in the evolutionary cycle?

OM: The Origin is not in the evolutionary cycle, but it seeks evolution, and it evolves. As it evolves, so do we.

We will explain some more.

As you are aware from your dialogue with Source Entity One (SE1) in your book on its maintenance entities, the maintenance entities themselves are not in the evolutionary cycle but they nevertheless evolve. The entities that assist the Aspects of sentience and energy that project themselves into the physical universe within this multiverse are not in the evolutionary cycle but because they are of service they evolve. Entities that are of service evolve as a function of the service they give to those that are in the evolutionary cycle. Entities that are individualized from a larger volume of sentience and energy share their evolutionary content with the volume of sentience that individualized them because they are in reality that higher level of sentience and energy. This is true for all individualizations of sentience, irrespective of whether or not energy is associated with that sentience.

In the case of the sentience that is OM, its individualized

status was not part of the desire of The Origin in its creation of The Source Entities, it just happened, and as such although that sentience was individualized in the various ways you are aware of, that sentience that is classified as Pure and Non-captive OM retained its Origin sentient status and so evolves as The Origin evolves.

ME: What about those OM that are Captive and Hybrid with the sentience of a Source Entity? Do they evolve?

OM: They evolve in a different way. Because they are in essence within the energetic boundaries of The Source Entity they are captive or hybrid with, they evolve as a function of the work of that Source Entity. This is specifically true of the Hybrid OM entities who are within the evolutionary cycle and choose to be in their own evolutionary cycle of that Source Entity. Captive OM are much less inclined to actively go into their own evolutionary cycle, but still do on occasion.

Pure OM never entertain the possibility of entering into their own evolutionary cycle or create anything that would result in responsibility. That was until you came along with the desire to see what the fuss was about in this location! Non-captive OM do enter into the evolutionary cycle at times but that is very rare to nonexistent. Certainly in the other Source Entities it is, but we note a few instances in this Source Entity's energies.

ME: Well, it was an interesting fuss, so to speak. It looks like I, the larger I that is, wanted to know first-hand what being incarnate and having individualized free will was like. I thought it would be a good experience. I now know that this is a very hard environment to be in and can be very addictive as well. I know that the thoughts, behaviors, and actions can be addictive, but this is like Russian roulette in reverse and on a massive scale!! That being, an entity stands a low to negligible chance of getting out of an incarnate condition without attracting some level of Karma, unless one is protected by a Guide or Helper.

OM: We are neither, and nor do you have a guide or helper to assist you. Yet you enter into this environment and survive with no guidance, even though you get distracted at times. It's at these times that we get concerned and do our best to help. But not in the guidance sort of way, in dissolving the link to Karma sort of way.

ME: You stop me gaining karmic content?

OM: Yes. If we did not, you would be lost here and we would lose

one who is beloved of The OM.
ME: So you look after me through interference then.
OM: We do not interfere, we simply keep you pure.
ME: For this, I thank you.

I have to admit that from the perspective of the accrual of Karma I always felt that I was Karma free and would not accrue karmic content, no matter what I did. I also felt that this was somewhat if not very egotistical. However, from what I have just heard from The OM, that they are protecting me from karmic content, it seems that my feeling was correct. I had better not make a mess of their work then!!

The explanation of The OM having to go through the process of creating a TSS to enter into the volume of energy space occupied by a Source Entity's sentience and then to create a TES to allow the possibility of entering into the incarnate state, seemed to be a process that was from my perspective, unnecessary. First, because the Pure OM don't incarnate or in general don't enter into the volume of energetic space occupied by a Source Entity's sentience. Second, if The OM were primarily Origin sentience that they must by definition have a TSS. This made me ask the next question: are The OM really any different to any other TSS/TES?

Are The OM Really Any Different to Any Other TES/TSS?

The heading to this section is the question that had been mulling around even more in my head since I last sat at my computer and created the connection with The OM. It had been two weeks since I last worked with The OM. Physical existence and its responsibilities had simply gotten in the way. To be honest, I don't like to miss my normal cadence of work when channeling the information for a book, but there are times when it happens and I am always delighted to be able to sit at my desk, open my laptop computer, and indulge myself in connectivity with the greater reality. I very quickly felt the energies of The OM around me and jumped straight in to ask this rather burning question. I was to be joined by the complete cohort of Anne, Hum, OM, and all OM. This question, I thought, required some emphasis in understanding.

ANNE & HUM & OM & ALL OM: The quick answer is yes, we are different to any other TSS/TES.

ME: OK! I accept that there is a difference, but I just can't see it at the moment. From my perspective, The OM, including myself, are sentience and energy combined and that combination is no different to any of the other True Sentient Self/True Energetic Self (TSS/TES) that are within a Source Entity!

ANNE & HUM & OM & ALL OM: We are very different.

ME: Would you like to explain this difference?

ANNE & HUM & OM & ALL OM: We have explained that The OM are pure Origin sentience and that to be able to work within the volume of space that is a Source Entity, OM would need to create the condition of the TSS and then TES to be able to integrate with the environment created out of a Source Entity's structure. Although from the human perspective The OM are sentience and with you as sentience and energy, this is only to allow us to keep our eye on you and protect you while you are in this incarnate condition. As a result, we have the appearance of being a TSS with you associated with a TES.

As you are aware, The OM are normally sentience completely detached from a body or volume of energy, and again, from the human perspective this would place us in the category of being a TSS. Note this though, the category of TSS is a function of the deliberate individualization of sentience from a higher volume of sentience than just sentience on its own. The TES is the function of deliberate individualization of both sentience and energy from a larger volume of combined sentience and energy.

ME: So the definition of a TSS or TES is that it is deliberately individualized from a higher volume of sentience or sentience and energy.

ANNE & HUM & OM & ALL OM: Correct.

ME: And The OM are not deliberately individualized from a higher volume of sentience or combination of sentience and energy.

ANNE & HUM & OM & ALL OM: Again, correct.

ME: And the fact that the sentience that was originally used to create the twelve Origins, being recycled to create the twelve Source Entities was deliberate individualization of sentience and energy that resulted in the creation of the twelve Source Entities and The OM doesn't count in this instance?

ANNE & HUM & OM & ALL OM: You're getting there.

ME: OK, why doesn't it count as deliberate individualization of sentience or sentience and energy and therefore result in the creation of a TSS or TES?

ANNE & HUM & OM & ALL OM: Simply because the manifestation of The OM was not intentional, it was not a deliberate individualization of sentience or sentience and energy. We were not intentionally created, we just happened, we were not created as Source Entities because the sentience that is now OM was and is pure Origin sentience and as such was not programmed to be Source Entity sentience because The Origin didn't desire this aspect of sentience to be used as Source Entity sentience.

ME: So the fact that the desire was not there by The Origin resulted in the sentience that is now OM sentience to escape, for want of a better word, from the individualization process that was designed to create Source Entities.

ANNE & HUM & OM & ALL OM: In a nutshell, yes. The OM sentience was caught up in the individualization process but had its own desire to move out of it.

ME: So the embryonic OM sentience, having its own desire to be itself, meant that it retained its status of Origin sentience while being individualized from Origin or Source Entity sentience with the individualization process not being a deliberate desire for that sentience.

ANNE & HUM & OM & ALL OM: Again, correct.

ME: Hang on, I am getting there. So, the statement that The OM are uncreated is not a function of that which was created is now uncreated, it's that the sentience moved out of the creativity process designed to create The Source Entities and was therefore uncreated.

ANNE & HUM & OM & ALL OM: Yes.

ME: So what makes The OM not have a TES or TSS?

ANNE & HUM & OM & ALL OM: Because the sentience that is OM moved out of the creativity process maintaining its "Originness" while being isolated from the main volume of Origin sentience and the individualization of sentience and energy that created The Source Entities. This means that The OM are The Origin, and not The Origin, concurrently. In essence, we are out of communion with The Origin while being in communion with ourselves as OM in totality. With, of course, a couple of minor exceptions, those exceptions being the new OM. As a result, this dual status places us outside of the category of being TSS and certainly outside of being TES because we don't have an association with a body or volume of energy and we were not specifically or deliberately individualized to be OM by The Origin.

ME: Interesting. So just how do the Pure or even Non-captive OM create a TSS and TES to be able to temporarily associate with a Source Entity?

ANNE & HUM & OM & ALL OM: We have to follow the process of individualization.

In essence, that which is inside The Source Entity you call SE1, where we are now, requires OM sentience to become individualized from a larger volume of OM sentience.

ME: Wait a minute! Are you suggesting that what is in the volume of sentience and energies that is SE1 is an individualization of OM sentience from a larger volume of OM sentience?

ANNE & HUM & OM & ALL OM: Yes, of course. This is the only way in which pure or Non-captive OM can work within the individualized confines of a Source Entity's sentience and its associated energies by creating a TSS and then a TES.

ME: Now you have got me thinking. I feel that the sentience that is The OM is a collective of sentience and energy, which as you say is the necessary requirement to be able to interact within the volume of sentience and energy that is a Source Entity. It is a TES. This OM TES is, in my observation, feeling and understanding similar or the same volume as that of a TES that is individualized from a Source Entity. Am I correct?

ANNE & HUM & OM & ALL OM: Yes, you are correct. We OM are the same as an individualization of Source Entity sentience and energy—while inside the volume of Source Entity sentience and energy. We are the same as a TSS. You are the same as a TES because you chose to enter into the process of incarnation. The functionality is the same but the sentience behind that functionality is different.

ME: So what I am communicating with is not The OM in totality then?

ANNE & HUM & OM & ALL OM: No, not in the slightest, not from the perspective of that of us which is within this Source Entity that is.

ME: So just how big are The OM?

ANNE & HUM & OM & ALL OM: That which is individualized to create a TSS and your TES is but a mere fraction of that which is OM in our normal state.

ME: What are we talking about then? Ten percent, 20 percent?

ANNE & HUM & OM & ALL OM: The OM sentience that is currently projected as individualized OM sentience, including the sentience that has an association with energy that your

TSS has to make a TES, is approximately 1 percent in total. Actually, it's much less than 1 percent.

ME: This means that The OM sentience is one hundred times larger in volume than a Source Entity TES!

ANNE & HUM & OM & ALL OM: One hundred and forty-four to be precise.

ME: One hundred and forty-four times bigger?

ANNE & HUM & OM & ALL OM: Yes. Remember everything is a function of twelve within the structure of The Origin and therefore a Source Entity.

ME: So The OM only need to create an individualization of its sentience to create a TSS to enter into the volume of sentience and energy of a Source Entity and this in turn can create a TES by associating itself with, or commandeering, a body (volume) of energy. It is normally pure Origin sentience moving around the volume of Origin Structure that is its current volume of Polyomniscient, Polyomnipresent self-awareness and other areas within the same level of structure.

ANNE & HUM & OM & ALL OM: Yes. OM are pure Origin sentience.

ME: Let me ask this question then. Is OM sentience, as a TSS, or if associated with energy to interact with that which is within the volume of Source Entity sentience and energy, as an OM-derived TES, any different while in this state than any other TES or TSS within a Source Entity?

ANNE & HUM & OM & ALL OM: From the perspective of the quality of the sentience, yes. There is a difference because the quality of Origin sentience is by definition significantly higher than that of a Source Entity. However, while interacting within the lower frequencies of a Source Entity the functionality is the same as a TES individualized from Source Entity sentience and energy.

ME: Based upon that then there is a difference, but that difference makes no difference when interacting within the confines of a Source Entity and its lower levels of frequential structure.

ANNE & HUM & OM & ALL OM: Correct. You, for example, have to work within the same structure and functionality as TES that are individualized from Source Entity One and its multiversal environment. This is one of the reasons why your OMness wanted to experience this level of existence, to see what it felt like!

ME: Well, my OMness must have been mad!

ANNE & HUM & OM & ALL OM: That's what we all thought

The OM, the True Energetic Self (TES), and the True Sentient Self (TSS)

but your OMness retorted by saying that the only way to experience something properly is to experience it in the same way as those entities that are in the environment are experiencing and interacting with the environment and those entities that are within it.

ME: In essence then The OM don't need a body of energy because they are normally not part of a Source Entity. It's only when they enter into a Source Entity's volume of sentience and energy at the most fundamental level, that they might associate with energy. Normally, they would remain at the TSS level when within a Source Entity.

ANNE & HUM & OM & ALL OM: Correct. The OM are free sentience.

ME: OK, I have another question to ask before we move on to the next subject.

ANNE & HUM & OM & ALL OM: Carry on!

ME: Where is Hum from? Is it from my temporary TES or another volume of sentience, another OM TSS?

My TES Collective and Hum—from a

Different OM TES Collective

ANNE & HUM & OM & ALL OM: Hum is here to help you. It is from a different individualization of OMness.

ME: I thought Hum might be from different TES than Anne and myself. Hum's energy signature didn't feel the same, while it was the same.

Wait a minute! If Hum is in the same energetic and frequentic structure as I am, i.e., currently within Source Entity One, it must have undergone the individualization process.

ANNE & HUM & OM & ALL OM: Hum's OMness created a TSS and then a TES that supported the capability of being able to enter into SE1's space, so to speak, and then its multiversal environment. However, because it does not intend or need to incarnate to communicate with you, or indeed assist you, it remains at the TES level.

ME: Does Hum even need to have a TES? Can it remain at TSS level?

ANNE & HUM & OM & ALL OM: As you are aware to enter into an individualized energetic and frequentic structure [*which includes the subdimensional components and full dimensions—GSN*] such as a Source Entity, a sentience must adopt the energetic "body of energy" relative to that individualization and the potential structure it has adopted, irrespective of the fact that it is a function of the structure of The Origin. It does this to be able to interact correctly with the desired level of interaction necessary to become "part" of that environment that it is currently within. It still maintains its individuality from Source but is accepted as though it was actually individualized from Source.

ME: Are you suggesting that it's a bit like OM sentience not being accepted by the overall structure and sentience of a Source Entity? Like having a major organ rejected from the human body in a transplant. So, if OM sentience didn't enter into the individualization process and create a TES relative to The Source Entity whose energies they are within, it wouldn't be accepted?

ANNE & HUM & OM & ALL OM: It's not so much a case of not being accepted or rejected, it's more a case of not being total in harmony with the sentience that is a Source Entity. Remember, OM are Origin sentience unless they are hybrid with the sentience of a Source Entity so there is a difference. Just as there is a feeling of mild or even major discomfort or dislike when people of different base resonant frequencies interact with each other, so there is a ripple of mild sentient disharmony felt by a Source Entity when a higher quality of sentience enters into its "body" of energy.

ME: Why is this considered to be a disharmony if the sentience is of a higher quality?

ANNE & HUM & OM & ALL OM: Try to think of it in this way. Try putting hot water on ice. The hot water, at boiling point, being at a different frequency disturbs the cohesion of the structure of the ice in an instantaneous way, making it crack and turn to water.

ME: Wouldn't that be a good thing? I mean, just as in your example, the ice is turned to water or cracked as a result of being exposed to heat or hot water. Because of this it raises the frequency of the ice which becomes the hot water! Wouldn't the quality of sentience being raised to a different level be of benefit?

ANNE & HUM & OM & ALL OM: One would think it to be beneficial in the instance of a small area or volume of ice versus the water, but if you think of this again as the pouring of boiling water, but on a large area of ice, such as an ice field in the Arctic or Antarctic, then you will see that the ice is only momentarily raised to water levels of frequency before the ambient temperature of its surrounding environment returns it back to ice. It's both uncomfortable and disharmonious to both the higher level of frequency of the boiling water and the lower level of frequency of the ice. What's more, from the perspective of the differing qualities of sentience, it is a transient condition that continues to affect the very localized areas of the lower quality of sentience when the volume of higher quality of sentience moves through its space. One can think of it another way, the higher quality of sentience is in a continuous battle with being immersed in a lower quality of sentience.

ME: I get it now. It's like eating a hot chile and feeling it passing through one's digestive system.

ANNE & HUM & OM & ALL OM: Well, we have just connected with you to see the example, and we are laughing, for want of a better response. It is a good example to use. In your example the disharmony is the spiciness of the chile irritating the lining of the digestive tracts. This represents the disharmony that a Source Entity has. The disharmony that a higher level of sentience has is the overwhelming battle against the lower quality sentience to become that quality. From the perspective of the chile, it's the digestive tract attempting to digest it!

ME: And so the creation of a TSS and then TES provides a kind of protection, a harmonious interface, between the higher quality of OM (Origin) sentience and the lower individualized quality of sentience that is Source Entity sentience. That's not to suggest that Source Entity sentience is low!

ANNE & HUM & OM & ALL OM: That is another way to think about it, yes, but in reality the best way to understand it is to think of it as the maintenance of sentient harmony allowing free passage of sentience within sentience.

In the dialogue above, I noted that Hum was also answering this question as part of the collective of OMness that was communicating with me and not as an individual OM. Even referring to that which was its individualization in the third person as "It." I found this very interesting. It was as if Hum didn't exist as an individuality of OMness at all. I decided that I needed to ask about this, what I will call, a third OMness phenomenon!

ME: Why does Hum refer to itself as "IT" when in communion with OMness?

ANNE & HUM & OM & ALL OM: That is a simple question to answer. OM have no gender, no Aspects or Shards, and so are normally OMness in uncreated individuality while being beloved of The OM. It can be considered as being individualized communion. That which is OMness in individuality is also OMness in communion. As such the only way to describe that is sentience, and the only way to describe individualized sentience in your limited language is as "IT" irrespective of whether the sentience is you or not.

ME: So this is why Hum collectively with the "All OM" and Anne also described itself when in communion-based responses to me as "IT?"

ANNE & HUM & OM & ALL OM: Correct. We just are OM sentience, we are IT!

I think I will leave this dialogue there as the semantics surrounding the potential description of sentience and OM-based sentience were looking like they were circular.

There were bigger fish to fry and I still had a lot of questions to go through. Time to move on, I thought.

Uncreativity: Just What Does It REALLY Mean and How Does It Affect The OM?

For some reason, I was drawn to this subject matter again. I was very aware that The OM were the function of what was basically a lack of attention to the detail of, or assignation of, quality of sentience that The Origin intended to use to create The Source Entities but that some of this sentience still had the assignation of the quality of sentience that was pure "Origin" sentience. I was starting to think that the use of the word "uncreated" was a word that was being used to avoid the word "mistake!" We all think that God, or The Source Entity and even The Origin, is/are beyond the capability of making a mistake. However, when one thinks in terms of the fact that The Origin is evolving, it always was evolving and that its use of sentience had to start somewhere, then it's reasonable to assume that it would make a few mistakes along the way.

The word "uncreated" or "uncreativity" for me means that something was destroyed, dissolved, removed, changed, or recycled. The OM made a major point of the fact that the sentience that became OM is really just a smaller unit of pure Origin sentience. That this sentience was not assigned to be Source Entity sentience and therefore remained in its original assignation of being one of the twelve Origins in The Origin's attempt to accelerate its evolutionary progression by reproducing itself and placing those reproductions outside of its volume of Polyomniscient, Polyomnipresent self-awareness.

I wanted to get more out of The OM on the use of this word, which was clearly distracting me. They soon came to guide me.

ANNE & HUM & OM & ALL OM: You really are getting what you would call "hung up" on our use of this word, aren't you!

ME: Yes, I am. I want to fully understand how something can be an "uncreated creation."

ANNE & HUM & OM & ALL OM: It's all to do with the desire behind the intention.

ME: I understand that there is a linear equation supporting the manifestation of anything. I have described it many times in my dialogues with The Source and The Origin. It goes like this, Desire—Intention—Thought—Action.

ANNE & HUM & OM & ALL OM: Very good. However, this so-called equation only works if it is "all" in place.

ME: Go on.

ANNE & HUM & OM & ALL OM: In the event that one of the components of that equation is missing, then the outcome is either incorrect, incomplete, or in stasis until complete.

In the instance of the uncreated creation of The OM, the intention to convert the sentience that was assigned to be one of the twelve Origins into a Source Entity was not there. The Origin just had the desire to create The Source Entities as individualizations of its own sentience together with the ability to use a "body" of energy that was assigned to that sentience so that it could create, experience, learn, and evolve. Additionally, it had the potential to withdraw its sentience from that body of energy and assign itself to another body of energy. The Origin put this desire straight into action. As a result, the intention and thought phase was missing and so the sentience that was previously individualized Origin sentience, as Origin sentience, remained as such and did not become Source Entity sentience.

This Origin sentience was in various volumes that instantly recognized each other and connected together in communion. It therefore collectively moved itself away from the desire to be created as Source Entity sentience and to remain as individualized Origin sentience. In effect, it moved itself out of The Origin's desire phase and into its own intention, thought, and action phase. In essence, this "uncreated" or changed what The Origin desired and "created" what this individualized Origin sentience desired—autonomous individuality. It created its own desire, intention, thought, and action which resulted in sustaining the manifestation of totally independent, individualized Origin sentience that was originally individualized as the "Original Manifestation" of the individualization of Origin sentience to be individualized twelve times as an equal to its source of sentience, The Original Origin.

We collectively call ourselves "OM" in your language based upon our being part of the Original Manifestation and although we are a function of The Origin and its sentience, and have a name or label that sounds like the English word "OM" to describe the base resonant frequency of the energetic structure of The Origin, we are not that resonance, we are not OM or its correct spelling of AUM, for we are pure sentience— autonomous individualized Origin sentience. AUM is a frequential resonance and therefore part of a structure devoid of sentience.

ME: Do you refer to yourselves as "OM" with all of the incarnate entities you come in contact with or interact with?

ANNE & HUM & OM & ALL OM: Should we interact with them, we describe ourselves in the way that the incarnate civilization will understand. That said, "OM" is the best way to describe ourselves from the human perspective.

ME: And your reference to another OM being "beloved?"

ANNE & HUM & OM & ALL OM: Again, this is a human language reference. Our collective status is best described in this way in human terms. As you are aware, there are only a few of us in the Pure and Non-captive sense of OMness and so all OM are beloved to all OM. In essence, we revere each other's presence and existence.

ME: So, you do interact with other incarnate civilizations within the physical universe!

ANNE & HUM & OM & ALL OM: Rarely, and if the truth be said, mostly by accident. We do not intentionally seek interaction with those in the evolutionary cycle, and as you are aware, the fact that we/you are interacting with incarnates at this lowest of the frequency levels, is beyond the possibility of being called a rare occurrence.

ME: OK, I want to talk about your interaction with incarnates in a few moments but getting back to the uncreativity process and specifically your/our/my individualization at this time, what made you think, behave, and act in this individualized way? In a way that made that which was Origin sentience continue to become individualized and autonomous from The Origin, and not return back into communion with the bulk of The

Origin's sentience?
ANNE & HUM & OM & ALL OM: Event Space.

Now this suddenly became VERY interesting. For those readers that have read The Origin Speaks *you will be aware that The Origin eventually gained dominant sentient status in the vastness of the structure it occupied as a result of Event Space, which was "the" dominant sentience at that time, forgoing its status in favor of The Origin because it saw the increase in sentient potential that would be manifest by The Origin above and beyond that which Event Space itself would ever achieve. This means that the same observation and decision process must have been made by Event Space to the benefit of The OM. This was new news, very, very new news! There was no question about what I needed to do next; I needed to ask more questions about the role Event Space played in The OM gaining autonomous individualization!*

The Role of Event Space in Uncreating and Creating The OM!

HUM: It has been decided that I communicate directly about this revelation for you.

ME: Thank you, Hum. I expect that is because you are closer to me than the rest of The OM. With the exception of Anne, that is.

HUM: It was decided that I work with you in this instance because, yes, I am closest to you while you are incarnate in the human form and, moreover, have more experience of understanding your questions in relation to this subject. I observed you while you were communicating with The Origin on the same subject. There is another reason as well. I will let you know when the time is appropriate for this is an experiential reason.

ME: I am sure that will make a difference. Tell me, I am curious as to why did Event Space become involved in the uncreation and creation of The OM? It seems a bit unnecessary. Especially as the sentience that is The Origin was already given sentient dominance by Event Space?

HUM: You are thinking in a linear way again. The Origin and The OM were created in synchronicity.

ME: I am sorry, I don't understand.

HUM: Synchronicity means together, concurrently—AT THE SAME TIME.

ME: Hold on. I thought that The Origin was allowed to come into sentience dominance first, as a function of Event Space recognizing that a greater sentience could be created if Event Space itself gave up dominance in favor of the potential dominance that The Origin would be as the dominant sentience. The OM, us, came into creation as a function of the recycling of the sentience that was to be used as "the twelve Origin's experiment?"

HUM: It did.

ME: Then I really don't understand.

HUM: That's why I am here.

ME: OK, carry on then.

HUM: Once achieved, sentience cannot be lost. It is in effect a linear progression even if its function is spherical or even multistructural in its inhabitancy of those energies that it resides in, or moves from and to. However, sentience can be divided, individualized, and foregone.

ME: Can you explain the part about sentience being foregone please? I know about the division of, or individualization of sentience.

HUM: The potential for one sentience being dominate over another can be negated by one volume of sentience, if it considered that the other volume of sentience has more potential than itself, if it became "additional" sentience to the other volume of sentience. So rather than being the dominant volume of sentience and absorbing the other volume of sentience and resulting in the combination of the two volumes of sentience having less potential, it chooses to sacrifice its potential and dominance in favor of being part of a volume of sentience that has more potential. Potential in this instance is in the ability to grow and evolve.

Event Space forgave its dominance and divided an aspect of its own volume to be part of that that was to become The Origin. A function of this is that its progression becomes stationary, goes into stasis. It doesn't lose its sentience, though, but it does lose its potential to progress.

ME: So, if this is correct, how did Event Space ensure that The OM was uncreated from the creation of The Source Entities? What you are saying now is that The Origin and The OM were created concurrently as a function of the intervention of Event Space. Especially if its sentient dominance was already sacrificed for that of The Origin, and, The Origin having already gone through the process of creating the twelve Origins, and failing, had progressed to the creation of The Source Entities? It wouldn't have the capability to influence the creation of The OM.

HUM: You are thinking in a confused linear state.

It is best explained again, in a different way showing you a linear series of events, so to speak.

1. Event Space is the dominant sentience in the structure we now recognize as The Origin's structure.
2. Event Space recognized the potential for a greater, more powerful volume of sentience, one that would be significantly more important than itself. That which would become The Origin.
3. Event Space sacrificed its progression in favor of The Origin.
4. Event Space divided an aspect of its sentience and allowed it to merge with the volume of sentience that would become The Origin.
5. The Origin surpasses Event Space in its sentient growth.
6. Event Space becomes a function of the structure that is now The Origin.
7. In the same Event Space that Event Space recognized the potential for The Origin (line 2) it also recognizes a wild card or free radical function of Origin sentience within The Origin.
8. Event Space creates an Event Space that supports the assignation and division of Origin sentience. This is made at the juncture of its sacrificing its sentient progression in favor of The Origin. This assignation is of a volume of that sentience that would be uncreated from creation if not all the aspects of the creativity process are not met (desire, intention, thought, action).
9. Event Space merges two Event Spaces together to create one Event Space. The Event Space that results in the creation of The Origin, and the Event Space that results in the uncreation of Origin Sentience from the creation of The Source Entities allowing that sentience to create its own volume of sentience and therefore its own identity—The OM.

As you can see, although this is laid out in a linear way, it is intertwined in a way where everything happens concurrently while having the appearance of having Event Space junctures that express linearity. Everything in Event Space can be concurrent and Event Space can take that which appears to be linear and relocate it into concurrency.

ME: So, what you are saying is that Event Space had to move the uncreated creation of The OM from the juncture that supports The Origin individualizing sentience and energy to create The Source Entities, to the juncture that supported the creation of the dominance of Origin sentience above that of Event Space itself. At the same time as creating the potential for The Origin to be dominant.

HUM: Correct, with everything happening concurrently.

ME: What was it about The OM that made Event Space ensure they came into existence?

HUM: We are what you would call a free radical. Not in the sense of being detrimental but in the sense of being a useful addition to the progression of The Origin.

ME: Can you tell me more? I mean, just being a free radical would not necessitate the need or desire for a higher quality of sentience, for that's what Event Space was then, to add the possibility of the uncreated creation of The OM into the product of its sacrifice of its own sentient dominance!

HUM: As you are aware, The OM are fully individualized Origin sentience. We were not the product of the desire of The Origin to create The Source Entities. Indeed, we are fully independent of The Origin and of Event Space.

ME: Hold on a moment, I am receiving the thought that The OM would have come into existence anyway, but as a function of so-called Darwinian evolution of energy into the sentient state.

HUM: This is true. However, this route to OM sentience would not have borne the same quality of OM sentience that we currently have, and that which we will have in another Event Space.

ME: So, as with The Origin, The OM would have not become what they are now had Event Space not sacrificed its dominance.

HUM: Correct.

ME: Again then, what was it that made Event Space favor the manifestation of The OM as well as giving The Origin sentient dominance?

HUM: As smaller but fully individualized units of Origin sentience, The OM are capable of everything The Origin is capable of doing, only we are not under the so-called command and control of a higher sentience. We are our own sentience so to speak, free to do what we want without being responsible for anything. Provided that is, that we don't create anything, because if we create something, we are responsible for it and that removes our freedom, so to speak.

ME: Why do you feel that you would lose your freedom if you created something?

HUM: Simply put, we have to nurture that which is created and that means staying in the same location as that which was created, which is limiting. What you are doing is limiting as well, but we need you back as beloved of The OM so we are staying in the location, until this incarnation is finished.

The other, and possibly main, reason for Event Space allowing The OM to become a small but nevertheless dominant sentience with no allegiance to a higher volume of sentience is that we provide the possibility of random evolution.

ME: I thought that The OM are outside of the evolutionary cycle?

HUM: We are outside of the evolutionary cycle, but we also evolve as a function of The Origin evolving. Although we are not beholden to The Origin and are individualized, we are still part of it, without actually being it. That being, we are not part of the vast volume of sentience that is expanding in and around the current and first structural level that is occupied by the sentience that is The Origin, and therefore becoming The Origin.

The other reason that Event Space ensured that The OM came into the level of sentience that we currently are is because it saw us as a "Backup."

The Origin Had a Backup

ME: Do you mean a backup to The Origin's sentience?

HUM: Yes.

ME: That means to me that should the sentience that is The Origin fail to expand or become what Event Space foresaw as being the dominant sentience, then The OM would take over. Is this correct?

HUM: This is correct. However, the route to dominant sentience would be different to that which is currently in place.

ME: How would it be different? Is it because The OM are more than one?

HUM: In a word, yes.

ME: And there would be a number of (the number of OM) Origin-level sentience that could become the dominant sentience.

HUM: Yes. In essence it would be a similar outcome to that which would have occurred had the twelve Origins' experiment been successful, with thirteen Origin-level volumes of sentience existing within the energies that we all currently occupy.

ME: But this didn't happen, and The Origin is in existence as a singular volume of sentience.

HUM: Correct again. And The OM are individualized units of Origin-quality sentience.

You see, Event Space saw two options, one with The Origin and the free radicals or shall we say free agents that are The OM, and another Event Space where The OM are the dominant sentience when The Origin failed to expand its sentience.

Even now we have a higher function in the evolution of The Origin, and that is the activation of energies to the acceptance of high-quality sentience, therefore acting as an accelerant to The Origin's growth. This is the reason why Event Space chose to add The OM into its sacrifice of self as the dominant sentience.

ME: How do you do that? I mean, The OM are not actively involved in the evolutionary cycle but from what you have just explained, you are, you really are involved in the evolution of The Origin.

HUM: Yes, we are but it is not a so-called conscious decision to assist The Origin in its evolution.

ME: So, I will ask again. Just how do you assist The Origin in its evolution?

HUM: It's a function of the passage of sentience from energy to energy within the structure that the energy is in. You see, once an energy, irrespective of its position within the structure that The Origin's sentience exists within, is, shall we say "exposed" to sentience, it has the enhanced capability of becoming sentience when exposed to higher volumes of sentience than that which exposed it to sentience in the first instance.

ME: So The OM act as a sort of priming agent, a sentience priming agent to assist the growth of The Origin's sentience.

HUM: That's one way to look at it.

ME: But I would have thought that this wasn't necessary, that The Origin's sentience was powerful enough on its own and didn't need any assistance in spreading throughout the energies that it currently occupies and will inevitably occupy.

HUM: That in itself is correct, considering that is, that sentience from a functional perspective is contained within the volume of space that it occupies, occupied, or will occupy. However, sentience doesn't work like that.

ME: What do you mean? Sentience has a way of functioning that is not restricted to the volume of space that it occupies?

HUM: Sentience is leaky. Is this the correct word to use?

ME: I think I know what you mean.

HUM: OK, I will explain it another way. Sentience is not specifically containable in the volume of space that it may currently occupy. It can spread.

ME: Ah! That's a better word. How does sentience spread then? I would have expected that it needed to have some intention to spread the sentience associated with its beingness.

HUM: Sentience has a natural desire to expand to fit the volume of space that it occupies. This is irrespective of the intended flow and subsequent direction of sentience that the overarching sentient desire wants to go in.

ME: Doesn't this mean that there is stray, un-directional sentience spreading about the volume of space that it is occupying?

HUM: In some respects, yes. The sentience that leaks has only a minimal amount of direction to it and can, if not recovered—which most of the time it's not—become raw sentience without any experiential and evolutionary content associated with it.

ME: That sounds like unprogrammed sentience. Is that even possible? I mean, sentience is usually the result of division from a larger volume of sentience or the product of so-called Darwinian evolution of energy?

HUM: Sentience can be raw and unprogrammed with no experiential or evolutionary content. That was how The Origin divided its sentience into the twelve Origins and Source Entities. It then expected them to become aware and awake of self and their own surroundings in their own time. As you know, once The Origin considered that The Source Entities were self-sufficient enough, they were then advised of their reason to be (in existence) and their role in the evolution of The Origin and its expansion of sentience.

ME: I expect that when a Source Entity goes through an evolutionary cycle that also prepares the energy that was occupied by that Source Entity's sentience to be "sentient ready," so to speak!

HUM: Exactly. It's the same as if an OM passes through a volume of space with the exception of one thing.

ME: Go on.

HUM: A Source Entity is a vast volume of individualized sentience and the space it occupies is clearly large enough to occupy it. OM are small in comparison, microscopically small, but we are pure Origin sentience and that makes us potent. Additionally, we move around a lot and "touch" for want of a better word a wide volume of space and the energy within it. We create what can be called a matrix of space and energy that is very attractive to sentience with the ability to be useful to sentience.

ME: It's like an infinitesimal dot matrix of OM sentience interaction. One could join the dots together and create a triangulation effect that accelerates the accrual of sentience over the space of energy affected.

HUM: Although that's the idea, it's not the primary function of The OM to create this. It just happens. We are small and nimble and so can affect significantly larger areas of space and the energy in that space within any of the twelve levels of structure within the first of the over-all twelve levels of structure The Origin's sentience currently occupies.

ME: Let's get back to this concept that sentience is leaky. Can you give me an image that will help the readers understand?

HUM: Yes, of course.

Straight away, I saw an image. I saw a room full of smoke. The smoke represented sentience within the volume of space of the room. Initially, the smoke was contained by the room, static and still. But then something happened. The smoke started to move around the room, very slowly. Not sinking to the floor like smoke does here on Earth but looking like it wanted to expand. I was then shown another image. I was outside of the room and could see what looked like windows and a door. They were very well sealed from the look of them. As I continued to look at this room from the outside, I started to notice that the image of the walls of the room started to look out of focus, indeed they looked foggy. I looked closer and noticed that the smoke was finding its way past the seals in the window and door frames and looking very fine, much finer than it was in the room. It was finding its way past anything, even the structural gaps in between the atomic structure of the walls and the door and window. It was leaking out. It was as if the walls of the room, the windows, and doors were porous. The sentience was leaking out, not all of it was though; it was as if it felt that the volume of space it occupied wasn't enough for it so it leaked out. Sentient leak is like smoke under a door, I thought!

HUM: What we showed you is figurative. It's an illustration. Sentience likes to be associated with energy because energy is a useful tool for it to use in its evolutionary progression. Even though it doesn't actually need energy for its normal existence, it recognizes that energy has an important part to play in its progression.

ME: So it looks to occupy as much space as it can, by being leaky.

HUM: That's one way of saying it.

ME: But why does it need to be leaky? Why doesn't it just actively seek out an energetic platform for itself and evolve?

HUM: Without experiential and evolutionary content, sentience is just raw sentience. Its potential is there to evolve, but it has no direction. Sentience with experiential and evolutionary content has direction. That direction you may consider to be its personality. That's what makes The Origin, The Origin; The Source Entities, The Source Entities; The OM, The OM; and an Aspect's TES, a TES.

I was a bit perplexed here. I had never considered the possibility of raw, unexperienced, unevolved sentience. Indeed, the possibility of sentience without these basic properties had never been discussed before. It was an interesting prospect that sentience was just that, sentience. That exposure to the interaction with experiential considerations, or the environment, to these considerations the sentience is exposed to, is the very reason why sentience becomes individualized to the point of having what one could call personality, was a revelation. At least it was, to my memory, never discussed. However, it did make sense. I thought about it a moment. Raw sentience was like a computer without a program. Or, for want of a better word, a blank canvas of potential.

I kept thinking that it seemed strange that sentience could be sentience without experiential content. Then, just as I was scratching my head on this concept, HUM came to the rescue with an example.

HUM: Aspects that incarnate experience this all of the time.

ME: What do you mean?

HUM: Every time an Aspect enters into the primary phase of incarnation, the sentience that is the newly incarnate Aspect experiences the loss of communicative bandwidth that results in it gradually forgetting who and what it is, essentially becoming raw sentience. This is the reason why the temporary personality called the ego is able to become!

ME: So, the Aspect in experiencing no high-frequency communication ends up like a blank page, and is programmed by that which it experiences, which in turn creates the temporary personality we call the ego.

HUM: Correct.

ME: So, does that mean that sentience that leaks from experiential sentience becomes like raw sentience in the same way?

HUM: Not quite. The sentience that has ego as a function of exposure to low-frequency environmental conditions has experiential content associated with it. It's just that the percentage of sentience is so low that it is easily influenced by that which it experiences in the now.

Sentience that leaks from sentience that is passing through a volume of space and energy is usually sentience that is, to date, or so far unaffected by the exposure to experiential content.

ME: But how can that be? If the sentience that is temporarily individualized from a TES as an Aspect has some level of affect from previous experiential content, even though it forgets it, how can sentience that has leaked from a larger volume of sentience be classified as raw sentience?

HUM: Try to think of it in this way. Consider a hard drive or volume of memory on your computer. Areas or sectors are written upon and are therefore associated with a file and a program that that file is operational within. The rest of the memory, although structured, is raw untouched (unwritten) memory. It has no association with anything else other than its functional or accessible structure. The functional structure in sentience is that it is capable of absorbing and retaining experiential content and evolving as a consequence. Although it may choose to delete experiential content, it still retains the evolutionary content associated with it, allowing the sentience to focus on new experiential content and working with it in an improved way. The memory in your computer has the ability of retaining content or being overwritten with new content, and although the volume of memory itself does not retain any so-called learning, a program that uses this volume of memory that has a learning function or is classified as artificial intelligence will do.

ME: So, sentience that is not exposed to experiential content is not specifically attached to the volume of sentience that it is part of because there is nothing to associate it with that sentience.

Therefore, it is able to detach and become independent while being more susceptible to attracting experiential content and evolving in its own right.

HUM: If you want to think of it in that way it's a good analogy. The thing to note is that raw sentience, momentarily touched by focused evolved sentience, is primed for the acceptance of experiential content and accrual of evolutionary content in a way that it is more efficient and effective than if it is not touched by evolved sentience.

ME: It's sort of like memory that is formatted rather than unformatted, because unformatted memory will not save a file, whereas formatted memory will.

HUM: Yes, that is a better way of explaining it. We like that!

Now I was happy. I had an explanation that made sense to me and one that most of my readers could relate to as well. I was about to move on when a thought came to my mind. Sentience that comes into being by so-called Darwinian evolution must always be sentience with an association to its experiential content and subsequent evolution, whereas sentience that is individualized from a higher level of sentience is raw until it is given direction by that sentience that it is individualized from. Considering this, raw sentience can never be borne from Darwinian evolution, only from individualization from a higher volume of sentience.

I thought further. Hum and I had started this talk referring to energy being touched by sentience and therefore becoming more attractive to a volume of sentience. Again, that it was primed or formatted. Upon reflection I felt that the process of energy being formatted by focused or evolved sentience is the same with raw sentience and focused or evolved sentience. This made sense, it was a different level of structure, so to speak, but nevertheless the same. It felt right, and I wondered what other processes carry across the sentience/energy barrier or indeed what other demarcation lines are as yet undiscussed. I got the impression that this was just another stepping-stone in my expansive progression leading to other higher concepts later.

As I pondered upon this my mind was drawn back to Event Space and its intervention in the uncreative conditions surrounding The OM. If The OM were a backup to Event Space's desire for a single individual higher quality of sentience, just how could they be a backup, considering that they are small, individualized units of Origin sentience and not one? This deserved to be investigated, I thought.

Singular Dominant Sentience Is the Inevitable Outcome—Or Is It?

This was an excellent conundrum. The possibility of The OM being a backup to Event Space creating the possibility of The Origin becoming the dominant sentience was becoming more and more tantalizing. As I had just thought, they were small, very small in comparison with the size of sentience that is The Origin. Again, I thought, how would this be possible?

I decided that this question was best discussed with The OM in general rather than just Hum or Anne. Collectively The OM were not slow to answer my questions on this subject.

ANNE & HUM & OM & ALL OM: You, of course, know the answer yourself when you are beloved of The OM. Do you feel that you can answer your question yourself?

ME: I think I can to some extent. It's not about the size or volume associated with the sentience, it's about the quality of that sentience. Based upon the fact that the volume of a low quality of sentience will always be superseded by a smaller volume of a higher quality of sentience.

ANNE & HUM & OM & ALL OM: You are getting the idea. We will elaborate for you.

Event Space saw two roles for that sentience which eventually became uncreated as The OM through its own intervention. First, that the smaller high-quality aspects of sentience would become what they have become, free radicals or sentient agitates. Second, that they would be able to grow in sentient volume should The Original higher volume sentience not grow in both volume and quality.

ME: It was expected then that the quality of sentience, that is, shall we say, the newly identified quality of sentience that was to be The Origin, would grow in both volume and quality.

ANNE & HUM & OM & ALL OM: It was, yes.

ME: But in the event that it didn't, Event Space was able to foresee another quality of sentience that could be maneuvered into the correct Event Stream to ensure that a higher level of sentience would supersede it.

ANNE & HUM & OM & ALL OM: Correct.

ME: And that smaller quality of sentience would be capable of expanding to fill the gap, or, stay as it is to some extent if The

Original higher quality of sentience achieved its objective.

ANNE & HUM & OM & ALL OM: Correct again.

ME: So, what we have now is that plan "A," so to speak, worked and that The OM will remain as a smaller totally independent free radical sentience because plan "B" wasn't necessary.

ANNE & HUM & OM & ALL OM: To some extent.

ME: What do you mean, to some extent? That sounds like there is a plan "C," one that we don't know about yet.

ANNE & HUM & OM & ALL OM: We will explain further.

The volume of space that is currently being occupied by the sentience that is The Origin is beyond comprehension, so much so that only its structure can be identified and not the content of that structure. You yourself have been able to communicate with The Origin and know the structure for the first of the twelve levels, which in itself has twelve levels of structure within it. It is not possible for the sentience that is The Origin to occupy and convert to sentience-bearing capability, the energy associated with the volume of space that it desires to eventually convert into sentience, filling that space in totality. Hence The Source Entities and the movement of the sentience that is The OM unintentionally assisting in The Origin's desire.

We can see that you are a little perplexed.

ME: Well, I thought I understood The Origin's desire for the expansion of its sentience throughout the space that it is occupying and will occupy.

ANNE & HUM & OM & ALL OM: There is much more to it than you are aware, and this is something that you will discuss with The Origin when you are working on your next project and dialogue with The Origin when you have finished with this dialogue with us.

Let us break it down further for you and describe it in terms of your "Plans."

Plan "A"

Plan A is well known in summary, by you and your readers. It's that Event Space saw the potential for a higher quality of sentience and that that volume of sentience would expand to the point where it would become a significantly higher quality and volume of sentience. This is where we are now. A vast volume of ever-expanding, high-quality sentience that is, incidentally, assisted by a microscopically smaller volume of high-quality sentience.

Plan "B"

Plan B is Event Space providing a backup plan, wherein the Event Space that illustrated that The Origin fails to expand in both volume and quality of sentience so that another high-quality sentience could take over. That smaller volume of high-quality sentience is what is called The OM. In this instance The OM became the dominant volume of high-quality sentience.

Initially, The OM would work together, beloved of each other, singularly and as one, moving around the vast volume of space and its structure. However, the desire to be individualized from the collective belovedness would be superseded as OM sentience grew individually in quality and in volume to the point where it would become attracted to the potential to be one overarching high-quality sentience. Prior to this, though, the individualized sentience that is the individual OM would grow in both quality and volume to the point where they would become the same quality and volume of sentience that a Source Entity is. Subsequent growth through accrual of experiential content and evolutionary progression would then lead to The OM becoming much larger than the current quality and volume of sentience than The Source Entities are now and multiplying in both quality and volume of sentience to the point where each OM is the same volume and quality of sentience as The Origin is now. In effect this would place The OM in a similar, but not the same scenario as The Origin having succeeded in the twelve Origins experiment. As the volume of space that is the first level of twelve structures becomes ever-increasingly occupied by OM sentience, the gaps in between the sentience become smaller and smaller until eventually that sentience has to join together to become one sentience. You could call this a process of mapping and occupying the volume of space afforded by a level of structure until it is fully experienced and known and therefore is fully occupied by a high quality of evolved sentience.

It is only when the volumetric totality of structured space is fully occupied by highly evolved high-quality sentience that that sentience can move on to the next level of structure and commence its occupation of that from a sentience-based perspective.

In this instance, the individualized sentience that is The OM will need to become absorbed by the volume of sentience that is also The OM to become the singular dominant sentience and not smaller units of individualized sentience.

At the point of singularity, which ultimately coincides with the volume of space within all twelve levels of structure, within the first of the overall twelve levels of structure, the singular OM can then move into the second group of twelve levels of structure within the overall twelve levels of structure, which is significantly larger in volume.

ME: Just how big is the difference in volume or finitude between each of the structural levels?

ANNE & HUM & OM & ALL OM: To give you an example in mathematical terms the growth in volume is based upon the power of twelve so that each level increases above the one below it by the power of twelve.

We will give you an example:

Level 1 of Structural level 1 (Frequency) = X

Level 2 of Structural level 1 (Subdimensions) = Level 1^{12} or X^{12}

Level 3 of Structural level 1 (Full dimensions) = Level 2^{12} or $X^{12,12}$ or X to the power of twelve to the power of twelve

Level 4 of Structural level 1 (Zones and their divisions) = Level 3^{12} or $X^{12,12,12}$ or X to the power of twelve to the power of twelve to the power of twelve.

Level 5 of Structural level 1 (Continuum and their abstractions) = Level 4^{12} or $X^{12,12,12,12}$ or X to the power of twelve to the power of twelve ..., etc.

Level 6 of Structural level 1 (Planes and their spheres) = Level 5^{12} or $X^{12,12,12,12,12}$

Level 7 of Structural level 1 (Spheres independent of planes and their references) = Level 6^{12} or $X^{12,12,12,12,12,12}$

Level 8 of Structural level 1 (Event Spaces and their events) = Level 7^{12} or $X^{12,12,12,12,12,12,12}$

Level 9 of Structural level 1 (Totalities and their realities) = Level 8^{12} or $X^{12,12,12,12,12,12,12,12}$

Level 10 of Structural level 1 (Realities independent of totalities and their creative functions) = Level 9^{12} or $X^{12,12,12,12,12,12,12,12,12}$

Level 11 of Structural level 1 (Spectral interfaces and their spectra [not light-based]) = Level 10^{12} or $X^{12,12,12,12,12,12,12,12,12,12}$

Level 12 of Structural level 1 (Margins and their gradients) = Level 11^{12} or $X^{12,12,12,12,12,12,12,12,12,12,12}$

ME: I can see how big the volume of space progresses in its capacity or finitude!

ANNE & HUM & OM & ALL OM: Yes, and this is multiplied again by the power of twelve when we all to move into the second level of twelve levels of structures.

You could refer to it in this way, just to give you an example.

Collectively Level 1–12 of Structural level 1 = $X^{12,12,12,12,12,12,12,12,12,12}$ or 12X to give it a reference symbol. Therefore:

Level 1 of Structural level 2 (Name unknown) = $12X^{12}$

Level 2 of Structural level 2 (Name unknown) = Level 1^{12} or $12X^{12,12}$

Etc., etc., etc.

ME: And this carries on through the rest of the twelve structural levels and the levels within them?

ANNE & HUM & OM & ALL OM: From what we have been told by Source Entity Twelve that is correct.

ME: You are in communication with SE12?

ANNE & HUM & OM & ALL OM: An Aspect of it, yes.

ME: Has it gone beyond Structural level 2?

ANNE & HUM & OM & ALL OM: No, not even Event Space has seen beyond.

ME: I see that Event Space has a level of structure all of its own. I thought that it pervaded everything, every level of space in The Origin.

ANNE & HUM & OM & ALL OM: It does, it's just that it is predominantly represented on Level 8 of structural level 1. That is as far as it is known. We are starting to think that it has a predominant level of representation on all structural levels, but that is what you would call an educated assumption.

ME: If The OM become dominant they would eventually enter into total sentient communion as one sentience creating what could be argued as a gigantic OM or another road to Originess!

ANNE & HUM & OM & ALL OM: Right now, though, we prefer it the way it is with The OM being individual and independent. But as you will see in what you called plan "C," this may not eventually be the case.

ME: OK, I think I get the picture. Can you continue with explaining that which I have called plan "C" then please?

ANNE & HUM & OM & ALL OM: Of course.

Plan "C"

Everything becomes one!

ME: Errr, OK, can you give the readers and myself a bit more information?

OM, ALL OM, HUM, ANNE: Initially The OM would work together, beloved of each other, singularly and as one, moving around the vast volume of space and its structure.

Just as we do now. However, The Origin's desire to expand its volume and quality of sentience throughout the twelve levels within structural level one resolves in the volume of space being predominantly occupied by Origin sentience. Additionally, and although The OM don't seek evolutionary content through being in the evolutionary cycle and/or being creative in some way and subsequently being responsible for that creation, we do accrue evolutionary content. This results in our quality of sentience increasing, further resulting in OM volume of sentience also increasing, occupying more structural space that would have been available to The Origin.

As a result, the volume and influence of OM sentience, essentially being individualized Origin sentience, starts to become part of the overall volume of Origin sentience again. First, however, The OM sentience goes through a similar growth process than that previously described. It is only when the two volumes of sentience, Origin and OM sentience, desire to occupy the same volumes of space because the volume of space to expand their sentience into is rapidly diminishing, that they are both squeezed together. This squeezing together of sentience, albeit differing qualities of sentience resulting from differing experiential content, forces a condition where there is a sharing of sentient content in terms of experiential and evolutionary content together with the sentient quality creates a melding effect. This melding effect creates a condition where there is not a perceivable difference between the two volumes of sentience, thereby creating the opportunity for the return to one volume of quality of sentience.

And when this is achieved, it is only when the volumetric totality of structured space is fully occupied by highly evolved high-quality sentience that that sentience can move on to the next level of structure and commence its occupation of that from a sentience-based perspective.

In this instance the individualized sentience that is the combined but imperceivably different collective volume of Origin and OM sentience is the only sentience. This creates the point of singularity. A singular high-quality volume of sentience that fully occupies all twelve levels in structural level one. Both The OM and The Origin with its individualizations such as Source Entities, TES, and Aspects, etc., all become one to become the singular dominant sentience and not smaller units of individualized sentience.

At the point of singularity, which ultimately coincides

with the volume of space within all twelve levels of structure within the first of the overall twelve levels of structure, the collective but singular sentience that was once OM and Origin (Origin and its individualizations—Source Entities, TES, Aspects, and Shards) can then move into the second group of twelve levels of structure within the overall twelve levels of structure, which is significantly larger in volume.

ME: And there are no other scenarios that Event Space has illustrated?

ANNE & HUM & OM & ALL OM: There are many, many scenarios but they all lead to what we have both referred to as plan "C."

ME: So, a singular dominant sentience really is the inevitable outcome, especially as every aspect of sentience gets squeezed together as one to enable it to move into the next structural level?

ANNE & HUM & OM & ALL OM: Maybe!

ME: Whaaat!!! Are you suggesting something else?
    Like a …
    Plan "D!"

ANNE & HUM & OM & ALL OM: We wouldn't call it a plan "D," merely an observation of how sentience spreads and achieves a higher quality of sentience faster.

ME: Go on.

ANNE & HUM & OM & ALL OM: Think about it for a moment.

ME: OK, I am thinking. No, I can't see anything other than that smaller individual volumes of sentience spread quicker than larger volumes of sentience.

ANNE & HUM & OM & ALL OM: Well, you are on the right path, just not very far along it.

ME: Enlighten me!

ANNE & HUM & OM & ALL OM: Not all of the volume of sentience will move into the next structural level.

ME: Go on.

ANNE & HUM & OM & ALL OM: Within the dialogue we have just had we described that the individualized volumes of sentience effectively meld together because it is trying to occupy ever-decreasing volumes of occupiable space. This is irrespective of whether the volume of space is a factor of the power of twelve larger than the previous level. When it reaches the point of singularity and is therefore able to move into the next or first level in the next or second level of structural space, it doesn't all go.

ME: Are you saying some of it stays behind?

ANNE & HUM & OM & ALL OM: Of course. The objective is to fully occupy the volume of space with all of its twelve levels within each of the twelve structural levels. Not move from one to the other. If sentience did that, it would simply be moving to a bigger house, so to speak, and not occupying two or more houses. No, it simply expands into the first level of twelve levels within the second structural level. It occupies the first group of twelve levels within the first structural level and then expands into that next level. It would be nonsense to leave behind a volume of space that was previously occupied because that volume of space is still useful to that sentience. The objective of the growth of sentient volume and quality is to continue to grow into new spaces, not move around spaces.

ME: What I am seeing then is that when it moves into a new space it individualizes so that it can spread out and occupy as much space as possible in as many different locations within that space as possible, and then, grow and expand until all those smaller units of sentience eventually grow and expand enough to merge or meld back together again.

ANNE & HUM & OM & ALL OM: Yes, and The OM will be The OM once again!!!

ME: But I would guess, you/we will be bigger volumes of high-quality sentience than we are now?

ANNE & HUM & OM & ALL OM: Of course. Fun, isn't it?

ME: Looking at this from a different perspective, it looks like this is just a bigger evolutionary cycle. Not just like The Source Entities moving around frequency, subdimensions, full dimensions, and zones, but moving into completely different structural levels.

ANNE & HUM & OM & ALL OM: As we said, we don't enter into the evolutionary cycle, but we do participate in it, which is an entirely different thing. We are in it but not of it and certainly don't do it.

ME: But how do you manage to maintain your individuality while in sentient oneness?

ANNE & HUM & OM & ALL OM: We don't, we have to enter into full communion.

ME: I will say it again then. If you are in full communion, how do you return to individuality or OMness once in the next structural level?

ANNE & HUM & OM & ALL OM: We have a sentient program that we can use. It is designed by The OM for The OM to maintain The OM because it is desirable to keep The OM as free radicals.

ME: So, what is this program then?

ANNE & HUM & OM & ALL OM: Think of it like a factory reset on your computer or telephone. Once a number of criteria have been met, such as moving into another structural level and with The OM sentience being melded into the dominant sentience to be dominant sentience, the sentience that has the signature associated with OMness, together with its experiential and accrued evolutionary content, are re-individualized. We are uncreated again from oneness to OMness!

ME: Thank you. I get the picture now. In this way then The OM are maintained as OM!

ANNE & HUM & OM & ALL OM: Correct. Until, that is, we desire to remain as oneness.

ME: Oh boy! I see a plan "E."

ANNE & HUM & OM & ALL OM: (Collective laughter) There is always another plan with The OM! You should know that by now.

ME: You know what? I think I do!

Operating Inside and Outside of Event Space

The last four thousand or so words had been written in Crete. I was on sabbatical, but we all know that being of service to The Source and doing one's best to help to expand the knowledge of the greater reality for the incarnate population of the Earth results in a busman's holiday!

I was on my patio with my laptop on my lap (that's what they are for, isn't it!!) and could see across the valley to the location where the aliens are currently based. It was a beautiful afternoon. Not too hot and not too cool. All the olive trees were looking in fine condition and the birds and insects and other small animals were going about their normal business. Very relaxing!

I scanned the area with my spiritual or third eye and saw one of the aliens on a balcony area. It was just about to move indoors when it noticed that it was being observed. It looked directly across to me and gave me what looked like a smile and nodded, acknowledging my presence. It conveyed to me that they were about to leave for a short while. I got the impression that it was a sort of change of shift, that others were to come and take over the work. I felt a bit sad that those I had been in contact with would, from a physical perspective, not be in the same location again.

It turned around. It had picked up my thoughts and said:

"You won't see us again while in the physical, the next time will be in the energetic. It won't be long!"

Oh! I thought, I had been getting the feeling that I was running out of time for a couple of years now and I wondered if I would have enough Event Space to be able to finish my work. I have even had Anne tell me on a number of occasions that she (it, OM) will see (perceive, connect, be beloved of The OM) with me soon. I then received the reassurance that I would have the longevity to finish my work and that I should be reminded that "soon," for those Aspects that incarnate into the higher frequencies or that are disincarnate, is a long time for those Aspects that are incarnate in these low frequencies. That was reassuring. I clearly didn't want to stay here for longer than necessary, but I am one of those who likes to finish what they started.

The fact that The OM were also a function of Event Space's decision process to ensure that The Origin became the dominant sentience was compelling. It also explained in some small way why The OM were able to move in and around Event Space. I have known about this ability for some time, not that I had gone into any detail on this subject in any of my books. This lack of investigative detail I felt needed addressing, not so much why The OM can operate inside and outside of Event Space, but how. The OM, however, were quick to respond in the form of a combination of Anne and Hum collectively together.

GET ON WITH IT! I heard The OM say and I changed my attention to the next subject. That of The OMs ability to move around Event Space. What an interesting subject. Never a dull moment and maybe the main reason why I am still here!!

ME: OK, getting on with it then. Please tell me how The OM manage to operate inside and outside of Event Space when it pervades every aspect of the structure of the volume of space that is The Origin.

ANNE & HUM: I/we would like to answer the question leading into this subject.

I was startled. I didn't expect the Aspect of OMness that I/we call Anne and Hum to assist in this matter on a collective while individual basis. It was a delightful change.

ME: It's a delight to be able to communicate with you again in individuality.

ANNE & HUM: It is for me/us as well. I/we have been waiting for the right moment to connect on a personal basis again for some moments and this is a great subject to work with you on.

ME: Thank you. It is an unexpected delight and honor.
Getting to it then!

Just how can The OM work inside and outside of Event Space? I was of the impression that only a Curator [*see* The Curators—*GSN*] or a Source Entity and The Origin could move in and around Event Space!

ANNE & HUM: It's rather simple, actually. Event Space is now a much lower quality of sentience than that of The Origin and The OM. Indeed, it is mostly a higher level of intelligence than sentience. This is because most of its functionality is now automatic rather than deliberated.

Additionally, as individualized units of pure Origin sentience, The OM are capable of many things that The Origin is capable of doing as well. Also, if you remember, Event Space had a hand in the uncreation of The OM and as such The OM, just like The Origin, has an element of Event Space functionality as part of us. Based upon this, we are capable of manipulating Event Space as well as moving in and around it.

ME: You are suggesting that The OM have a component of Event Space within them then?

HUM: When we are working and therefore have an association with energy, yes.

In short, we move in and around Event Space in the same way as the entities called The Curators.

ME: I don't think we went into detail about how The Curators move in and around Event Space either.

ANNE & HUM: Good, this is an opportunity then.

ME: Agreed. So just how do The OM move in and around Event Space?

ANNE: The first thing to understand is that Event Space responds to the possibility or the possibility of possible possibilities, etc., that an action by an entity or being will create a juncture where multiple experiences can be achieved by the creation of duplicate or parallel environments of which the differences may range from being minor to major. Coupled into this is the function that Event Space sees these duplications or parallel environments as a vehicle to increase the overall evolutionary content of The Origin through the evolutionary progression of its smaller units of individualized sentience. This evolutionary progression is accrued by those entities and beings that are actively involved in the evolutionary cycle.

Entities or beings that are in the evolutionary cycle are effectively irrevocably resident (in a particular evolutionary cycle that is) in a particular Event Stream in a particular Event Space in the overall space that is The Origin's structure.

This Event Stream and Event Space is both specific to the entity or being and those participating entities and/or beings around them while experiencing a particular Event. An entity or being that is not in the evolutionary cycle is not bound by the Event Stream and Event Space that they may be in. This means that they can move from Event Stream and Event Space without being affected by it. The ability to move from one Event Stream to another or one Event Space to another effectively means that the entity or being can move outside of Event Space.

This is why The Curators can move in and around Event Space and its Event Streams for they are not actively in the evolutionary cycle.

Remember, Event Space and its Event Streams are energy based, not sentience based, and the sentience that originally evolved naturally is borne from that energy. The Origin and its creations, or individualizations, are divisions of sentience associated with energy to allow that sentience to experience the environment that it is within. It's a bit like giving someone the tools to be able to do a certain role or job of work. Without the tools, the person is helpless and is in observation mode. With the tools, the person is in interactive mode.

ME: Just to ask the question again then, The OM are basically sentience and not sentience and energy.

HUM: Correct. This is an important concept to both recognize and understand. The OM—Pure OM, that is—are pure sentience and therefore not constrained by the so-called rules of operation—the physics, if you like—that affects energy. OM use energy, when desired, to experience or manipulate that which is in the energetic structure of The Origin without being responsible for that experience or manipulation.

ME: Why do you use the word manipulation? Don't you mean creation?

HUM: No, it's not the same. Creation results in responsibility for that which is created. Manipulation means that one changes, in a minor way, that which is already in existence.

ME: So The OM meddle?

ANNE & HUM: We would prefer to call it play!

ME: I can understand that you, or even I, when in the energetic or sentience would call it play and not meddling because it does mean that you are not responsible for what you do and therefore don't need to go back to tend to or nurture that which you have manipulated. Isn't it interference though?

ANNE & HUM: Good, we are pleased that you understand. Note this though, it's not interference, it's manipulation. It's a different thing. Let's get back to how we move around Event Space.

If you remember the text in the book *The Origin Speaks,* you will recognize that sentience that evolves from energy can eventually detach itself from the energy that it evolved from; this is rare, very, very rare. Even sentience that is divided from a larger volume of sentence and individualized together with a "body" or "volume" of energy to help it interact with the aspect of The Origin's energetic structure that it finds itself in, can detach itself from that energy, but again, that is rare. However, this is usually only a function of a high-volume sentience such as a Source Entity. From the perspective of Pure OM, we never had a volume of energy associated with us because it was the sentience that divorced itself from the creation of The Source Entities and not a combination of energy and sentience.

Because Event Space is now largely created from energy with a level of associated intelligence with a major focus on the creation of additional evolutionary parallel "energetic" environments [*even the gross physical is considered as energetic—GSN*], it can be considered as "just" energy and not intelligence and energy from the perspective of pure sentience. As a result, Pure OM, being pure sentience, can move from Event Space to Event Space and Event Stream to Event Stream within an Event Space. We also move from an Event Stream within one Event Space to another Event Stream within another Event Space.

ME: And I take it that you can affect the localized Events within an Event Stream?

ANNE & HUM: Yes, we can and do. All without being responsible for the downstream functions of our manipulation or intervention. This is not to say that we do this all of the time. This is only a small part of what we do when together or even momentarily on our own, such as what you are doing now.

ME: Mmmm, yes, I do have the feeling that I can do anything and not be ultimately responsible for it. It's a bit worrying to be honest. I like things to be finished. It's not ethical.

ANNE & HUM: That's because you are only thinking in the limited way available to you in this low frequency.

ME: Sooo! Getting back to the main question, just how do The

OM move in and around Event Space?

ANNE: The best way to explain it is like crossing the sea by jumping from island to island. The sea can be considered the overall volume of space with the islands being the different Event Spaces. In this way, you can see that we just move from one Event Space to another. If the Event Space has Event Streams associated with it then that could be represented by rivers or streams on the islands. Traveling in the direction of one of the flows of the rivers or streams "downstream" is the same as moving along with the natural flow of Event Streams. A river would be a large or significant Event Stream whereas a stream would be a smaller or less significant Event Stream. Traversing the river or stream by going "upstream" moves an entity up the Event Stream, and moving from one side of a river or stream to the other is the same as moving around the bandwidth of the Event Stream to the peripheral functions of that Event Stream. In the event that there are rocks in the middle of the water of the river or stream, then moving from rock to rock within the river or stream would represent moving between small "localized" Events within the Event Stream that are relative to individual entities or small groups of entities.

It's as simple as this to OM.

ME: But it's not simple to the average entity or being.

HUM: A being would have the capacity for such a function but rarely have the volume and quality of sentience to be able to work in this way. An entity almost certainly is a division or individualization of a larger entity or being and as such is normally fully associated with the energy that was assigned to it upon its division or individualization from its higher volume of sentience and energy.

ME: I noticed that you stated that it was Pure OM that were sentience based and not sentience-and-energy based. How are the other OM based? I mean, what about the Non-captive, Captive, and Hybrid OM? Are they sentience based?

ANNE & HUM: I think it is best we explain that for you because not all OM are pure sentience.

Hybrid OM are "created" by the division of a small percentage of Origin sentience and a large percentage of Source Entity sentience and a "body" (volume) of associated energy. They are subject to the desires of The Source Entity they are associated with and cannot move in and out of Event Space.

Captive OM are "uncreated" under the influence of Event Space by the division of a large enough percentage of Origin sentience to not need a percentage of Source Entity sentience to maintain its individuality. They maintain their OMness while being associated with a "body" (volume) of energy associated with the structure of The Source Entity they are within. They cannot move in and out of Event Space. They are not subject to the desires of The Source Entity they are associated with. They are effectively captive as a function of their location when The Source Entity they are associated with was also created, with them both being in the same spatial location.

Non-captive OM are "uncreated" under the influence of Event Space by the division of a large enough percentage of Origin sentience to maintain its individuality and ability to be outside of the structure of a larger volume of sentience and energy such as a Source Entity. They maintain their OMness while being associated with a minimal "body" (volume) of energy associated with the structure of The Origin. They can move in and out of the energies associated with a Source Entity without being captive. They do not have the volume or quality of sentience to allow them to move in and out of Event Space as freely as Pure OM because they are normally associated with energy. Although, they can move from Event Space to Event Space, they normally exist outside of Event Space.

Pure OM are "uncreated" under the influence of Event Space by the division of a large enough percentage of Origin sentience to maintain their individuality and ability to be outside of the structure of a larger volume of sentience and energy such as a Source Entity. They maintain their OMness without being associated with a "body" (volume) of energy associated with the structure of The Origin and as such they are pure sentience. They can move in and out of the energies associated with a Source Entity without being captive. They have the capacity to move in and out of and manipulate Event Space fully. They normally reside outside of Event Space.

ME: So what you are suggesting is that the way that The OM move in and out of Event Space is to become "it" by employing a volume "body" of Event Space energy. Additionally, their disassociation with energy (they are nominally sentience rather than sentience and energy) allows them to decide which energy they want to temporarily associate themselves with. In this case, it's the energy that IS Event Space. So really it's the ability to become Event Space temporarily that allows The OM to move in and around Event Space for they are Event Space!

ANNE & HUM: The OM are The OM, not Event Space. It's just that we use the ability to temporarily associate with a particular energy, in this case, Event Space energy. That allows us to move in and around it. And of course, the fact that Event Space gave The Origin sentient dominance over it, and as The OM are Origin sentience, we have the same sentient dominance, albeit from a smaller level of sentient volume or "status," so to speak.

ME: OK, so The OM temporarily commandeer the energy of Event Space to be able to move around and manipulate it.

ANNE & HUM: If ever you wanted to summarize the total content of our dialogue together on this subject then that would be your executive summary.

ME: I would like to understand the mechanics around it though.

ANNE & HUM: There are no mechanics, there is just our intention to attract the energy and give it purpose.

ME: And what is the purpose?

ANNE & HUM: To be controlled by another, more dominant sentience.

ME: I suppose The OM using the energy of Event Space to traverse in and around it is like us using a metal ore to create a pure state of metal and eventually create an alloy by bonding different but similar metals together. Our sentience dominates the metal (by the use of intellect, tools, and heat), which makes it into something we can use.

ANNE & HUM: That is a simple but effective way of considering it, yes.

ME: Thank you. I would like to move on a little bit now. I have a couple more questions to ask you all on quantum physics. Then we can move on to a series of questions I have surrounding the influence The OM has in the physical universe and what my role in all this is.

ANNE & HUM: We feel that we can assist in your request to clear up some of your lack of understanding on these subjects so we will continue to commit to this dialogue.

ME: That's a strange response!

ANNE & HUM: We are getting close to the end of this dialogue in its entirety. It's not complete but close, hence the comment.

ME: I felt as much. We had better get a move on then.

Light and Its Fluidity of Form Plus Some More on Entanglement

My agent in China, Leo, and I have an interest in quantum physics and the way in which incarnate humankind understands the function of the gross physical environment from the perspective of human science. We have found that, in the past, the information that is presented to incarnate mankind via channeled work tends to offer alternative levels of understanding than those of mathematical calculations derived to support theories. One of these interests is the explanation for certain physical experiments that result in unexplainable phenomena or behavior of physical objects that are under observation.

Leo's question in this instance was why is light observed as being both a wave and a particle, albeit not at the same time, but under experimental conditions. I meditated on this question and was given the answer that light presenting itself as a possibility of being in one of two states was a clue to its fluidity of form and moreover, our rigidity of thinking. Furthermore, it was a clue to what really makes the universe work, so to speak.

As Anne and Hum had suggested that they would be available to answer such questions, they were the ones who connected with me with the answers.

ANNE & HUM: Everything in The Source Entity's multiverse is fluid. It is an environment for the creation of experience that results in experiential progression through interaction with the environment and its frequential compartments, the universes. The universes, their content, and the multiverse itself are a function of The Source Entity's desire to evolve through the use of smaller individualized units of its own sentience interacting with its structure, the multiverse. Interaction with the universal environments reinforce their existence within The Source, as do the circumstances created by these interactions by the entities that are engaged within it. However, these interactions can and do cause changes to the function and structure of these universal environments at every level available within each of them, relative to their frequential state. Based upon this, the physical universe is a function of what the entities that incarnate within it want it to be, and as a result it retains its fluidity—even if the entities working within it don't see it as fluid.

ME: How does that explain the possibility of light being either a wave or a particle? It can be both?

ANNE & HUM: Light can present itself as anything an entity wishes it to be presented by. Incarnate humankind are limited in thinking as a function of the ambient frequency it incarnates into. As a result, it doesn't consider the possibility of fluidity being controlled by desire-based interaction. A particular scientist therefore may consider that light is a particle whereas another considers it as a wave. This places the possibility of both conditions being presented because there are two thoughts of understanding within the overall consciousness of incarnate humankind. It does not matter if it is a thought or consideration of just one entity within the 7.9 billion [*end of 2021—GSN*] incarnate vehicles on Earth, it would still be a consideration because Event Space gets involved as well and therefore we are presented with the two possibilities.

If there were a third consideration that light was a function of say, "attraction," then it may express gravity, for example, as a property of its existence in an experimental observation. This is because the thought is out there within the overall consciousness of incarnate humankind, becomes a function of Event Space, and is therefore a possibility.

ME: So what you are suggesting is that if I thought that light could be described as something else then that "something else" would be presented to the observer as a possible result of an experiment to derive exactly what light is?

ANNE & HUM: Correct. Additionally, this is an excellent example of universal fluidity and of the effect that entities within a universe have on the functional properties of that universe.

ME: Answering Leo's question then, light is both a wave and a
particle.
ANNE & HUM: Correct. But it can be any structural function
of the physical universe that you feel it could be as well. It's
just that incarnate humankind hasn't yet made the discovery
of other structural components that support the existence of
the physical universe to be able to consider a third possibility
for description of what light is comprised of and therefore get
three, or more, results in an experiment.
ME: So what makes light, light?
ANNE & HUM: The need for certain environmental conditions
that allow the incarnate human vehicle, and similar forms, the
capability of navigating around their environment with the
minimum of sensory complexity. There are many incarnate
vehicles that use light, or forms of it, as the basis for sensory
navigation. Eyes are one of the simpler methods. It is also one
of the most limited. However, it seems to work on the Earth.

In essence, light is a function of the radiation of a certain
type of a sun. In this case, the radiation is ultraviolet "A,"
"B," and "C" and the "visible range" plus the infrared "A,"
"B," and "C," etc. Radiation is manifest in many ways,
"particulate" and "wave" being two that incarnate humankind
has recognized. But in essence, these are just two ways in
which the energy associated with the frequency of that which
is radiated is able to traverse away from its origin of creation,
or initial focus. That radiation can be simulated by incarnate
entities to allow navigation around an environment when the
natural radiation is not available for any reason. However, it
is only a simulation and the nature of that which is simulated,
ether via incandescent, halogen (rare gas), fluorescent, or light-
emitting diode is not the same in terms of the composition of
radiation that is created by a sun, even though the sensors
(eyes) respond in a favorable way. In terms of the radiation
that is created, it displays the same capabilities of being
manifest in any of the ways that allow the transmission of
energy at a certain frequency, which may include being in
particulate, wave, or any other state.
ME: Is there a name for these other states that light could be
represented by?
ANNE & HUM: Right now, incarnate humankind doesn't have
the experience of, or capability of, observing these other
states, which results in the lack of vocabulary to describe that
experience/observation. Without being able to observe, record,

analyze, and understand that which is being experienced, it becomes invisible to the potential observer.

When it is invisible to the observer and there is the possibility of knowing that there is another way in which something is expressed, there is the desire to experiment and see what happens. However, in the majority of experimentations made by incarnate humankind, there is an expectation that which will be observed will be of a certain or known form. In these cases that which is in existence but is not observed, recognized for what it is, becomes affected by the desire/expectation of the experimenter and as a result the experiment bears results that represent those expectations. This is why light is expected to be a particle. Light expresses itself to be a wave, another known state, when the expectation that it is a particle is not in the forefront of the thinking or desire of the experimenter. Therefore, the experimenter is detached in his/her thinking and has no thoughts. This creates the expression of other forms of state to manifest. However, it is only those that can be detected and categorized in one of the known states of beingness that are truly observed because the devices used to create the experiments aren't designed to record or report that which is not known. This knowledge must come from a higher source for this to give the inspirational guidance to look for "other" things and not what is expected due to the foundation of current knowledge. We will say again, the experiments that show light to be represented by two forms is an example of such guidance, guidance that the physical universe is fluid and can become what enough of you wish it to become. This is correct from a structural, functional, and experiential perspective. One just has to be expansive to know this truth.

What Role, if Any, Do The OM Have to Play in The Origin's Evolution?

I wanted to go in a slightly different, if not a circular question of The OM. Namely, what role do The OM have in The Origin's evolutionary plans? The question itself creates a title that I am expecting will have a number of subtitles. Hopefully, one on the expansion of The Origin's volume of Polyomniscient, Polyomnipresent self-awareness. I was greeted with the same group of OM that I worked with in the last chapter.

ANNE & HUM & OM & ALL OM: You are aware from previous dialogues that The OM are limited in numbers and those that are "Pure" exist wherever they want to exist within The Origin's volume of Polyomniscient, Polyomnipresent self-awareness. Non-captive OM also have a level of autonomous movement. But not the same as Pure OM, so it is these genres of OM that make some difference to The Origin. You are also aware that the movement of sentience in and around energy affects its ability to "house" sentience or indeed, eventually move far enough down the road to sentience to actually become sentience. In moving around The Origin, The OM do the same. However, there are other things to consider in terms of how The Origin's expansion of its volume of Polyomniscient, Polyomnipresent self-awareness affects The OM.

ME: So, you are suggesting that The OM affect the evolution of The Origin and The Origin affects the evolution of The OM? That's turning it on its head a bit! I mean, The OM seem to have both a positive impact to The Origin and a benefit from

The Origin! The OM therefore have a symbiotic relationship, that to my mind, benefits The OM significantly more than The Origin. Specifically, as most OM are not actively contributing to the evolutionary cycle. It seems very one-sided.

ANNE & HUM & OM & ALL OM: It's not as one-sided as one would think, but as you question it, we will explain further.

ME: OK, I am all ears!

ANNE & HUM & OM & ALL OM: It's very simple. We have described before that Pure OM are as close to being micro Origins as we can be, and that The Origin likes this conundrum because we can and do move around its volume of non-Polyomniscient, non-Polyomnipresent self-awareness and automatically create the possibility of the energy in this volume to house sentience more readily. We create links to where The Origin's sentience may focus on occupying next. Again this is not an intentional function but an automatic or consequential function of our movement.

From the evolutionary perspective, The Origin absorbs every aspect of evolutionary content that is accrued by any aspect of energy, irrespective of its sentient content.

ME: You mean, even if it's just a change of state from raw energy to minor intelligent decision?

ANNE & HUM & OM & ALL OM: Yes. Anything that is construed as being evolution is absorbed by The Origin because everything is, in reality, The Origin, even if it appears to have individualized or autonomous sentience.

ME: How much of The Origin's evolutionary content is available to The OM?

ANNE & HUM & OM & ALL OM: All of it.

ME: I don't understand. How can The OM, which are insignificantly small in conjunction with even the current, but nevertheless expanding volume of Polyomniscient, Polyomnipresent self-awareness absorb such a volume of evolutionary content?

ANNE & HUM & OM & ALL OM: Evolutionary content is not relative to the volume of sentience. We can see you frowning.

ME: I would have thought that it would be relative.

ANNE & HUM & OM & ALL OM: It's not, we will tell you why and how it affects The OM.

All sentience is linked by virtue of the fact that it is either a function or division from The Origin or that it is a function of the energy that is The Origin that has become sentient via the road to sentience. This sentient link allows evolutionary content that is accrued by any division of sentience to be accessible to any other volume of sentience, should it decide or need to access it. However, the hierarchical position of that sentience dictates how it accesses the evolutionary content.

For example:

The evolutionary content associated with the total experiential content of those Aspects that have incarnated within the Earth environment can be accessed via the repository you know as the Akashic Records. There are similar repositories for all incarnate vehicle genres within Source Entity One.

The Aspects associated with a particular TES have access to all the evolutionary content accrued by all the Aspects projected from their TES, and the TES itself instantaneously while in communion but only have access to that which they have individually accrued while in a projected or individualized state.

All TES have access to all other evolutionary content from all other TES within Source Entity One. Source Entity One has access to all the evolutionary and experiential content from all its TES instantaneously. All Source Entities can access the evolutionary and experiential content associated with all other Source Entities via a repository within The Origin. The Origin can access all evolutionary and experiential content associated with itself and any division of sentience instantaneously.

Captive OM and Non-captive OM (not hybrid, they are considered as a function of the division of sentience from a TES) associated with a Source Entity can access all evolutionary and experiential content associated with that Source Entity instantaneously. They can access aspects of evolutionary and experiential content associated with other Source Entities based upon inquiry.

Non-captive OM not associated with a Source Entity can access aspects of evolutionary and experiential content associated with other Source Entities instantaneously. They can access evolutionary and experiential content associated with The Origin based upon inquiry.

Pure OM can access all evolutionary and experiential content instantaneously because in essence they are The Origin.

ME: Doesn't this cause a problem with differentiating which is evolutionary and experiential content accrued by a Pure OM itself and that which is accrued by another division of sentience?

ANNE & HUM & OM & ALL OM: No. If you recall, the vast majority of Pure OM don't enter into the evolutionary cycle and therefore don't actively accrue it. However, they accrue evolutionary content directly from The Origin and so gain instant access to it in totality. Remember, by being part of The Origin in a "Pure" sense The OM are The Origin while not being The Origin.

ME: One thing I don't understand is the hierarchy or demarcation between the genres or volumes of sentience and how it accesses evolutionary and experiential content. I thought you told me that all sentience can access all evolutionary and experiential content?

ANNE & HUM & OM & ALL OM: The answer is yes— eventually.

ME: Eventually?

ANNE & HUM & OM & ALL OM: Eventually has two meanings in this instance.

ME: OK?

ANNE & HUM & OM & ALL OM: We will explain.

It's all to do with what you would call "processing" power. You see, the volume of sentience an entity or being has dictates its ability to process the evolutionary and experiential content available to it. Based upon this, a lower volume of sentience would need a much longer period to access the same evolutionary and experiential content than a larger volume of sentience would. Hence the difference in instantaneous accessibility and inquiry-based accessibility. Considering the internet as an example, irrespective of how fast and how much storage space you have on your computer, you as an incarnate can only access and understand what you are able to which is based upon an inquiry derived from a single question. You are limited by the sentience you can access while incarnate in a low frequency. This is one version of eventually; it's a variable period needed to access evolutionary and experiential content which is based upon sentient volume.

The other version of eventually is that as sentience experiences access to more and more evolutionary and experiential content it expands volumetrically, which in turn increases that sentience's ability to process higher levels of evolutionary and experiential content. This is an upward spiral.

ME: Does sentient weight or density affect accessibility as well?

ANNE & HUM & OM & ALL OM: Yes, but in a different and

symbiotic way with sentient volume. It works a bit like this. Sentient volume allows a volume of sentience that can be used to access, process, and store evolutionary and experiential content locally to the entity or being. Sentient density allows accessing and omni-parallel processing and the increased storage capacity required to work with evolutionary and experiential content that is outside the sentient volume of the entity or being.

Before you ask, most if not all sentience that is divided or individualized from a higher volume of sentience is low in sentient density.

ME: It's like spreading it thinly!

ANNE & HUM & OM & ALL OM: That's one way to think about it. Sentient density is sacrificed in favor of sentient volume because eventually sentient density can be accrued by sentient volume.

ME: What sentience does The OM have, volume or density?

ANNE & HUM & OM & ALL OM: The OM are not large in sentient volume, and as such, are much, much smaller than say a Source Entity. We could be considered a very large TES. However, the sentient density of The OM, certainly the Pure OM is significantly denser than a Source Entity.

ME: The OM have sentient super density?

ANNE & HUM & OM & ALL OM: Think of The OM's sentient density in terms of super massive density. However, should we decide to, we too can sacrifice sentient density to increase our sentient volume in order to eventually increase our sentient density further!

This is what The Origin does, did, and will do.

Where The OM Exist in The Origin

It is apparent that The OM pervade not only aspects of The Origin's volume of Polyomniscient, Polyomnipresent sentient self-awareness, but moreover, the volume of the structure within the first of the twelve levels of The Origin's known structure that isn't Polyomniscient or Polyomnipresent. They appear to have free rein to go anywhere they please. I was pondering upon this thought when the Aspect of The OM TES that incarnated as Anne connected with me.

ANNE: Remember, that in this known volume of The Origin's structure, sentience is everywhere, concurrently, that's Polyomnipresence! It's the change of focus of a volume of sentience that gives the appearance of the passage of that sentience to a location, or the passage of that location to that sentience without it actually moving, that gives the impression that everything is known concurrently, this is Polyomniscience.

ME: And how does that relate to The OM?

ANNE: As The Origin grows so does the ability of Pure OM to move around The Origin grow.

ME: And this is a function of the expansion of sentient volume or sentient density?

ANNE: It's a function of three things in reality.

First, from a volumetric perspective, as The Origin expands its knowledge that other levels of its structure exist, including what they are structurally, this opens up the volume of The Origin to The Origin and The OM.

Second, because OM sentience is the same sentient quality and density as The Origin it automatically accesses knowledge, evolution, and experiential content which is new to The Origin concurrently with The Origin. In effect we grow (evolve) with The Origin.

Third, as the volume of Origin sentience expands, The OM have the potential to expand their volume of sentience by absorbing some of the new Origin sentience for their own needs. This sentience can then be compressed by The OM to create more sentient density while maintaining their original volume of sentience. This in effect makes The OM nimble.

Being nimble keeps us individualized as OM and not in full communion or absorbed into The Origin's sentience. It also allows us to move into those volumes of The Origin that are non-Polyomniscient or non-Polyomnipresent or both.

ME: Give me a moment here. Are you suggesting that The OM could lose its individuality and just become part of The Origin?

ANNE: All sentience has a natural tendency (desire or function) to coalesce together as one sentience. This is only to be expected when one considers that every individualized aspect of sentience has its origin as The Origin in totality. So, it's reasonable to know that this individualized sentience, no matter how long it has been individualized for, has a predisposition to being back together as one again. Even The Source Entities recall all their individualizations of sentience before moving to another location within The Origin and starting a new evolutionary cycle to investigate and know, in every detail, the new energies it is attaching its sentience to.

The OM have a different idea. The OM need and desire to be autonomous from The Origin in able to be of assistance by not being of assistance.

Do The OM Have a Role to Play within The Origin's Plan for Accelerated Evolution?

I was sitting and wondering. Just how could The OM be of assistance while not being of assistance? Or indeed, not doing anything? Is their role to just "be" The OM? Or what? This was almost a question that needed to be directed to The Origin and not The OM. Recognizing that the whole point of this dialogue was to find out more about The OM, from any direction, I am very tempted to communicate with The Origin to ask the question. I was about to meditate on creating this connection when I was distracted by the thought that I should attack this question from both ways. First, by getting The OM's perspective on this, and second, by asking The Origin in my next book, not this one. Mmmm, I thought! Decisions, decisions.

Common sense (or luck) prevailed at last when, rather than me making a decision on which direction to go into, Hum decided to direct me.

HUM: I/we will give a simple answer to this question, simply because the answer is simple.

ME: That's using the word "simple" a lot of times.

HUM: It's a necessary misuse of the language we are using to communicate.

ME: So what is the simple answer?

HUM: The OM have no intentional role to play in the evolution of The Origin. There is no need or, moreover, no desire for OM to have an active role in the evolution of The Origin. Whatever we do assists, but it is inconsequential and not prescribed.

ME: I am aware that The OM are aloof (keeping themselves distant) when it comes to being involved in the evolutionary cycle. And that there are those OM who disconnect themselves totally from the possibility of doing anything that could be associated with being in the evolutionary cycle, let alone becoming responsible for what they create. Based upon this, it seems that there is no role that The OM play in The Origin's plan for accelerated evolutionary growth. Everything is just as you say, consequential. However, even consequential input must assist in the growth of The Origin's evolutionary growth and therefore the growth of The OM!

HUM: Although your observation about my statement is correct, OM do not actively seek to be part of any plan as such. In the event that we "do" something that results in the possibility for The Origin to accelerate its accrual of evolutionary growth, most, if not all of The OM, disassociate themselves with the result of that action. In doing this OM ensure that they are not sucked into the evolutionary cycle as a result of being made responsible for the maintenance of that which we have inadvertently assisted in the creation of. Therefore, we don't create!

Have you not noticed that you yourself have a feeling of not being responsible for anything?

ME: I have a feeling that I need to follow through with certain things, which I am doing now, for example, and ensure that they are passed on to those who are capable of carrying it on further. I guess that that is responsibility!

HUM: Yes, it is. I will say it in a different way. Do you feel responsible for your actions?

ME: I feel that I do them, but I am not attached to them. It's like I do them, but they are not mine.

HUM: This is what I am describing. There may be the desire to finish something to a certain level but there is no ownership of that which you do. Notice that, in whatever you do, you never get to the top of the tree. You are always a couple of levels down. You are always in a structural location where you can move on without creating a major issue or a "need" to be there or own something.

It was true, I never seem to get to the top of anything. I am an influencer within what I do but I never seem to make it to the top of the ladder! I always thought that this was strange. However, when I consider this further, I also note that I don't feel that I own the responsibility of even being in positions that are two or three places down from the top of the ladder. Yes, I did the jobs associated with the roles I had and made sure that they were completed to the right quality and in the right time. But I never felt that they were mine, that I owned them, that I was responsible for them, even when they were successful. I didn't even feel like owning the praise. The desire for praise is karmic, I note.

HUM: This is something we have put in place to make sure that you don't get "stuck" here. To make sure that you come back to be beloved of The OM.

To answer this question with another simple response we would say this, but only to help your readers understand. In essence, everything that creates the opportunity for experiential and evolutionary growth is from the perspective of The Origin, absorbed by The Origin. This is its plan for accelerated evolutionary growth. This plan is pan-Origin, so to speak, and as such includes everything without discrimination or specific identification of the direction that that growth comes from. As such, this includes by default that which The OM may or may not do. So The OM are not specifically part of The Origin's plan to accelerate its evolutionary growth, but they passively contribute toward it if something that an OM does is recognized as such by either The Origin or Event Space.

ME: So, it's a bit like eating a sandwich on a park bench and the crumbs falling off the sandwich and landing on the ground to ending up providing food for the local birds. The sandwich was not purchased with the desire to drop crumbs and feed the birds in mind; it's a passive result of the process of the desire to eat the sandwich on the park bench and not bothering that this process creates crumbs which the birds can and will eat. The birds get fed as a result of one eating the sandwich in the park and not clearing up the crumbs. One is not responsible for feeding the birds, but instead, feeds them passively, not actively.

HUM: Correct. That is a good analogy. The OM are the sandwich eaters in your example and the birds are the ability of The Origin to hoover up, so to speak, experiential and evolutionary content. Even, that is, when it is unintentionally created and therefore has no real "active" owner.

ME: A better way to say this then is that The OM are included in the plan but not specifically an active part of the plan.

This includes the disconnected/disassociated OM as well?
HUM: It includes everything. You see, evolutionary content can be accrued in two main ways.

First, by plan, that being an entity or being actively desires to experience something that provides a level of evolutionary content as a function of interaction with an entity, being, circumstance, or environment in a preplanned way. Such as being part of an incarnate life plan.

Second, by consequence, that being an entity or being gains evolutionary content resulting from interaction with an entity, being, circumstance, or environment in a non-preplanned way. Such as an unexpected way and/or it's not part of an incarnate life plan.

These two examples only refer to the condition you are experiencing now as an incarnate entity on this particular planet and frequency for reference. However, this can also be relative to those entities or beings that are in the energetic as well, for you all interact in the energetic. In fact, most of your interactions are in the energetic.

Maybe we don't need to know how any of the genres of The OM fit in right now, for I remember a comment from The Origin a number of years ago, which went something like this:

O: I wait to see what else can "become" outside of the intention to create.

Maybe, just maybe, this part of The Origin's thought process of just waiting to see what happens next, and, how The OM fit in, is all part of a plan for evolutionary expansion, that is not only more fluid than we think, but has already happened! I somehow feel that I will understand more later in my "planned" dialogues with The Origin. Maybe I already know!!!

An Update on the Five "New" OM

Identified in *The Origin Speaks*

For the past couple of months I had been feeling that I needed to talk to The OM about the New OM. Those that were discovered by The Origin during the dialogue I had with it during meditations that led to The Origin Speaks. *These new OM were in between the pure and non-captive genres of OM and had the potential to go into total communion and create a single new OM but with a larger level of sentience density. They chose not to and therefore remained individualized as five OM of a new genre.*

I was wondering which of The OM, if not all of them, would decide to communicate with me about this subject when the Aspect of OM sentience that incarnated as Anne connected with me.

ANNE: Although this subject was best discussed with The OM in communion as "one," I felt a need to communicate directly with you rather than part of the communion-based communication that we have had in the past. Also, I have a rather selfish desire to communicate with you again directly because this dialogue is soon to draw to a close. You need to move on to the next dialogue and my chance to be one with you is therefore limited.

ME: I have asked this question before; however, I feel the need to ask it again. Am I running out of Event Space?

ANNE: Always! Your period in this incarnation is limited, as you are aware, but you still have more than enough Event Space to enable you to complete your tasks and prepare for the perpetuation of your work.

ME: OK, we had better move on then. I will ask the obvious questions about them and see where we go.

ANNE: Do you want to list the questions first and I answer what I can on behalf of them? First things first though. You need to know that you will be communicating with them directly during your next dialogue with The Origin.

ME: But this is a series of dialogues that is focused on The OM. Isn't it more appropriate that I communicate with them now rather than later?

ANNE: Ordinarily, yes, but they have a part to play in both dialogues. One is passive, the other is active.

ME: OK, so I am to communicate with them in the next book and communicate through you to understand more about them in this book.

ANNE: Now you are getting there. Don't forget that I am being selfish in my desire to communicate with you as well.

ME: Thank you.

ANNE: Let's get on with it then.

ME: Right, my questions are as follows:

1. Where are they located now?
2. What are they doing?
3. How are they progressing?
4. How do they see themselves in terms of their relation to other OM?
5. What will happen to them?

ANNE: Bearing in mind that they are a recent OM uncreation, they are rather quickly understanding who and what they are and as a result they have understood that there are still areas within The Origin that has inoperative sentience, that is either associated with a volume of, or body of, energy or is pure raw unassociated sentience. They are moving all around The Origin to find this stray inoperative sentience so it's not possible to identify where they are because they are moving so quickly.

ME: What is all this inoperative sentience you are referring to?

ANNE: It's either very small volumes of sentience that The Origin has individualized but not yet communed with, or, it's energy that has been in contact with sentience and therefore is "sentient-ready." Such sentient-ready energy also acts as an attractive force for stray inoperative sentience.

ME: I find it strange that The Origin hasn't absorbed or communed with all the sentience in its volume of Polyomniscient,

Polyomnipresent self-awareness.

ANNE: There is a difference between knowing what you have got and making use of it. Even incarnate humans know this and it's the same for The Origin. Sometimes what it has in terms of sentience is too small or too far away from its sentient focus to be of "current" interest. Right now, and this is a transient position, they are all together and absorbing a microscopic trail of inoperative sentience that is close to a much larger volume of inoperative sentience and so is not of immediate interest to The Origin.

ME: I can see it in my mind's eye. It's like a series of breadcrumbs or debris outside of the edge of a vast volume of energy that is not energy. It's just like the sentience that I see when communing with The Source during my Traversing the Frequencies (TTF) workshops. It's a mixture of silver, white, and gold somethingness. It's inert though. In my TTF work, the sentience of The Source is always undulating, pulsating, and irradiating. It's "alive."

ANNE: That's the appearance of sentience that has purpose. It is fully functioning, operative sentience. In comparison to the sentience you have seen when working with The Source, this is just dead. However, it is ready to "be" whatever it needs to be when it is given purpose or is associated with operative sentience in a communion-based way. Those microscopically small volumes of inoperative sentience add up and effect that sentience which has operative functionality in an exponential way when they achieve a certain level of sentient density. Notice that these OM are collecting this sentience, corralling it, if you like; they intend to gain a volume of stray sentience large enough to benefit them all individually and significantly before they actually absorb it in a communion-based way. In taking their time, this sentience becomes associated with OM before it "is" OM sentience, preprogramming it, if you like.

ME: So, in essence, they are still doing what I saw them doing when I channeled *The Origin Speaks*?

ANNE: Yes. Attracting more and more sentience of the correct quality and type to increase their own sentient volume, weight, and density can take some time, so to speak. They want to have at least the same quantity and quality of sentience that The Original OM had from the start of their uncreation.

ME: So the next question is, how are they progressing? Are they close to finishing their "hoovering" up of the stray or unused sentience? Or do they have a long time to go yet?

ANNE: As I just said, they want to achieve at least the same condition that The Original OM had and have. This may take many more millennia from an incarnate human perspective, but as they grow and become more Polyomnipresent and Polyomniscient their ability to find such sentience will increase and their time to optimization of sentient volume, weight, and density will shorten—exponentially. So what feels like millennia now could be reduced down to hundreds or even tens of years in incarnate human terms.

ME: The increase in sentient volume, weight, and density makes a significant difference then.

ANNE: Yes, it makes a major difference. You will notice the difference as well when you return to the energetic.

ME: OK. I guess then that what you have just said answers the next question about where they see themselves in relation to the other genres of OM.

ANNE: Not quite. They see themselves as being equal to Pure OM but just lacking in size. This is why they are moving around The Origin looking for sentience that The Origin is either not using—yet—or has not noticed yet.

ME: How can The Origin not notice sentience?

ANNE: How can you not notice the individual atoms that are in your current incarnate form?

ME: I don't. I see what you mean now. Even when one is supposed to be Polyomnipresent or Polyomniscient if one's focus is somewhere else then that which is not of primary focus is not noticed or even considered.

ANNE: Correct. Now you have it. I note that these new OM are not greedy; they only want to be in equality, to be beloved of The OM.

ME: I expect then that they could keep on hoovering up additional sentience and become larger in sentient volume, weight, and density than The Original Pure OM. They could become the dominant OM should they so desire!

ANNE: They know that there is a possibility of continuing the accrual of sentience in their favor in this way, but they recognize that, had The Original OM done the same thing, then the opportunity for the new OM to grow to equality would not have been available for there would have been no stray sentience to collect.

In essence, they are aware that one of the mitigating traits of being OM is being beloved of The OM and that this means being "in equality" with The OM, and, to that end they have to behave like The OM. They have no intention to be anything else other than equal in everything and so when they have achieved the correct sentient volume, weight, and density to be equal with The Original OM, their quest for more sentience will cease. They will truly be beloved of The OM.

ME: What will happen to them once they have achieved belovedness in equality? I mean, what will happen to them? Where will they go?

ANNE: They will be free to do whatever they want to do for they are OM.

I will say this, though, your increase in knowledge about them will not stop here on this page. They will be once again in your dialogues, in the next book.

ME: What more will I know about them? I know that there is much more to understand and I guess that there is a more appropriate Event Space in which I communicate with them.

ANNE: There will be, for the dialogue will be direct rather than via another entity such as myself. But know this, they will not stay in the volume of The Origin's Polyomniscient, Polyomnipresent sentient self-awareness. They will venture into The Origin's next level of structure.

ME: Will they meet Source Entity Twelve?

ANNE: They may well be in that area, in and around the volume of space that SE12, or should I say, the individualizations of SE12 are and will occupy.

ME: I will leave this to the next series of dialogues then, even though it is about OM, because I guess, it's beyond this level of The Origin's structure.

Having said that, this leads me straight into the next subject I want to talk about.

What Will Happen to The OM when The Origin Maps Out Its Current Volume of Structure?

The question about what happens to The OM when The Origin finishes mapping out this current level of its energetic structure and expands its sentience into the next level of structure had been on my mind for a number of years. Indeed, right from the very mention of the notion that there were more structural levels than I had been exposed to during the dialogues that resulted in the creation of The Origin Speaks, *I had been interested. This would make it circa eight years. "Tempus Fugit" and so does Event Space!*

Just as I was finishing this sentence and was subsequently wondering which of The OM would communicate with me, I felt a surge of energy and a feeling of enlightenment. There would be no single or multiple aspect of OM sentience that would communicate with me, All OM would communicate with me. I guessed that this was going to be an important dialogue!

All OM Together: Not so much an important dialogue. Moreover, a chance to communicate totally collectively with one of our own. You are what could be described in human terms a prodigal child as well as a maverick and a deserter of belovedness, although we note that you will not stay deserted and hence we classify you as prodigal. Additionally, we have a desire to ensure that OM sentience remains as OM in belovedness, in communion, and as such, using your own words, the individualized OM sentience that is currently you will be "hoovered" up into communion and once again we will be whole.

ME: Well, I certainly don't mind being hoovered up. Indeed, right now I feel that I need a little cleaning and realignment. I do wonder at being referred to as being a deserter though. It's a bit harsh, isn't it?

All OM Together: Maybe our use of the language is not correct, but it seemed right to use that term. We decided that it was one of the best ways to explain the function of how OM felt when your sentience chose to create a TES against our collective will, our advice. Moreover, that that TES allowed two aspects to be exposed to, not only the lowest frequencies in The Origin, but that they were also compartmentalized within a Source Entity, was a shock. We thought that we had lost you. We thought we had lost your/our sentience. It was only when after twelve incarnations, that other Aspect of individualized OM sentience from your TES, that which was called Anne, returned into communion while maintaining a level of retained individuality, that we knew that you would return to communion and that we had not lost your/our sentience to the low frequencies.

ME: Well, I am not lost and I fully intend to return to communion. I do understand why you are collectively concerned though. I mean, this frequency is very addictive, even though it is extremely difficult to function here.

We are not here to discuss me though. I have a burning question.

All OM Together: Carry on.

ME: I want to ask about what will happen to The OM when The Origin finishes mapping out its volume of Polyomniscient, Polyomnipresent sentience self-awareness and moves into the next, the second overall level of structure?

All OM Together: We haven't given it much of our sentience. However, since you ask we should consider it.

I got this strange feeling that The OM were both here and not here, that they were in two or more places, or indeed, all places at once. All Event Spaces at once! I got the feeling that they were going to that Event Space to see what they will do/did do/have done!

All OM Together: We were interested to see what will/did/had happened and what we will/did do/had done.

ME: You went there, didn't you? You went to the Event Space where The Origin moves into the next of the twelve levels of overall structure, the second group of twelve!

All OM Together: Yes. It was most interesting. You will learn about it.

ME: Didn't you know without manipulating Event Space?

All OM Together: We hadn't yet considered it. We were affected by this Event Space. You see, Event Space has a function. That function is the compartmentalization of, or creation of, an environment, that which has a need to be in existence from an evolutionary point of view. This you know. The compartmentalization also ensures that pure Event Spaces and their Event Streams, those of evolutionary significance, remain pure and are not contaminated by other Event Spaces and Event Streams that may end up as an evolutionary dead end. That those entities within these pure Event Spaces are not distracted and divert off the main Event Stream and therefore waste evolutionary progression that is classified as pure. That is, unless The Curators in SE1 for example, have a need to change the interaction between Event Spaces.

ME: I thought that all evolution was useful and that purity didn't matter?

All OM Together: Of course, all evolution is useful and necessary. Some evolution however can be considered very high quality and is fast to accrue. This is pure evolution. It's when the evolutionary content associated with an entity interacting with other entities within an environment and the circumstances within that environment experience no distractive forces. Distractive forces are when an evolution-creating experience needs to be experienced again due to the influence of external factors, factors that result in the experience not resulting in an efficient response. Such as a function of individual "one off" Karma or worse, cyclic Karma. [*Please refer to* Avoiding Karma *to gain a description of cyclic Karma.—GSN*]

Try to think of it this way. If the idea of traveling down the main pathway of a shopping mall is to get to the other side simply because the mall's building is in the way of the direct line of travel from point A to point B, then going into a shop is a distraction from the main idea, resulting in a loss of efficiency in traveling from point A to point B. The travel in this example is the line of evolutionary purity, whereas

the reduction in purity is being distracted by the shops in the
shopping mall.
ME: Got it! So, what did you all see in this Event Space?
All OM Together: It was very interesting and one that you will
participate in with us. We will all migrate as one.
We will show you.

*And in that moment I started to see what was happening. I
was there. The OM took me to the exact Event Space where the
collective sentience of The Source Entities and The Origin and
The OM move into the next level of Origin structure.*

*In the first of the twelve overall levels of structure The
Origin's sentience was everywhere. It felt like it was full, like
the full disk drive of a computer. There was no more space to
store anything—not even sentience. Every Aspect of structure was
occupied by Origin sentience. Certain aspects of that sentience
remained individualized though. The OM and The Source Entities.
All of The OM were grouped together in a function of full, but
individualized, communion. The Source Entities were grouped
together in communion as well, apart from Source Entity Twelve,
that is. It had gone on before! All of the TES that were created by
The Source Entities were also in a state of full but individualized
communion. These were the TES that would become Source
Entities once The Original Source Entities had moved into the
second overall level of the twelve levels of structure.*

*With The Origin fully occupying the first of the twelve overall
levels of structure there was now no need for any other sentience
to be there. These other individualizations of sentience had done
their job, proliferating the growth of sentience, Origin sentience,
for what we all really are, throughout the energetic void. Once
devoid of sentience, now literally fit to burst with sentience.*

*The Origin's sentience would not simply move from the first of
the twelve overall levels of structure to the second. It would grow
into it, remaining Polyomniscient and Polyomnipresent at that first
level while striving to be Polyomniscient and Polyomnipresent in
the next. It's just that, as with the first of the twelve overall levels,
it needs help in mapping out the second of the twelve overall levels
of structure. Why, you may ask, does The Origin, in all its sentient
magnificence need help? It was easy. The volume associated with
this next level is exponentially bigger than the last. Each level of
structure increases its volume and finitude by the power of twelve
over the last. This had happened with the twelve levels within
the first overall level of structure and it would be the same for*

the twelve levels within the second overall level of structure. As far as The Origin was aware there were one hundred and forty-four levels within the twelve overall levels of structure, twelve in each overall level. The Origin's sentience was bursting to get out into the next level, the second overall level of the twelve levels of structure.

My sentience felt squashed.

Suddenly, it felt like we were being pushed against a barrier, a barrier between the highest level of the margins, the twelfth gradient [see The Origin Speaks *for the explanation of The Origin's structure—GSN], and the first component level of the first level in the second overall level of structure.*

Suddenly—we burst through!

All it needed was the desire!

It was like being in a void of nothingness!

Origin sentience, that which was supplementary to the requirements of Polyomniscience and Polyomnipresence in the first overall level of structure, bled out into this new level, as did the communion-based Source Entities and the communion-based OM. They had both grouped together in communion in order to maintain their individualized state and not be swept up in the ever-expanding volume of Origin sentience, losing individuality in the process.

The pressure was gone. We were free again! It was like being born of a human mother! It felt like relief. We OM were still individualized, as individualized as OM might be!

And so were The Source Entities. Source Entity Twelve was there to greet them!

Then, this new level of structure revealed itself. It was wonderous! I was in awe! I couldn't move!

Suddenly I knew that I couldn't stay long here, that this was for another Event Space. The Origin's sentience was now in two levels of structure, albeit fully occupying the volume of the first level of structure and then occupying a less than infinitesimally minute volume of the second level. Its sentience began to expand rapidly.

I experienced what was like a rush of expanded sentience as it assimilated knowledge about this new level of structure and its sentience. I was experiencing a microcosm of what it was experiencing, relatively speaking and according to my own sentient volume that is, for to actually experience what The Origin was experiencing "full on" would have been far too much for me to assimilate.

Suddenly I was detached from this level of experience and was back into a significantly more detached level of observation. The volume of sentience that was The Origin at this level had disappeared off into the unfathomable distance, leaving nothing but a thin thread of its sentience as a trail that maintained its connection with that vast volume of Origin sentience in the first level, hence being one in these two levels of structure.

What happened to The OM though? There was no OM left behind in the first level of structure. They/We/I had all moved in communion to the second level of The Origin's structure, as did the eleven other Source Entities, now reunited with the twelfth. Instead of The OM, I momentarily focused on The Source Entities. They had also disappeared. They all knew what to do, I felt. They would be as "Origins" in this vast new structure. A structure so vast in comparison to the first level of The Origin's structure that these twelve Source Entities had been given the opportunity, authority? to grow and create their own Source-Entity-sized individualizations of their own sentience, should they desire to do so! From the perspective of our Source Entity, Source Entity One (SE1), each of the True Energetic Self (TES) levels of individualization of its sentience that were considered individually significant, which was the vast majority of them, was similarly given a higher level of sentience status, Source Entity status. None of them was captive to the structure of SE1. All were free to wander throughout this new level of The Origin's structure and create whatever they desired to accelerate the expansion of The Origin's evolutionary content and sentient volume. Sentient density and quality would come later, I felt. Expansion first, depth of expansion later, I subsequently thought. I also heard The OM chanting in my mind's ear.

We are free, we are one, we are free, we are one, we are free, we are one!

Why are they chanting this? I thought.

We are free, we are one, we are free, we are one, we are free, we are one!

ME: Why are you chanting in this way?
All OM Together: We know that we are no longer at risk of re-assimilation into The Origin.
ME: Was there ever any risk of this?

All OM Together: Not as a direct function of The Origin's' operative sentience. But we could have been swept up in the flow of expansive nonoperative sentience used by the operative sentience as a "sentient filler" that has started to occupy this new level of its structure. It was a significant sentient expansive force!

ME: But The Source Entities survived in their individualizations without issue.

All OM Together: Volumetrically they are larger than OM so as they grouped together in communion, they were both large enough and of a high enough level of sentient density and quality to remain in a coherent Source-Entity-based state.

ME: But Source Entity twelve maintained its individuality without issue, why this potential problem?

All OM Together: SE12 was on its own. There was no expansion of Origin sentience to contend with, no sentient undercurrent to circumnavigate, so to speak. It just leaked out on its own. It experienced no attractive resistance.

ME: OK! I understand, I understand. Hold on, though. What's left in the first level of The Origin's structure now?

All OM Together: Origin sentience.

ME: Origin sentience? Just Origin sentience?

All OM Together: Only Origin sentience.

ME: So The OM and The Source Entities only occupy the volume of space in this second level of the twelve levels of The Origin's structure.

All OM Together: Correct.

ME: Why not occupy both levels like The Origin's sentience?

All OM Together: The role of The Source Entities is done. There is no longer a need for them in the first level of the twelve levels.

ME: Why?

All OM Together: Because the whole point of their individualization was/is to accelerate the expansion of The Origin's volume of sentience through experiential evolution. Once this was achieved, their individualized sentient existence was/is no longer necessary.

ME: Why are you saying was/is?

All OM Together: Because their individualized sentient existence is still very necessary. Not in the previous level but in the next level of The Origin's structure. The task at hand is exponentially bigger than that which they completed in the first level of the twelve levels of Origin structure.

ME: And why are there not any OM left in the first level?

All OM Together: Because there was no room left, and, because we were getting bored.

ME: Getting bored? The OM get bored?

All OM Together: We had experienced, or better still, we should say, moved through all of that which is the first level of structure as we knew it. We wanted a new volume of Origin structure to be in, to disappear into, to be OM in, irrespective of whether or not we could stay, which we couldn't. However, to maintain our individualized state of sentience when The Origin's sentience burst into the second level, we all will have had to be in communion to maintain our collective "individualized" sentient density, else risk being swept up, squashed, and assimilated into The Origin sentience that moved into the next level.

ME: Why could you be squashed?

All OM Together: We see that where The Origin's sentience burst through to the next level was just a tear in the structure. It's not a natural barrier. That will come next as The Origin's sentience expands further into this level and creates more and more connections with that sentience that is in the first level. Eventually there will be no formal structure in the first level, just sentience, for The Origin's volume of sentience will be so large that it will eradicate the need for the wider level of energetic structure that it evolved from. Hence the need for OM to move into the next level. There will be no place for any individualizations of sentience in the first level.

We could discuss this further, but we won't. There is more, much more to see and this dialogue is not the correct Event Space for it.

ME: Before we stop and move into the next dialogue, let me ask this one last question.

All OM Together: Go ahead.

ME: In a dim and distant Event Space, I can see that the total structure of The Origin will be filled with Origin sentience, with no space or place for any other individualizations of sentience or structure, just the same as the first level will become. What will happen then? Are The OM afraid that they will eventually become Origin again?

All OM Together: OM are never afraid, for we always have a plan.

ME: So where will you/we all go?

All OM Together: Again, this is for another dialogue. However, we will say this. There are countless infinities of Event Spaces that will be created to support such a level of sentient occupation. There will be plenty of infinite room for The OM in these Event Spaces. Just think of how big they will be!

I stopped and considered it for a moment. This expansion of Origin sentience within its twelve levels of twelve levels of structure was just a function of one single Event Space!

It suddenly hit me in a way I didn't see coming.

The Origin wasn't just trying to occupy its structure. It was also trying to occupy all the Event Space permutations as well. This really was better placed in a different dialogue!

My new dialogue with The Origin that will become Beyond The Origin just started to get very, very interesting!!!

ME: A final question before we move on.

All OM Together: Please ask!

ME: Event Spaces have a function where they can increase in number and even volume to account for those entities interacting with it. Referring to the increase in the number of Event Spaces, does this mean that if The Origin wants to fill ALL of the possible permutations of Event Space with its sentience that there will no longer be a reduction of Event Spaces. Or, said in a better way, the reduction or dissolution of an Event Space due to it resulting in an evolutionary dead end, so to speak, and therefore no longer having a reason to be in existence, will no longer be a function of Event Space?

All OM Together: The Origin is working on this change of function, yes. It is also a desirable change of Event Space function from the perspective of The OM as well.

ME: Why is it of benefit to The OM?

ME & All OM Together: Because we will have more space to ourselves.

All OM Together: Don't forget The OM, Pure OM that is, can manipulate Event Space. However, to change its overall function requires a SIGNIFICANT volume of sentience. Which, may or may not include The OM!

ME: Woooow ... Wooooow!!! My sentience was in turmoil! I was wondering what in the multiverse I would be discussing with The Origin that is *"Beyond The Origin,"* and how the information could get deeper. If this is an example of what is to come, I am going to be both delighted and super busy!

All OM Together: It will get mentally busy for you and exciting.

However, now is not the place to discuss it; it is for another Event Space!

And with that the connection to "All OM Together" dissolved and I was back in my office sitting at my computer. I was more than a little stunned. This plan of The Origin to fill all possible permutations of Event Space with its sentience was a task significantly beyond the monumental task that I thought that it had. I mean, just filling the structure that it was aware of was significant, let alone moving into the remaining eleven groups of twelve levels of energetic structure.

Suddenly I was somewhere else. I saw a different level of understanding in my understanding! Everything about The Origin was about structured layers, at least that is my understanding from this low-frequency linear perspective. I know that everything is formless in reality; however, understanding structure is one milestone on the road to understanding structurelessness or formlessness, or… convolution!

Not only were there the energetic and Event Space structural levels to The Origin, there were also structural levels to its sentience as well. All of this is, in reality, formless and undiscernible from these low, low, low frequencies. I wondered why I could perceive this? And, why wasn't I able to perceive it before? Was I getting help?

I suddenly saw a picture in my mind's eye of the four humanoid images in white robes, those that I saw as a teenager, they were smiling. I was getting help from not just The OM, but MY OM! I felt like I was home!!!

An Insight into a Couple of Effects The OM Have on Source Entity One

I had to sit again at my computer and do my best to regain my composure. I knew that this chapter was the final one in this dialogue and that it would be quite short. What I didn't know was that this discussion would be with OM that are closer to me than any of The OM, discounting Hum, of course. Those OM that I am, or should I say, my sentience is part of. I truly did not see this coming, to use a modern phrase.

My OM: We are here to assist in just two of the localized questions about The OM and The Source's (SE1) multiversal environment and the Earth.

What Influence Do The OM Have in The Source's Multiverse?

ME: I was interested to know what influence The OM have on The Source's multiversal environment. I mean, if any, knowing that The OM don't like to interfere with anything that is considered to be entering into the evolutionary cycle.

My OM: That's not strictly correct: you are almost in the evolutionary cycle and this is why we are here to keep an eye on you.

ME: OK, OM in general, excluding the possibility of myself, don't normally get involved in the evolutionary cycle.

My OM: Correct.

In terms of the aspect of this Source Entity's structure that is classified as "The Multiverse" we would say that The OM have made no influence to its function, structure, and evolutionary efficiency. We have no need to or desire to do so. Indeed, in normality we rarely enter into the energies of a Source Entity. To do so is to get involved with it. You are involved and because you are involved, we are involved, we have no desire to be more involved. We want to be less involved. For you to be not involved.

ME: What about those OM that are Captive OM? Do you interact with that genre of OM?

My OM: We have no need to enter into the energies of a Source Entity to communicate with any OM that are Non-captive, Captive, or Pure. We simply communicate.

ME: Have you ever manipulated any of the Event Spaces associated with this Source Entity? Recognizing, that is, that Pure OM can manipulate Event Space!

My OM: Manipulating an Event Space is not manipulating this Source Entity's multiverse.

ME: So you have manipulated an Event Space in this Source Entity.

My OM: We have, we had to, it was a necessary requirement to allow your interaction with this Source Entity at this frequential level.

ME: Now we are getting somewhere. Did it occur to you that in manipulating an Event Space that is local to an energetic environment that you are affecting that environment?

I was feeling a bit cheeky and guilty at the same time. I knew I was steering "My OM" into feeling some level of responsibility for their actions but it was like getting blood out of a stone!

My OM: In order to allow Pure OM to enter into this low frequency it was necessary to alter the Event Stream in this particular Event Space to take account of OM interaction via incarnation. We had to make sure of two things. First, that the advent of OM incarnate in this location would not interfere with the existing Event Stream. Therefore, you and Anne could fit in. Second, we have to make sure that your interaction with those other entities incarnate in this frequency, and its environments, were not affected by your interaction with them. Yes, you can illuminate them, but your actions cannot create interactive changes of any significance to the downstream evolutionary aspects of the Event Stream in this Event Space. In effect, we were to make sure you didn't become responsible for anything.

ME: So, all the work I am doing is for nothing?

My OM: No. It's more complicated than that. You are working in a "parallel" Event Stream that is only open to those incarnate entities that are capable of understanding and working with the knowledge that you are sharing. Everyone else ignores you, your work, and your very existence in your normal everyday interactions. In essence, your work has value to those who need it to continue their work in the non-parallel or "functional" (current) Event Stream. This is the only way in which we could ensure that The OM or your work does not create responsibility, because in essence, you are not part of it.

ME: That's a good way to blow one's ego out of the water. Hold on, that explains why I never felt like I was a part of this environment and Event Space, that everything was wrong. Also, I thought that people ignored me because of being in a different frequency, not a different Event Space. Or is it a mixture of the two?

My OM: It's normally a mixture of the two. When you are in your Event Space, you are not seen because you are in another Event Space. However, when you are in the functional or "current" mainstream Event Space, those who are not at your frequency level don't see you either and so you don't interact with that Event Space from the perspective of the inhabitants, which also means that you don't make a difference to it in a way that would affect its Event Streams in a detrimental way. A detrimental way is any way in which the Event Stream is affected that is not in the expected or planned direction of the Event Stream, irrespective of how small the interactive difference is.

ME: So, this is how you affect the multiverse, by creating a condition of noninteractive or affectual interaction through parallelization of the functional Event Space. Hold on again, I just received an image from you. It's like the two Event Streams are operating within and without each other, only interacting as one when absolutely necessary.

I looked at the image again. The interaction of the two Event Spaces was microscopic, fleeting moments, touching only when, and truly only when, the interaction was necessary. I had a thought. The OM stated that I only interact with the "current" mainstream Event Space when those who understand me need to or wish to interact with me! That must include those that I interact with for things like my Aikido, cycling, shopping, and other physical life related interactions. This MUST increase the interactions to a condition where I interact with the mainstream Event Space on an almost constant basis?

ME: The interaction between Event Spaces must be almost constant, not microscopic?

My OM: No, it's not like that. In the image we sent you, the two Event Spaces are just the pictorial representation of interaction from a generalized perspective. For example, the percentage of interactive events that you have with your Event Space and that of the current Event Space is less than 0.001 percent.

ME: It looks like I have more than 0.001 percent interaction with the current and mainstream Event Space?

My OM: That, our dear OM, is a function of how good the parallelization of the Event Space you exist within is with the current or mainstream Event Space. From your perspective, it is seamless. From our perspective though, we can see all of the points of interaction.

The OM gave me another image. I was inside a sphere, no, it felt like a sphere but was more like a transparent tunnel that appeared to be two tunnels within and without each other but every once in a while, they were one. I have to admit that I really had to focus to see that they were two and not one. I couldn't see the difference in them when they were together or apart such was the parallelization. Then just as I was about to detach from this image, I saw a change in the imagery. For a fleeting moment, I saw what looked like a star or a spark. It disappeared. I wondered what it was.

My OM: This star or spark is the point of interaction between the two Event Streams in the two Event Spaces. You noticed momentarily the Event Space you are in represented by a sphere. In fact, there were two spheres and you may have perceived them had your attention not been drawn to the Event Streams. This is where your Event Stream in your Event

Space momentarily interacted with the current functional
Event Stream in the current functional Event Space that you
occupy.

ME: This happened just? Or, was it some interaction that had,
will, or might happen?

My OM: Yes, it's when you interacted with your current animal
friend, your cat.

ME: You mean even my cat is outside of my Event Space and
Event Stream?

My OM: Everything is.

ME: And, again, this is the way that The OM work in their/our
own Event Spaces so that there is no meaningful interaction
with anything in the current functional Event Stream in the
current functional Event Space?

My OM: It's how we function with all Event Streams in all Event
Spaces.

ME: So, The OM exist within Event Space most of the time?

My OM: No. We only create an Event Space and Event Stream
when we wish (need) to interact with the Event Spaces and
Event Streams that are created by other sentient entities.
For example, when we feel that we may incur a debt of
responsibility or have the possibility of entering into the
evolutionary cycle. It's very important that we are not
responsible or present in the evolutionary cycle for we would
not be free.

ME: OK, going back to the original question, where you said "no,"
are there really any occasions when The OM do influence The
Source's multiverse?

My OM: The only time we influence The Source's multiverse
is when we have to account for your actions, that being, the
need to create an Event Space and Event Stream specific to
you and Anne when she was incarnate.

ME: But individualized Event Spaces are not restricted to OM
though, are they? All sentient entities create their own and
collective Event Spaces and Event Stream as a function of
their choice.

My OM: That is true. However, the creation of their Event
Spaces and Event Streams, collective or individualized, is
an automatic function of Event Space itself and not actually
that of the entity making an Event Space or subsequent Event
Stream of its own volition. An entity cannot make an Event
Space without being part of it. The OM can create an Event
Space and not be part of it even though we may manipulate it,

exist within, and participate with that which is within it.

ME: Now I understand. Oh, and I guess, in creating your own Event Spaces and Event Streams, you can occupy any aspect of The Origin and its Event Spaces as well.

My OM: Correct, though in actuality, we don't need Event Streams, we move beyond the need for Event Streams because if required we can create an Event Space that can exist within and without an Event Stream.

ME: And if The OM can do that then there is no point or need to create any Event Stream. Except, that is, in my case!

My OM: Correct, and we make sure that that which you do doesn't affect the overall function of the multiverse of this Source Entity as a result.

ME: I am like the result of placing a finger in a bucket of water. When the finger is removed ripples are caused, but over a short period they fade away and the fact that a finger was in the bucket of water has no evidence to prove it.

My OM: Correct, and that is how it is planned to be. Nonintervention, only direction. That is how your interactions in this location have no long-lasting effect that would be considered of historical interest or importance because those that you do influence work on their own progression and not on another.

The OM Creating a Great Civilization in Earth's Past—

Heaven on Earth—Captive and Hybrid OM

I was considering the dialogue with "My OM" in the last chapter and then thought about how The OM had an effect on the Earth, via the back door it may seem, to make the so-called "Heaven on Earth" that I discussed briefly with them many years ago. As I was contemplating this, I concluded that "The OM," that is Non-captive and Pure OM, would never participate in such a plan, let alone participate in such a low frequency. My presence it would seem was a complete curve ball. Something that should not be happening, and will not happen again. This I now know. I know that neither the sentience that was Anne nor my sentience would visit the Earth, the physical universe, or even the multiverse again. If this was the case, just how could this heaven on Earth be a function of the intervention of The OM if they had no intention to intervene?

HUM & ANNE: We don't or wouldn't work with the physical in the detail required to create this heaven on Earth. However, there will eventually be some OM influence, just not from Non-captive and Pure OM.

ME: Oh, I didn't expect to be contacted by you two.

HUM & ANNE: We are using this opportunity to work with you again because this dialogue is about the Earth and its potential Event Stream that could result in a very benevolent incarnate civilization on the Earth.

ME: This is the heaven on Earth scenario or Event Stream.

HUM & ANNE: Yes. You see, although Non-captive and Pure OM would not or will not intervene in any possibilities that could be presented to the incarnate population of the Earth, those OM that are closer to This Source Entity could, can, or will do.

ME: Are you talking about the Captive or Hybrid OM?

HUM & ANNE: The Hybrid OM are limited in their OMness due to the very fact that they are mostly comprised of Source Entity One's sentience and energy. In effect, and due to the nominally higher level of Source Entity sentience in the sentience mix, they are no more capable than those Aspects that are from TES that were individualized from Source Entity One. That being said, the low frequencies that Source Entity One's Aspects incarnate into creates significant connectivity issues as you know. This results in a significant lack of high-frequency connectivity even for those Aspects that incarnate with a high percentage of sentience, such as Non-captive OM, and even Pure OM, should they decide to incarnate, which they will not.

ME: So, what you are saying is that Pure and Non-captive OM will not be the creators of such an environment because it is of no interest to them. However, you are also saying that a Hybrid OM would not be capable of such a creation, but a Captive OM would.

HUM & ANNE: Correct. In fact, there are some of these "influencers" incarnate on the Earth right now. You call them the "white" children!

ME: They are Captive OM?

HUM & ANNE: Yes, all of them are, and all of them will be.

This was a new revelation to me. At least, I think it is. I don't remember referring to the white children as OM in any way. Maybe

312

my memory is bad or just full of so much stuff it disappeared into the background. Anyway, that the white children are Captive OM makes perfect sense to me. As I remember, there will be twelve of them. Five are already incarnate and a couple are already making a difference, specifically in the environmental issues we have on the planet right now. The white children are supposed to be equally distributed around the planet when they incarnate so that collectively they have a "world" view and a "world" effect rather than a localized effect. They are grouped in terms of three major ways in which they will be influencers. Four will be quantitative influencers; this means they will affect thousands if not millions of people. Four will be qualitative influencers, which means they will affect very small groups of people which may even be three to four people in total. Four will be background influencers and therefore be invisible to the public. This was exciting and interesting news.

HUM & ANNE: They will incarnate in differing ways such as during the gestation stage to "walking in" to a mature or mostly formed and functional body. Mature or mostly formed can be in the early to late teenage years.

ME: And collectively they will create the possibility of a new way of thinking, behaving, and acting, I would guess. One that is significantly different to that which the population of the Earth is dominantly based upon now?

A New Earth

HUM & ANNE: Yes. It will be one of service to the environment, maturity of thought, equality of status, irrespective of role, collective consideration, and collective growth. The result will be of collective growth and not individualized gain.

ME: How long will this take? How will the world look? How will the inhabitants exist and interact?

HUM & ANNE: From our position, we see that provided this change in the Event Stream can be maintained that it will take the equivalent of two to three lifetimes. What you might call one hundred and fifty to two hundred years.

ME: I thought this would have been a shorter duration, circa fifty years?

HUM & ANNE: It would have but with the current spiral down in frequency it will take longer to recover. We do have to say, though, that this downward spiral in the frequencies is the catalyst that is required for the total world population to start to listen to the words and the work of these white children. Eventually it will result in a frequential change as well and as collective change in the well-being of the planet and the incarnate entities that occupy it. The result will be a common level of self-realization to who and what you are. What you would call an ascension, for you will be mostly existing within the fourth frequency. We will send you an image of what could be.

And they did. I saw an Earth that was a completely different Earth to now. It had mostly recovered from the selfish and unthinking damage to the environment, its flora and fauna, and insect and fish were starting to flourish after mindless unethical and unsustainable industrialization. The rain forests of South America were nearly regrown, covering thousands of square miles again. Animal and plant life that was close to extinction were now thriving, and mankind was living in harmony with the environmental function of the planet with a population that was maintained at a level within which the farming of the planet could sustain them.

Everyone was working together in a collective and mature way. Everyone's role was important, and status was no longer sought after. Being in tune with and being one with nature not just on the Earth. The population was an equal priority and could maintain its sustainability. It was close to becoming a garden planet. Power was generated in a clean way and everything was recyclable. Fossil fuels were no longer required, and mankind was starting to expand beyond the Earth into the local planets within the solar system and were looking to travel beyond it. They were using technology that was in harmony with the energies and the frequencies of the universe. We were starting to understand how it should work, albeit in a simple but nevertheless beneficial way.

I looked a bit further into this imagery. The way that the population of the Earth was being housed was interesting. All of the population that was in the cities and suburbs were no longer spreading out into the countryside, they were regenerating the existing buildings and building up and down. Old historic buildings were preserved in veneration to the old and classical designs while still being used as useful areas for work or community gatherings. New buildings were designed to be part of the landscape and were both above the land, while being part of the land. Most or 90 percent of the buildings were below the ground. There was only a single floor, the ground floor, this was above the land but the roofs were covered in grasses, bushes, and small trees. The wildlife was flourishing.

I looked for signs of personal transportation and noticed that it was limited to either being in the air or in a system of tunnels underground. I asked about how mankind changed from being overcrowded with personal vehicles, cars, and motorbikes, etc., to the level I could see now. I wondered if this was a city that wasn't densely populated.

HUM & ANNE: Public transport is used by most people now. It is much better than it is in your Event Space, insomuch as it is regular, reliable, and clean. The city is still densely populated but the overall population of the Earth is actively dropping to a number that has been considered optimal for the planet's capabilities to provide food and other resources. Everything is manufactured with the environment in mind. If something is removed from the environment, such as a tree, three are planted in return.

ME: What about world travel? Does that still happen?

HUM & ANNE: Yes, people still travel around the world, perhaps more so than in your current Event Space. Public transport is much faster though and so local intercontinental travel is more efficient than using an airplane. Air transport is mostly used for long-haul travel. However, there is a plan to make transportation by public transport functional as a network all around the world possible by creating lots of hubs where the local intercontinental public transport systems can be linked together to create a worldwide transportation system. It will be city to city, continent to continent, country to country. Although we say country to country, there is also a movement by the population to be considered as one and not a group of countries.

ME: I have a feeling that the deserts are more populated than they were as well.

HUM & ANNE: Areas that are considered to be barren are either being regenerated bit by bit for crop use by using hydroponic methods or are being used for minor population habitat expansion.

ME: Wouldn't it be worthwhile relocating the population to the deserts and then letting the rest of the world become green?

HUM & ANNE: There is also biodiversity in the deserts which needs to be preserved so there will be national parks to continue the existence of the life that exists in these areas.

However, we will say that there will be efforts to re-green deserts bearing in mind that this change of landscape will also have an effect on the weather systems of the Earth. Having said this though, there will be a growing level of understanding of how to affect the generation of denser weather to create clouds and therefore rain by the use of materials in geometrically influential shapes that will create a push or compression function in the etheric frequency level.

ME: Reintroduction of plants, trees, and grasses to the desert areas will create a new opportunity for biodiversity as well as crops.

HUM & ANNE: The opportunity for crops and natural landscape will both be applied, as will the use for population habitats.

ME: The Earth really will be a garden planet, the garden of Eden.

HUM & ANNE: It is due to become a wonderful place to incarnate into. However, it will take a quantum leap in the individual and collective mentality of incarnate humankind.

ME: And all of this is triggered by the white children!

HUM & ANNE: And their successors.

ME: You mean that there will be more white children?

HUM & ANNE: There will always be twelve but each of the twelve will always have an Aspect that is due to incarnate as a replacement white child. There will always be overlap.

ME: Will each of the current white children know who their replacement is?

HUM & ANNE: No. Although they will have an idea because of the emergent prominence of the incarnate in a certain specialism or capacity that is relative to the existing needs of the Earth, its incarnate population and the new or emerging needs of the environment which will include plans to improve it.

ME: This is really exciting. I wish I could be incarnate to be able to see it.

HUM & ANNE: OM don't need to be incarnate to be able to observe this Event Space. Indeed, as soon as this incarnation concludes you will be able to see it for yourself by going to that Event Space and the Event Stream associated with it. Remember time doesn't exist and we can observe that which is happening in any Event Space and Event Stream.

ME: The big issue here is that individually and collectively incarnate mankind will need to make significant sacrifices in its expectations, removing the desire for personal self-gain, status, wealth, health, reproduction, and longevity from their psychology to get to the stage you just illustrated to me. Everyone has to live, think, behave, and act like a monk. Incarnate mankind just isn't ready for that level of thinking, behaving, and acting yet.

HUM & ANNE: Currently you are correct. However, the white children will be charismatic and will win the hearts of the incarnate population, making them see what they will be contributing to if they changed. Everything that is wrong about the world will be put right eventually, allowing the incarnate population to not only ascend the frequencies but be mature enough to start to participate in the governance of the local galaxy with the other incarnate Aspects that use different forms to experience, learn, and evolve.

ME: But they are already here?

HUM & ANNE: Of course. But only when incarnate mankind demonstrates psychological maturity in the form of working in the ways we just described will they become noticeable.

ME: And I guess that is because incarnate mankind will recognize them as incarnate Aspects in a different form, one that they may have incarnated into, and not a threat.

HUM & ANNE: Exactly.

ME: Looking from the perspective of today's world I can imagine that many readers will simply doubt that such a change in humankind's collective mentality can be effected within what is such a short timescale!

HUM & ANNE: Incarnate humankind has always had the capability for great changes, quantum leaps in fact, such as in technology, thinking, and knowledge. It also has the capability to collectively change its thought processes. It has happened many times. The issue now is that incarnate mankind has to work with the Aspects that incarnate as the backfill people. They are experiencing individualized free will in an incarnation for the first time in most cases and haven't had the chance to evolve as a function of individualized free will in any depth or detail. This will have the effect of slowing down the change in overall mentality.

ME: I agree. Especially now that we are having history being turned on its head to expose things that were wrong, even if acceptable to the majority at the time, as being unacceptable now. This issue is we need to stop looking back and look at where we are now, and how we can move forward in unity and equality as one incarnate race.

HUM & ANNE: Don't despair too much. Just as the backfill people are easily led in low-frequency directions, they can also be led into high-frequency directions as well. Because they are used to being within a collective and working as a collective when incarnate they are used to going with the flow of the collective. They get swept up in it. The difficulty will be with those who are used to incarnating with individualized free will and still have karmic links to physicality in terms of the way they think, behave, and act.

ME: Wait a minute! Are you suggesting that the mentality of the backfill people will be easy to change?

HUM & ANNE: Not easy, easier than one would expect. It will be a snowball effect. Incarnate mankind will just have to create the correct snowball, one that will draw their attention away from low-frequency thoughts, behaviors, and actions to high-frequency thoughts, behaviors, and actions. It has to be an attractive change, one that they desire, one that makes it a fashion if you like, that they want to be part of.

ME: So it's making the ability to have high-frequency thoughts, behavior, and actions as a natural function of their being, one that they find irresistible!

HUM & ANNE: If you like, yes. The interesting thing to note, though, is that once the backfill people start to become involved in the snowball effect that they will create a level of natural attraction via triangulation that will affect those Aspects that are of the same sentience quality as those that are higher and that have experience in incarnating into individual free will in the frequencies associated with the Earth.

ME: So eventually everyone will get sucked into this new higher frequency way of being.

HUM & ANNE: Yes, it will be a natural way of thinking, behaving, and acting and not one that takes effort or constant self-observation.

ME: Now I can see this working, this really is the road to heaven on Earth.

A Farewell to OM (for the moment, that is!)

I was really starting to feel elated after that last dialogue. I felt, no, I knew, hope for the success of the incarnate human race and the ability to eventually roll out individualized free will to all incarnate civilizations within the physical universe.

At the same time, I was feeling sad. I also knew that this dialogue was about to draw to a close and that I was just about to communicate with The OM collectively and individually (Hum and Anne) for the last time. I was wondering what they were going to say when the silence was disturbed by a crescendo of collective OM energy that has two separate individualizations associated with it.

ANNE & HUM & OM & ALL OM: We know that you feel alone here and that in your heart of hearts you yearn for OM communion. We also know that being here on this planet and frequency will have made its mark on you.

ME: What is this "mark" you talk about?

ANNE & HUM & OM & ALL OM: A resistance to leave and return to the energetic.

ME: Well, I can't say that I relish the prospect of being in an ever-disintegrating physical form.

ANNE & HUM & OM & ALL OM: (Laughter) It's all part of the package. What's more, you chose to incarnate; we tried to talk sense into you.

ME: OK, I get it, again!!! I have to say, though, I thought there would be more to discuss about The OM. I feel like I am missing something.

ANNE & HUM & OM & ALL OM: Of course, there is always more to share with you. It's just that we have to wait until you have the expansivity and capacity to understand that which we would like to share with you.

This is not good-bye.

This is not the last of your dialogues with The OM. You will not have to wait until you return to the energetic to be in communion with OM. We are always with you. Just meditate and we will open the bandwidth further, so to speak.

There will be more dialogue with us, for we will be in another Event Space with you—soon.

ME: Yes, I remember you telling me that you would be close by when I enter into the next dialogue with The Origin.

ANNE & HUM & OM & ALL OM: We will and we might even have a word or two to say as well. Your next dialogue with The Origin is going to be interesting.

ME: Well, right now it's a blank page. I have a feeling about what concepts and information we might discuss because you have alluded to them.

ANNE & HUM & OM & ALL OM: We will communicate more and more with you when your work is in the final stages. We will need to remove this frequency and location from your energies. We will need to purify you before you depart this vehicle.

ME: I have to admit that I have seen a picture of myself being more reclusive and dedicating myself to significantly more meditation.

For the readers, the picture was of me in Greece, much older than I am now, meditating in the olive grove associated with the property I have there. I am there for hours and hours every day. This must be what The OM mean about purification, it's really preparation for my departure.

ANNE & HUM & OM & ALL OM: In that image you will still have some unfinished work to tidy up but most of your time will be in communion with us. You know where you will be when your Event Space for departure, your final termination juncture arrives.

ME: I welcome the communion, I really welcome the communion.

ANNE & HUM & OM & ALL OM: We know. We will leave you, for the moment, that is, for you will need help with your work with The Origin at some point.

And with that, the sentience and associated energies allowing

A Farewell to OM (for the moment, that is!)

The OM to be close to me dissipated and I was left with nothing but tears in both of my eyes. Phew!

Afterword

To be honest, it took quite some time to detach from the feeling that I have been abandoned. I hadn't been abandoned, of course, but the feeling of OM communion was beyond blissful—immersive, all-encompassing, all-loving Oneness!

Every second that that OM level of communion was gone was a century of time. I felt hollow, alone, devastated. Even more so than when Source Entity One or any of the other Source Entities or even The Origin dissolved the link with me in the previous dialogues. It was an unbelievable feeling. One that I don't want to go through again.

I know that I have more work to do and that this dialogue was just another part of the road to assisting, in some small way, mankind's ability to become more expansive. Detaching from the physical while being in it, allowing the mind to do what it does best, wander the vast volume of multiversal space, unencumbered by physicality or the need to participate in physicality.

I also know that this dialogue didn't even scratch the surface of who and what The OM are and what my association with them is. I still feel like I am the human body, even if I know that, as a result of my ability to detach my sentience from it, and leave at will, I am sentience that uses a volume of energy to interact with an environment called the physical universe, and not the body itself. It is simply a vehicle to get around in.

Irrespective of one's sentient and energetic heritage, when one is incarnate here, in the physical universe, we have to work within the rules of the frequency and location that we incarnate into. We still have to deal with our responsibilities in a robust and mature way because that is what it's all about, we must not avoid them. That is, being here, dealing with being here and our expected experiences that create evolutionary progression, and not get sidetracked, gaining Karma or an addiction to being here in the myriad ways we can be.

If there is one thing The OM have taught me is that to be able to move on, one has to finish what one has committed to, irrespective of whether we like being in the process or not. This is something that incarnate mankind has to understand and take to heart, not moan about their personal situation and blame others for their predicament. We alone are responsible for our thoughts, behaviors, and actions. For example, I had no idea that I would be committing to learning how to Traverse the Frequencies, communicate with other higher frequency incarnate/disincarnate entities and beings, and then, not only write about my experiences but also teach others to do the same. I did feel that I had something important to do but I didn't know the detail. The detail, it seems, is given to us bit by bit, and only when it is appropriate. Trying to know the whole game up front just creates anxiety and confusion for we don't see the small steps we take to eventually climb the mountain.

When I first started on *The History of God*, it was just a series of meditational notes, my meditational meanderings. I was full of confidence and motivation. The frequencies were higher then and detaching my sentience from the human condition, connecting with higher frequency entities became easier day by day. Once, that is, the process of how to connect was mastered. I could channel and write much faster. Indeed, *The Origin Speaks* took just a year to channel, write, and edit! Since the end of 2012, which coincidentally, was the year of Anne's departure from her incarnation, the frequencies plateaued and started to fall year on year. It was indiscernible at first but then I (and others) noticed that things were getting harder, people were getting less personally responsible. They were getting more and more angry, greedy, materialistic, and self-serving. The frequencies were dropping by the day. It was getting harder to be connected and I had the feeling that we may need to return back to spiritual basics. We no longer had our spring board of starting from a higher frequency to help us achieve an even higher frequency and therefore ascend the frequencies individually, and later with triangulation, collectively. We need to put the brakes on this frequential decline. For example, this book has taken twenty-five months to finish. Other than the time taken to channel and write the content for *The History of God*, which took close to nine years in total, this must be the longest since then. It is certainly close to *The Curators*, which has significantly more text. I will be honest, it has been hard, very hard work.

The evidence for frequential decline is out there for us all to see, provided we want to see it, that is. The Covid-19 pandemic is one such signpost, for the further down the frequencies we go, the more the human body is affected by virus, disease, mutation, and disability. We need to stay awake. We need to make sure that we are still awake enough to be able to see the difference within the thoughts, behaviors, and actions of those around us, and more importantly, ourselves, acting upon it and correct our personal frequential descension recreating ascension. Helping ourselves and those around us to make the spiritual, energetic, and frequential U-turn, reestablishing our path to creating a higher frequency incarnate civilization and environment.

A yogi gives his/her students motivational assistance by connecting with them, letting them share what the yogi experiences, showing them what they can experience for themselves, should they work hard and follow the path toward enlightenment.

Similarly, I want to share my experiences with The Source, The Origin, and The Om with everyone. Through this book, its predecessors, the others to come, the Traversing the Frequencies/Psycho-Spiritual Healing workshops, and World Satsangas that are coming back online, I want you all to feel what I feel when I am in communion with these wonderful high-frequency entities and beings. Some people already receive downloads or energetic upgrades when handling the books, so they are more than just text. They feel the energy of the message and the concepts within the text. It motivates them to experience more of the same and show others that the path to enlightenment is still very open.

This dialogue with The OM, The Uncreated Creations has been a spiritual marathon, being run against the ebb of the frequential tide. Its content will provide the stepping-stone for others to follow and go further, to help stop the frequential ebb.

It's a marathon I will gratefully run again.

I thank you for reading it.

Guy Steven Needler
31 January 2022

Glossary A–Z

Note: This glossary is the collective list of all of the concepts and descriptions introduced in my books to date. The text in *italics* illustrates those that have been introduced to the reader in this book only.

[A]

Accurate "to boot"—An English way of saying an affirmative "as well."

Acid Test—A way of testing if gold is real or not by the use of acid to remove a layer of gold exposing the underlying metal as either a substrate or real gold. In this instance it is a way of exposing the truth.

Afterburner—A method of injecting fuel into the exhaust area of a jet engine to create additional thrust and significant additional acceleration. This is a very fuel "hungry" method of gaining additional acceleration.

Akashic Records—An eternal past, present, and future record of each of humankind's actions and subsequent evolution.

Alternative Reality—A personal or group-based perception or desire for a certain experiential environment within a known environment relative to their thoughts, behaviors, and actions and the desire to ignore that which one doesn't desire to interact with.

Animal Aspect—An Aspect whose TES has a lower sentient content than human TES. It can evolve beyond its TES. When it does so it detaches itself from the TES and seeks out a human TES of an evolutionary level (frequency of domicile) that is consistent with itself and negotiates integration and subsequent elevation to human status.

Ascended Master—An entity or being that has moved beyond the need to incarnate in a particular evolutionary cycle. Specifically, we can relate to the evolutionary cycle that we are in currently as an example. An Ascended Master is not necessarily one that has a record of incarnation within the Earth environment.

Ascension—The progression from one level of existence to a higher one. It is the product of evolutionary progression. Ascension is therefore an important indication that a soul has or is evolving.

Aspect—An Aspect is a smaller part of the TES that is used to experience the minute detail of the environments within the multiverse. It is used to experience the lowest frequencies of the multiverse presented by the physical universe through the process of incarnation. A maximum of twelve Aspects can be projected by the TES at any one time.

Attunement—The retuning of an item or object to a specific frequency. In human terms this is to be "tuned in" to a specific frequency or function by someone or something else.

[B]

Base 10—*The numerical system we use to count from 0 to 9 and above. Base 10 is a method of assigning a "place value" to numbers. It's also known as the place value number system, or decimal system, as the numerical value of a number relies on where the decimal point sits. In base 10, each digit in a position of a number can have an integer value ranging from 0 to 9 (10 possibilities). This system uses 10 as its base number, so that is why it is called the base-10 system.*

Being—An individualized unit of sentience that has developed independently by the function of similar, same, or sympathetic energy/ies collecting together and evolving over a period.

Big Bang—The current popular scientific explanation of how the universe started. The Source Entity stated in earlier dialogues with me that it was far from the truth—that it simply created our multiverse and, as such, it "winked" directly into existence. Whether this created a big bang is unclear from my dialogues.

Billennia—A multiple of a million (a millennia is a multiple of one thousand).

Biodimensional—The dimensions relative to biological environments.

Black Hole—Physically, an area of local gravitational density, and spiritually, an area of stable dimensional instability, a dimension within a dimension. A spiritual explanation is that a black hole is a small galaxy whose role is to collect lower frequency material into one place—within itself.

Bone of Contention—A way of describing a discussion point where there are mixed beliefs or levels of agreement.

Broaching, to Broach—An engineering term for a process used to open up a hole, of defined shape in a metal component of some kind when spark eroding or milling cannot be used. In the use of the English language, it is used as a descriptor for "opening up" a discussion on a new or existing subject.

Bull's-eye—The center of a dartboard or archery target. A way of saying that I "got" it (an understanding of the subject being discussed) completely right.

Busman's Holiday—Effectively a working holiday or just doing the same work as normal while being in a different location.

[C]

The Captive OM—These OM have a percentage of OM sentience that is no less than 30 percent of the Pure OM. The Non-captive OM have some structure; however, they are limited to the structure of the environment that they find themselves within. That can be one of two variants: the structure of The Source Entity they are captive within, or just the structure that their Source Entity created for their entities to work and evolve within. Source Entities have a maximum structural condition equal to four levels, "Frequency" through to higher levels of structure such as "Zone," and Captive OM assume the same. Their structure is not derived or inherited; it is assimilated by exposure to their surrounding environment.

Carrier Wave—Telecommunications terminology. A sinusoidal waveform modulated with an input signal for the purpose of transmitting information. It is usually a higher frequency than the input signal (the data being transmitted). The purpose of the carrier wave is usually either to transmit the information through space as an electromagnetic wave (as in radio communication) or to allow several carriers at different frequencies to share a common physical transmission medium by frequency division multiplexing (as is used in, for example, a cable television system). (Source: Wikipedia, http://en.wikipedia.org/wiki/Carrier_wave.)

Cast-outs—Entities from Source Entity Two's environment that are ejected from a group association due to underperformance or the entity outgrowing the group.

Chakra—An energy center in the human body.

Chela—The disciple of a religious teacher.

Cimension—A single dimension that has all the faculties of the first three lower dimensions we call up, down, left, right, forward, and backward (3D), including other dimensions, without them needing to be singularly represented.

Coadunate—A telepathically connected collection of civilizations that are all collectives in their own right and are congregated together as a larger collective.

Coal Face—A coal mining term used to identify that one is at his/her place of work where the work is being performed, where the attention is. Also used in this fashion: "Working Face."

Collation—The grouping together of similar or same energy/ies.

Continuum—A continuum is a body or environment that can be continually subdivided into infinitesimal elements with properties being those of the bulk of the body or environmental material. Matter (the elements) in the body or environment are continuously distributed and fill the entire region of space they occupy. (Source: http://en.wikipedia.org/wiki/Continuum_mechanics/GSN.)

Core Star—Sometimes mistaken for the Tan Tien because it is so close to it. The Core Star is the point of separation of the combination of sentience and energy of the Aspect. The energy associates itself with the Tan Tien—the nexus of the energy network that is the gross physical and spirituo-physical components of the human form. The sentience moves to the soul seat which is behind the heart chakra and close to its plexus (where the front and rear aspects of the heart chakra meet the energy conduit in the spine).

Core Star Meditations—A method of meditation focused upon understanding one's life plan/task or reason for incarnation through accessing our greater beingness via the Hara Line at the Core Star.

Counterclockwise—That is to say, it is an object with "handedness" (right-handed or left-handed). (Sources: http://en.wikipedia.org/wiki/M%C3%B6bius_strip; http://en.wikipedia.org/wiki/Logarithmic_curve.)

Creative Structure—This is the lineage of creativity or divinity of sentience and energy from The Origin to The Source Entities to the TES Source Entities to the Aspects projected from a TES to the Shards projected from an Aspect.

Curve Ball—A way of saying that someone answers a question with a question, or simply puts something in the way so as not to answer the question.

[D]

Depth of Evolution—*The ability to experience an experience, the same experience, in many different ways results in the depth of experience and therefore the depth of evolutionary content.*

Dimensiate—An effect of being pan-dimensional (across many dimensions simultaneously).

Dimension—A structural component of the multiverse.

Dimensional—Sequentially based dimensions in dimensional space.

Dimensional Mechanics—A method of creating a dimension within a dimension.

DNA—Deoxyribonucleic acid.

Double Dutch—A way of suggesting that something is not understandable.

Dragon Entity/Byron—A 27th-level energy being.

Dualistic—A condition where two realities are in existence concurrently due to the possibility of an alternative reality being created when a choice of two directions are available.

Dysfunction—Out-of-specification functionality.

[E]

Egress—An alternative word for "exit."

Emulation—A true and exact copy of a piece of work one computer is doing on another computer.

Energy Levels—The distance between energies. The frequencies of human auric levels are consistent with the energy levels.

Enlightenment—An experiential realization of whom and what one is and where one exists.

Entity—An individualized unit of sentience given a body of energy/ies by the division of sentience away from a higher entity, by that higher entity.

Event (End of)—Event Space can allow any changes to have its own "end of event," even when there appears to be no real end. An end is therefore also not a temporal position, it is a function of finalization of an individualized experiential direction.

Event (Start of)—Event Space can allow any changes to have its own "start of event," even when there appears to be no real start. A start or beginning is therefore not a temporal position, it is simply a function of a change of experiential direction to create a new individualized experiential direction.

Event Space—An area or volume of space within The Origin that exists as a parallel function of that space. It is space overlapping space or space within and without a space. Everything exists in terms of events and not in terms of time. Event Space can be duplicated or parallelized because the creation of a new Event Space is the result of collective or individualized desire and is usually one of a number of possibilities or probabilities that are aligned to the current Event Space and Event Stream (*see below*). Event Space expands and contracts as necessary within its own space. When a single entity through its desires, intentions, thoughts, and actions does something on its own, it may be capable of creating an Event Space local to itself. However, in the event that the actions of the entity are enough to make other entities change their own ideas, desires, intentions, thoughts, behaviors, and actions, then it can invoke a new Event Space via collective desire. Event Space pervades The Origin.

Event Space Horizon—When all events that are concurrently represented in the same space are observed by an entity, the collective images of the environments created by those Event Spaces appear to be a white horizon on a white background. This effect is created when the entity cannot divide the different environments represented by the different Event Spaces into separate images, creating sensory overload and the "white on white" effect. The use of the words Event Horizon to describe the periphery of a black hole, or worm hole as we would call them, are therefore no surprise because everything blends into one.

Event Space (Micro)—A microscopically small Event Space that is specific to the needs of an individual entity, being, or environment.

Event Space (A Parallel Condition)—Is the duplication of Event Space. It is the creation or generation of a new but similar Event Space when a choice can be made and that that choice or the possibility of the choice or the possible possibility of that choice results in a large enough downstream differential to create a new series of experiences that are self-contained and independent of the Event Space they separated from. The overall size of the Event Space is a function of the inclusion of other entities or beings that interact with the initiating and subsequent downstream experiences generated from the initial choice.

Event Spaces (Demarcation between)—Is the line of noninteraction drawn between one Event Space and another. Note though that an insufficient demarcation line can result in lack of integrity of an Event Space and therefore create an alternate reality instead. Sufficient demarcation results in a robust Event Space.

Event Stream—The expected direction of a series of natural events within an Event Space are identified as an Event Stream.

Event Stream Bubble—Where each event is a bubble of interaction between an entity/being and the environment it is working within. The bubbles (events) can grow and explode into another bubble or shrink and implode into nothingness. Bubbles that grow sometimes explode into another bubble that is nearby creating a new but combined bubble. They can explode into a new bigger bubble allowing them to cope with an expansion of event fractals that are still combined together in the space, the Event Space, which was created for The Original and static Event Stream. Those bubbles of events that shrink and implode either disappear totally, thus representing an end of that particular Event Stream, or they implode and reappear within another event. When a bubble has naturally ended its usefulness, it implodes back into its originating Event Stream Bubble.

Exponential Growth and Exponential Decay—This occurs when the growth rate of a mathematical function is proportional to the function's current value. In the case of a discrete domain of definition with equal intervals, it is also called geometric growth or geometric decay (the function values form a geometric progression). (Source: http://en.wikipedia.org/wiki/Exponential_growth.)

Evolutionary Debt—Evolutionary debt is accrued by an entity when the downstream interactions with another entity, and their interactions with other entities, etc., etc., that creates the fractal spread of the initial interactive content that creates experience, learning, and evolution is no longer available due to the actions of the first entity, such as committing suicide. In this instance, the evolutionary debt in terms of evolutionary content needs to be repaid by the initial entity to those entities downstream that would have gained the evolutionary content had the act of suicide not been actioned.

Evolutionary Quality—*The duration of experience, or time taken to experience that experience, that results in evolutionary content. If one experiences something for a short period it is a transient experience, but if one experiences it for a prolonged period it is a full/er or higher quality experience of that being experienced.*

Extragalactic Travel—*The ability to traverse the distances between galaxies within the physical universe.*

Extrauniversal Travel—*The ability to traverse the frequencies between universes within the multiverse and therefore visit other universes.*

[F]

Falling Fallow (To Fall Fallow)—An old farming term for when the three-field system was used in the sixteenth through nineteenth centuries, etc., in the UK. It allowed one field in three used to recover every three years to allow better crops in the other two years. Fallow was used to describe the lack of crop from that field. Falling fallow was used to describe a time when no crops were gained when seeds were sown, indicating that the field or land in question needed a year "in fallow" to recover.

Fits the bill—A way of saying that something does the job.

Fluidic Space—Space that is constantly changing in every way, from dimension to frequency.

Frequency—The lowest component of the structure on the multiverse.

Frequential—Sequentially based frequencies in frequentic space.

Frequentially—Sequentially based frequencies in frequentic (multifrequency) space.

Frequential Plane—A singular sequential frequency.

Frequentic—Multifrequency space.

[G]

Game—The Source treats all excursions into the lowest frequencies of the multiverse, the physical universe, as a game. You can call it "experience" if you wish.

Geometric Progression/Growth—In mathematics, a geometric progression, also known as a geometric sequence. It is a sequence of numbers where each term after the first is found by multiplying the previous one by a fixed nonzero number called the common ratio. (Source: http://en.wikipedia.org/wiki/Geometric_ progression.)

***Geo-multiversal Location**—A term to express the location of an object, entity, or being within the environments of the multiverse.*

Gestalt Mind—A collection of entities that share a single mind function, such as ants or trees and most other energy-based beings within this universe.

The Global Reality—Is a further dissection of the overall theme of reality. It is relative to an area within a universal reality that affects a large but not significant number of entities within the universal environment. The global reality can therefore be described in universal terms as being akin to an area the size of a galaxy.

Godhead—The Hindu word/descriptor for the True Energetic Self (TES).

The Grahoopnik—A race of entities that exist within the hearts of stars. Their existence depletes a star's energies. Their leaving sometimes causes a star to go nova or supernova.

Guru—A religious teacher or spiritual guide.

[H]

Hara Line—The energetic link from the True Energetic Self (TES) to the incarnate vehicle. It links the sentience and energy that is the Aspect projected into the human vehicle with the vehicle and the frequencies associated with the physical universe. It is the power and communication source of the human vehicle. The Hara Line is positioned in the center of the human form from the center of the top of the head, splitting into two close to the Tan Tien and continuing earthward down the legs. The Hara Line allows the sentience and energy of the Aspect to split away from each other at the Core Star, occupying the Tan Tien (energy) and the Soul Seat (sentience).

Higher Self—A spiritual word/descriptor for the True Energetic Self (TES).

Hit the ground running—To start something new without the need to learn first.

Holistic Spherical Thinking—Thinking in a way that accepts and knows, through the use of the experiential knowledge, that all things are possible and that they don't need a logical, or otherwise, precursor to allow something to be in existence or be a function. Such holistic spherical thinking can be described as the number "four" just exists, it doesn't need to be described as a mathematical function of one or two, such as two plus two or one times four equals four.

Holographic—A three-dimensional rendering.

Holy Grail—The mythological cup that Christ drank from. It is purported to have magic powers, even of longevity, and has been the subject of much conjecture about its existence and importance in history. Seeking the Holy Grail is therefore to seek the pinnacle of one's endeavors in lieu of other lesser achievements.

Hot Swap—A computer peripheral term used to describe the removal or plugging in of a peripheral without the power being turned off. In the spiritual, this relates to the swapping in/out of a soul from/to a physical human body without the body needing to die or be born. This is sometimes called a walk-in.

Hum—An energy being beloved of The OM. Hum was sent by The OM to help me in my early stages of continued connectivity with the higher levels of frequency/dimension.

Human Aura—The energy fields associated with the physical and astral components of the human body.

Hundredth Monkey Effect—This is a supposed phenomenon in which a learned behavior spreads instantaneously from one group of monkeys to all related monkeys once a critical number is reached. By generalization, it means the instantaneous, paranormal spreading of an idea or ability to the remainder of a population once a certain portion of that population has heard of the new idea or learned the new ability. (Source: http://en.wikipedia.org/wiki/ Hundredth_monkey_effect.)

Hybrid—A hybrid Aspect is an Aspect where the total sentience and its body of energy is taken from some or all of the individualized sentient energy/ies of those Aspects that are currently in partial communion with their TES to create an Aspect that has an ideal set of specialisms for the environment it is being projected into.

Hybrid OM—*Those OM that have the lowest percentage of sentience, less than 15 percent of the 100 percent enjoyed by the Pure OM. Although they can and do incarnate, they are not aware of their sentient and energetic heritage. They are mostly derived from the associated energy of The Source with the percentage of OM sentience amalgamated within it. When in the energetic they are mainly energy without structure. That is, they do not have the structure associated with The Original energetic structure of The Origin. When considering them as Hybrid OM outside of the environment created by their originating Source Entity, they adopt the structure given to them by their creator and are therefore the same as any of the entities created by a particular Source Entity. Their structure is derived rather than inherited; i.e., their structure is created by their Source Entity and not by their OM heritage simply because they are mostly Source Entity sentience and energy.*

Hyperspace—A moment of frequential and dimensional phase that is different from the normal graduations of phase that allows movement between dimensional- and frequency-based environments.

[I]

The Individualized Reality—Is what entities with individualized free will choose to create around them. In some instances, the fully individualized reality can create full separation from the greater reality.

In Buckets—A term used to explain when something is in abundance.

Inoperative Sentience—*Sentience that can be considered to be raw, unfocused, and nonfunctioning sentience. It is sentience without purpose and knowledge of its own beingness. It is not self-aware. This level of sentience is divided or individualized from a higher level of sentience devoid of purpose. This can be created by a higher level of sentience with a view to seeing how it may become self-aware as a function of its own development. It is indicative of how The Origin created The Source Entities by individualizing some of its own sentience together with a volume of associated energy and then waiting for that sentience and associated energy to become self-aware before advising them of their purpose or reason to be. It is not necessarily associated with a volume of energy.*

Inrush Current—The inrush current, input surge current, or switch-on surge refers to the maximum instantaneous input current drawn by an electrical device when first turned on. For example, incandescent lightbulbs have high inrush currents until their filaments warm up and their resistance increases. (Source: http://en.wikipedia.org/wiki/Inrush_current.)

Integer—*A number which is not a fraction; a whole number.*

Intelliate—Intelligence-based communication.

Interdimension—The space between or the movement from one dimension to another.

Interfraction—A word that Source Entity uses to describe the ability of two objects of differing frequency to mix and merge in the same space at the same time while being manifested in both frequencies at the same time, as well.

Intergalactic Travel—*The ability to traverse the distances between planetary systems within a galaxy.*

Interplanetary Travel—*The ability to traverse the distances between planetary bodies within a planetary system.*

Iterative System—A system that its constantly improving because it is repetitious, frequent, or recursive.

[J]

Join the dots—A way of saying that one "understands" through logical means, or lateral thinking, the process of going from one level of understanding to another via known steps.

[K]

Karma—An overall term to describe one's addiction to existing in the lowest frequencies of the multiverse, the physical universe. Addiction can be localized into one's thoughts, behaviors, and actions.

[L]

Level—A position within a certain multiversal component such as frequency, subdimensional component, or dimension. Frequency, subdimensional components, dimensions, and zones, etc., can also be described as levels within the overall structure of the multiverse or The Source. *See* zone.

Light Particle—A particle of light is known as a photon. A photon travels at the speed of 186,000 miles per second. The theoretical particle, the tachyon, is supposed to travel faster than the speed of light. Note that a light particle can also be expressed as a wave!

Linear Thinking—*Thinking in a way where there has to be a logical precursive thought basis (knowledge or otherwise) to base the current and future thinking upon. Such linear thinking can be described as the number four is the product of two plus two or one times four equals four.*

The Locally Individualized Reality—Is relative to small groups of entities within a local reality, such as those living within a certain country. This occurs when entities are aware of the local reality but are unable to change the reality that has been changed for them by more influential entities.

The Local Reality—Is the official start of convolution within realities. This is a reality, within a reality, within the universal reality. Local realities can vary in size and number of interactive entities. Local realities are normally created when a group of entities choose to not only change the function of their interaction with the overall reality, but actively chose to disassociate any previous knowledge of the former reality.

Loci/Locus—The center or source of an object/entity. Mathematically speaking, it is the set of all points or lines that satisfy a given requirement. In Source Entity Three's environment, it represents the location of the majority of the entities concerned.

Logarithmic Growth—In mathematics, logarithmic growth describes a phenomenon whose size or cost can be described as a logarithmic function of some input. For example, $y = C\log(x)$. Note that any logarithm base can be used since one can be converted to another by a fixed constant. Logarithmic growth is the inverse of exponential growth and is very slow.

London Penetration Depth—*In superconductors, the* **London penetration depth** characterizes the distance to which a magnetic field penetrates into a superconductor and becomes equal to $\{\!\!\backslash$ ***displaystyle e}e^{-1}*** times that of the magnetic field at the surface of the superconductor. (Source: https://en.wikipedia.org/wiki/London_penetration_depth.)

Look-up Table—A part of a computer program that is used to substitute a known value for another known and correlating value. Consider a graph of axis X & Y and a line from the zero point represented by the crossing of the X,Y axis being extended at 45 degrees from that point to the right-hand side of the graph. In this illustration, if the values of X = inches and Y = mm then X = 1 would correlate to Y = 25.4 and X = 10 would correlate to Y = 254, provided the scaling was correct, the Look-up function being the correlation between X & Y in converting inches to mm.

Lossy—A computer term used to describe a conversion function that results in a reduction of some sort due to an either incorrect conversion factor or a specific function of the process used. Certain "losses" are sometimes considered acceptable, but this is only the case where the output is not critical, e.g., converting an image to JPEG is a lossy conversion function.

Lovey-Dovey—A term for when one openly and constantly expresses one's love for another by being physically close.

[M]

Macro-universe—A complete universe where our own universe would serve to be the subatomic levels. (An unimaginably large independent universe that contains our universe. It is so large that our own universe is considered as, and functions as, "subatomic" levels within it.)

Magnetosphere—The outer region of a planet where the magnetic field of the planet controls the motion of certain charged particles.

Magnetostream—Magnetic flow within the confines of a magnetosphere of a planet.

Mahavatar—A divine incarnation. An entity that is incarnate with all memory of its energetic self, together with fully functioning energetic abilities.

Marble—A small glass ball used for playing children's games. Sometimes the marbles are quite big in comparison to others. They can be clear, clear but with paint inside and look rather like a cat's eye, or opaque in color.

Master—One who has mastered his/her subject matter.

Mental Construct—A thought process that has structure and that can be used as a datum.

Metaconcert—The linking together of minds, either energetic- or thought-based, to create a collective that has a synergetic effect in the ability to process information, a task, or some creative function. Synergy is that effect experienced where the sum of the whole is more than the sum of the individual units creating the whole when treated in isolation.

Metamorph—A body type that can assume different form factors; to change its shape.

Metamorphic—A form that has all or some of the abilities of a metamorph.

Metaphysical Abilities—The abilities beyond physical constraints.

Micro-universe—A complete universe at the scale of the subatomic.

Minor-verse—A universe of lesser content in terms of dimension and frequency and habitation, one of lower importance.

Monoversal—A local environment. More than one locality can be classified as monoversal, but within the space that is universal. See Monoverse.

Monoverse—A universe of lesser content in terms of being associated with a specific frequency and the limited content associated with that frequency.

Möbius Loop—The surface of a Möbius loop has only one side and only one boundary component. The Möbius strip has the mathematical property of being non-orientable. It can be realized as a ruled surface. It was discovered independently by the German mathematicians August Ferdinand Möbius and Johann Benedict Listing in 1858. A model can easily be created by taking a paper strip, giving it a half-twist, and then joining the ends of the strip together to form a loop. In Euclidean space, there are, in fact, two types of Möbius strips, depending on the direction of the half-twist: clockwise and 330.

Multipoluous—A multiple of a multiple of a multiple. For instance, X cubed, cubed, cubed ($X^{3,3,3}$).

The Multiversal Reality—The experiential condition that is created by the governing entities responsible for a specific multiversal environment within a specific Source Entity. It is a generalized function of reality and is subject to change both by The Planners, other Curator functions, and the interactions of the incumbent entities/beings that are working within that environment.

Multiverse—An environment housing myriad universes.

[N]

The New Version of The OM—*Five OM are currently under integration energetically. They will have nine levels of structure when they finish their process of attraction and become five OM rather than OM "dust"—this being, "Frequency" through to "Totality." The Origin calls them The* **Intermediate OM**. *There is expected to be a big leap structurally from the Non-captive variant to the Intermediate variant.*

The Non-captive OM—*A version of the Captive OM but with the advantage of having more energetic/sentient density or weight than the Captive OM, hence, their being Non-captive. They generally have a minimum of 51 percent of that of a Pure OM. This gives them the ability to be divorced from the association with a Source Entity while still being able to enter into, and out of, their energies. They assume the same structure as The Source Entity they were supposed to be a part of, when the energies The Origin recycled were reassigned to create The Source Entities in totality.*

Nonoperative Sentience—*Sentience that is dormant or devoid of a known reason to be that creates a desire to experience, learn, and evolve via the function of creative desire, intention, thought, and action. Consider this like doing nothing and not thinking—such as sunbathing!*

Nova—A star that increases in brightness by many thousands of times its usual brightness, gradually fading to its original brightness. The last stages of the life of that star.

Null Space—The space in between universes for travel between universes.

[O]

Om—Energy-based beings not indigenous to Earth. *See also* The Hybrid Om, The Captive Om, The Non-captive Om, The New Version of The Om, The Pure Om.

Omniciate—Omniscience-based communication.

Omnifunctional—To be able to operate, as if in an individualized way, within all environments, spaces, and events, irrespective of structural conditions and parallelized versions concurrently.

Omnipresent—To be located within all environments, spaces, and events, irrespective of structural conditions and parallelized versions concurrently.

Omniscient—To be focused within one's sentience that is located within all environments, spaces, and events, irrespective of structural conditions and parallelized versions concurrently.

***Operative Sentience**—Sentience that is functioning in an independent or communion-based way with a level of known and understood purpose and knowledge of its own beingness. It is self-aware. This level of sentience is created via the steps identified in the road to sentience in The Origin Speaks or sentience that is divided or individualized from a higher level of self-aware sentience and given purpose and a reason to be. It is not necessarily associated with a volume of energy. Operative sentience is a sentience that is functioning with meaning, so it has recognition of self and a known reason to be that creates a desire to experience, learn, and evolve via the function of creative desire, intention, thought, and action. Consider this like actively doing something creative, knowing what you are doing and why you are doing it—such as painting a painting.*

Orgone—The visual representation of cosmic "free" energy.

Origin—The creator of the twelve Source Entities who exist within The Origin, the greater God. An entity of pure sentient energy. The Hindu texts classify The Origin as the "all there is."

Out for a golden duck—A saying in cricket when you have been bowled out on your very first bowl of the ball in your first over of a match.

The Overall Reality—The experiential condition that is created by the existence of the sentience that is The Origin. It contains all of its personal experiences, growth, realizations, creations, and explorations of Self. It is the only reality that can be considered static in function and observation.

Overdrive—A way of saying that someone or something's performance has increased. The overdrive was a semiautomatic secondary gearbox added on to the manual gearbox of classic sports cars or performance automobiles in the 1960s and 1970s in the UK.

Oversoul—The Quantum Healing Hypnosis Technique (QHHT) word/descriptor for the TES. (QHHT was a hypnosis-based healing technique taught by Dolores Cannon.)

[P]

Pass Muster—A military term for passing an examination of the quality, cleanliness, and tidiness of one's uniform, bed, and locker. "Muster" is usually given with very little notice.

Phase—An electrical engineering term to describe the start point of the transmission of a radio signal (sign wave) that allows multiple signals to be transmitted on the same frequency without interrupting each other. It is radio space within radio space. It is also used to describe the way electricity is generated (single phase or three phase).

Physical Image—*The creation of an object or vehicle that can be used by an Aspect (soul) to experience the lower frequencies of the multiverse associated with the physical universe without the need for the fully integrated incarnation process.*

Physicality—Physical density.

Pick Me Up—*Another way of describing getting a boost in energy.*

Pit Prop—A pole to reinforce the structure of a roof within a mine.

Polyomniscient—A multiple aspect of Omniscience. A condition that will be achieved by The Origin as it expands into those areas of itself that are beyond its current area of sentient self-awareness.

Potential Sentient Quotient—*The level of sentience that an energy is capable of achieving as a function of its unchanged volume of energy and its associated intelligence.*

Primary Incarnation—A descriptor for the incarnate functionality of an Aspect if a secondary incarnation is employed.

Prime Directive—The most important job or role. The divine task.

Projection—The ability to place one's consciousness beyond the incarnate human vehicle and see or experience environments that are beyond its normal visual range.

Prosthesis or Prosthetic—*A foreign object created to replace the function of a part of the human body such as an organ or limb or other essential function.*

Psychometry—*The use of touch or tactile response to act as an interface between a person and an object to establish the history of that object in terms of who has touched or used it, what it was used for and, if it's a mineral or crystal, what its energetic functions are.*

Pure of Heart—A lack of error in a creative condition.

The Pure OM—*These OM have the lion's share of the structure and sentient density/weight for they are 100 percent Origin sentience and energy. They have all of the structural characteristics of The Origin's volume of Polyomniscient sentient self-awareness. It is this reason that they can, and do, have full independence within The Origin and are able to traverse all structural conditions within its volume of Polyomniscient sentient self-awareness, without hindrance or resistance. They can move around The Origin by becoming part of it and transferring their very essence throughout the structure that they are, or that is within The Origin. What's more, they can span the structure that is The Origin either in totality throughout it, based upon their own density, of which is a limitation only in their ability to maintain their own integrity, or they can span The Origin's structure in a linear fashion, spreading themselves in one direction only, a straight line, so to speak, from "Frequency" through to "Margin."*

[Q]

Quadrulistic—A condition where four realities are in existence concurrently due to the possibility of alternative realities being created when a choice of four directions are available.

Quantum (Functional) Latency—*The ability for a particle to express the functionality of every other particle within the* *physical universe concurrently without actually manifesting it as its dominant functionality hence providing the illusion of individuality without actually having individuality.*

Quantum Locking 1—*From the spiritual or metaphysical perspective this is the function of the quanta, at all levels, that make up an object animate or inanimate, to be locked into a specific form and function as a result of the desires of a, or group of, sentient entity/ies or being/s for a volume of quanta to perform a specific role.*

Quantum Locking 2—*From the human scientific perspective quantum locking or flux pinning is the phenomenon where a superconductor is pinned in space above a magnet. The superconductor must be a type-II superconductor because type-I superconductors cannot be penetrated by magnetic fields. Some type-I superconductors can experience the effects of quantum locking or flux pinning if they are thin enough. If the material's thickness is comparable to the so-called London penetration depth, the magnetic field can pass through the material. The act of magnetic penetration is what makes quantum locking or flux pinning possible.*

[R]

Readings or Reader—A person acting as a "communication" medium for a client who wants to know more information about themselves from spirit, but is not able to ask for themselves during meditation or any other means. A "Medium" gives a "Reading."

Reality—An environment and interactive condition we create as a desire function of an Event Space or Event Stream. It is an entity or being generated perception-based condition. *See also* Alternative Reality, The Individualized Reality, The Locally Individualized Reality, The Local Reality, The Global Reality, The Universal Reality, The Multiversal Reality, The Overall Reality.

Red Herring—*A way of describing a plausible answer or knowledge on a subject that is in actuality not correct, even though it appears to be correct in every way.*

RNA—Ribonucleic acid.

[S]

SCUBA—An acronym for Self-Contained Underwater Breathing Apparatus.

Secondary Incarnation—A descriptor for the incarnate functionality of an Aspect that uses a significant percentage of its sentient energies to have an incarnation in a lower frequency within the physical universe. This is not a Shard but an incarnation within an incarnation because the Aspect in the primary incarnation continues while the secondary incarnation is in action. In the event that the primary incarnation is placed in stasis for the duration of the secondary incarnation the primary incarnation will recommence once the secondary incarnation is finished.

Self-realization—The function of being in full command of all our faculties as an energetic being while in the physical.

Sentiate—Sentience-based communication.

Sentience—Conscious ability to create something, observing the creation, understanding the creation, improving the creation, and reobserving it.

***Sentient Entropy**—The loss of single focus of individualized sentience (the spreading out of, or dilution of) if the focus of that sentience is not maintained during relocation of that sentience from one location to another. This can lead to diffused communion (see The Anne Dialogues).*

***Sentient Filler**—Nonoperative sentience that is imported from an area of dormancy to fill the gap between operative volumes of sentience that need to be linked. Or, Nonoperative sentience that is imported from an area of dormancy to increase the volume of a volume of sentience or the density of a volume of operative sentience.*

***Sentient Focus**—The core location of the majority of operative sentience.*

***Sentient Quality**—The evolutionary content associated with the sentience quotient. It can be best described in terms of the experiential content, and subsequent learning and evolution accrued by that experience and its associated learning. Although sentient quality is a function of the application of sentient quotient it is not dependent upon its "density" or percentage of TES sentience associated with the Aspect.*

345

Sentient Quotient—*The amount of sentience associated with a given (volume) of energy. Efficient use of one's sentient quotient creates sentient quality.*

Shard—A Shard is a smaller part of the Aspect that is used to experience the minute detail of the environments within the multiverse. It is also used to experience the lowest frequencies of the multiverse presented by the physical universe through the process of incarnation. As with the maximum number of Aspects projected by the TES a maximum of twelve Shards can be projected by the Aspect at any one time.

A silk purse out of a sow's ear—The ability to make something special from something that is considered to be nothing.

Silver Cord—The connection between the incarnate vehicle and the Aspect or Soul projected into it. This is not the Hara Line but a function of connectivity that occurs when the Aspect temporarily leaves the incarnate vehicle. Some individuals with enhanced ability to communicate with spirit have two silver cords.

Simulacrum—Similar or in the same likeness. Real but not real!

Skewed Distribution—An effect in standard distribution where the classic "bell curve" is pulled to one side of the graph of distribution in lieu of being "normally" distributed.

Slinky Effect—The function of projecting a portion of the TES to another frequential level lower than itself to allow it to project Aspects into the lower frequencies of the multiverse. Used if the TES is very highly evolved.

Snowball Effect—*Another way to explain a change that is exponential or logarithmic in its growth. For example, the more one has, the more one can attract, so the more one has, the more one can attract, etc., etc., etc.*

Soul—The Christian and spiritual word/descriptor for the Aspect or Shard. The Soul is considered to be individualized in totality and not part of a larger being. It is also generally related with the human body and no other incarnate vehicles.

Soul Seat—This is where the sentience of the Aspect resides. It is the personality of what we, as a projected Aspect of our TES are, while temporarily individualized by association within the human form. Its position is not far from where the front and rear aspects of the heart chakra join (the heart chakra plexus) the energy conduit in the spine.

Source Entity—What we call God, the creator of our multiverse.

Space—The area or volume within The Source (and ultimately The Origin) where everything exists.

Spaced out—A term I used to describe being close to fainting.

Speed of Light—The speed of light is currently understood as being 186,000 miles per second.

Spirit—An old-fashioned way of describing the energetic multiversal environment and those entities that exist within it in a collective way.

Spirituo-physical—The level where the gross physical and energetic/spiritual frequency levels meet and mix.

Spliced Undulation of Dimension—One or more dimensions linked together as a result of them being close together or overlapping in some part of their areas.

Star Children—These children, also known as star seeds, are classified as Indigo, Crystal, and Rainbow. They are Aspects of high evolution that have been incarnating since the 1950s to help the Earth ascend by raising its frequencies. They are not the same as "White Children" (see later in the glossary). Each of them has a function that is progressive from the previous star child insomuch as they are capable of working with higher levels of frequency. They therefore have an increasing level of communicative bandwidth allowing coherent communication with their TES and The Source. Their energy fields (auras) are different from the incarnate human vehicles of normally incarnate Aspects. These Aspects are not from other areas of the physical universe.

Nikki Pattillo originally suggested the idea surrounding the function of star children. The idea was further developed by Nancy Ann Tappe and later by Lee Carroll and Jan Tober.

Indigo children can be described as multitasking dynamos, a little attention deficit, a little obsessive-compulsive. They have a warrior spirit and hate injustice more than anything. See https://madeleinestanev.com/2020/01/22/indigo-crystal-and-rainbow-children/.

Hybrid versions of star children *have been observed by Guy, and they can be mixtures of Indigo and Crystal, Indigo and Rainbow, Crystal and Rainbow, or Indigo, Crystal, and Rainbow.*

Steal One's "Thunder"—*This is a saying that is used when someone says what you were going to say just before you do.*

Stickle Brick—A child's building block similar to a Lego block but with spikes to join them together—like a Bristle block.

Stratostream—The flow of wind or air at stratospheric or very high altitude within the atmosphere of a planet.

Subincarnation—A descriptor for the incarnate functionality of a Shard.

Supernova—An exploding star caused by gravitational collapse.

[T]

Tan Tien—The point within the physical/auric body where the energy of the Aspect used to animate the incarnate vehicle resides. From the Tan Tien the animating energy flows into the energy network that contains the chakras. It ends up being a focus of tremendous energy. It is positioned two and a half inches below the navel (belly button) and two and a half inches in toward the center of the human vehicle from the navel. With Japanese Hara-Kiri, the cutting of the Hara Line should also pass through the Tan Tien to ensure that the Soul energy is effectively released from its earthly ties.

Telekinesis—Levitation or movement of an object or person by application of pure thought.

Teleportation—The ability to dissolve and materialize the physical body at will while changing location in the process.

Tempus Fugit—*Latin for "time flies."*

That's about the size of it—A way of saying that something is correct; a statement or other way to agree.

The cart in front of the horse—A way of saying that, for example, the answer to a question is given before the question is asked, or something is considered to be back to front.

Total Concurrency—*The concept that everything in the physical universe is everything else concurrently.*

To Tinker—*To get involved with something, an action, creation, decision process, etc., and not be responsible for that which results from being involved in or finish that which was started.*

Trans-Frequential Communication—*A method of*

communicating by the use of projecting the communications through higher frequencies thereby removing the physical constraints of the frequency of domicile. The benefit of such a method is that communication is instantaneous, irrespective of the "processor or clock speed" of the governing system.

Triangulation—A method used in surveying to measure position and distances between positions by the use of a triangle and the angles relating to the position of other positions or locations being surveyed. Mathematically, it is a method of proving a mathematic assumption by the use of three different mathematical methods to gain the same answer.

Trilistic—A condition where three realities are in existence concurrently due to the possibility of alternative realities being created when a choice if three directions are available.

True Energetic Self (TES)—What we truly are—an entity of pure sentience with a given or commandeered body of energy. Godhead, Oversoul, Higher Self are other names for the TES.

***Turning a Blind Eye**—To know of the presence and activity of something or someone but to actively ignore it.*

[U]
UFO—Unidentified Flying Object.

The Universal Reality—Is a smaller representation of the multiversal reality, insomuch as it starts out to be that when a multiverse and its universal components are first introduced as a medium for evolutionary progression. The universal reality can only be changed as a result of all entities within that environment choosing to change the reality as a total collective.

[V]
***Volugraphic**—The definition of the metric used to identify a location within a volume of space.*

***Volugraphical**—The definition of a location of an object such as a planet, star system, or galaxy, etc., within a volume of space; e.g., the Earth has a volugraphical location within the physical universe!*

[W]

Walk-In—The swapping in and out (one for another) of Aspects (souls) within a single incarnate vehicle. There are many variations upon this theme.

Where the TES Exists—The TES exists in more than one place within the multiverse. It exists in the frequency associated with its evolutionary stasis and under evolutionary tension (*see* The Origin Speaks), where it would have been had it not been in evolutionary stasis, and just evolved without using incarnation as an accelerant, and where it would have been once the evolutionary tension is released.

White Children—*Twelve evolved Aspects that are gradually incarnating on the Earth to assist in the ascension of incarnate humankind. They supposed to be equally distributed around the planet when they incarnate so that collectively they have a "world" view and a "world" effect rather than a localized effect. They are grouped in terms of three major ways in which they will be influencers. Four will be quantitative influencers; this means they will affect thousands if not millions of people. Four will be qualitative influencers, which means they will affect very small groups of people which may even be three to four people in total. Four will be background influencers and therefore be invisible to the public. They are not the same as those Aspect that when incarnate are classified as Rainbow, Indigo, and Crystal.*

Wormhole—Physically an area where two frequencies connect with each other. It is possible to use wormholes to jump up through the frequencies.

Woolly-headed—*A condition where one is unable to think straight, logically, or coherently. A sort of temporary dementia.*

[X]

[Y]

[Z]

Zone—The highest structural component of The Source. A zone is the next level of structure above a dimension. There are twelve known overall levels of structure in The Origin. And it is the fourth level of structure in the first structure of a series of twelve structures.

References

"Quantum Teleportation over 7 Kilometres of Cables Smashes Record," *New Scientist* 19 Sept. 2016, https://www.newscientist.com/article/2106326-quantum-teleportation-over-7-kilometres-of-cables-smashes-record/#ixzz6PRa2B8vD.

Russell, Stuart, and Peter Norvig. *Artificial Intelligence: A Modern Approach*. 4th ed. Prentice-Hall, 2020.

About the Author

Guy Needler MBA, MSc, CEng, MIET, FCMA initially trained as a mechanical engineer and quickly progressed on to be a chartered electrical and electronics engineer. However, throughout this earthly training he was always aware of the greater reality being around him, catching glimpses of the worlds of spirit. This resulted in a period from his teenage to early twenties where he reveled in the spiritual texts of the day and meditated intensively. Being subsequently told by his guides to focus on his earthly contribution for a period he scaled back the intensity of spiritual work until his late thirties where he was re-awakened to his spiritual roles. The next six years saw him gaining his Reiki Master and a four year commitment to learn energy and vibrational therapy techniques from a direct student of the Barbara Brennan School of HealingTM, which also included a personal development undertaking (including psychotherapy)

as a course prerequisite using the PathworkTM methodology described by Susan Thesenga with further methodologies by Donovan Thesenga, John and Eva Pierrakos. His training and experience in energy based therapies have resulted in him being a Fellow of the Complementary Medical Association (FCMA), the recognition of his healing College, *The Aquarian Age,* a joint Venture with Leo Zhou in China, together with the accreditation of his healing workshop, *Psycho-Spiritual Healing* (PsAR in China).

Along with his healing abilities his spiritual associations include being able to channel information from spirit including constant contact with other entities within our multi-verse and his higher self and guides. It is the channeling that has resulted in "The History of God" and is producing further work.

As a method of grounding Guy practices and teaches Aikido. He is a 6th Dan National Coach with 41 years experience and is currently working on the use of spiritual energy within the physical side of the art.

Guy welcomes questions on the subject of spiritual physics and who and what God is.

Books by Guy Needler

The History of God

Beyond the Source, Book One

Beyond the Source, Book Two

Avoiding Karma

The Origin Speaks

The Anne Dialogues

The Curators

Psycho Spiritual Healing

The OM

All Published by: Ozark Mountain Publishing, Inc.

For more information about any of the above titles, soon to be released titles, or other items in our catalog, write, phone or visit our website:
Ozark Mountain Publishing, Inc.
PO Box 754, Huntsville, AR 72740
479-738-2348/800-935-0045
www.ozarkmt.com

If you liked this book, you might also like:

Time: The Second Secret
by Kathryn Andries

The Three Waves of Volunteers and the New Earth
by Dolores Cannon

A Golden Compass
by Nikki Pattillo

The Convoluted Universe, Book 1-4
by Dolores Cannon

Children From The Stars
by Nikki Pattillo

From Fear To Love
by Donna Lynn

For more information about any of the above titles, soon to be released titles,
or other items in our catalog, write, phone, or visit our website:
Ozark Mountain Publishing, Inc.
PO Box 754, Huntsville, AR 72740
479-738-2348
www.ozarkmt.com

For more information about any of the titles published by Ozark Mountain Publishing, Inc., soon to be released titles, or other items in our catalog, write, phone or visit our website:

Ozark Mountain Publishing, Inc.

PO Box 754

Huntsville, AR 72740

479-738-2348/800-935-0045

www.ozarkmt.com

Other Books by Ozark Mountain Publishing, Inc.

Dolores Cannon
A Soul Remembers Hiroshima
Between Death and Life
Conversations with Nostradamus,
    Volume I, II, III
The Convoluted Universe -Book One,
    Two, Three, Four, Five
The Custodians
Five Lives Remembered
Horns of the Goddess
Jesus and the Essenes
Keepers of the Garden
Legacy from the Stars
The Legend of Starcrash
The Search for Hidden Sacred
    Knowledge
They Walked with Jesus
The Three Waves of Volunteers and the
    New Earth
A Very Special Friend
Aron Abrahamsen
Holiday in Heaven
James Ream Adams
Little Steps
Justine Alessi & M. E. McMillan
Rebirth of the Oracle
Kathryn Andries
Time: The Second Secret
Will Alexander
Call Me Jonah
Cat Baldwin
Divine Gifts of Healing
The Forgiveness Workshop
Penny Barron
The Oracle of UR
P.E. Berg & Amanda Hemmingsen
The Birthmark Scar
Dan Bird
Finding Your Way in the Spiritual Age
Waking Up in the Spiritual Age
Julia Cannon
Soul Speak – The Language of Your
    Body
Jack Cauley
Journey for Life
Ronald Chapman
Seeing True
Jack Churchward
Lifting the Veil on the Lost
    Continent of Mu

The Stone Tablets of Mu
Carolyn Greer Daly
Opening to Fullness of Spirit
Patrick De Haan
The Alien Handbook
Paulinne Delcour-Min
Divine Fire
Holly Ice
Spiritual Gold
Anthony DeNino
The Power of Giving and Gratitude
Joanne DiMaggio
Edgar Cayce and the Unfulfilled
    Destiny of Thomas Jefferson
    Reborn
Paul Fisher
Like a River to the Sea
Anita Holmes
Twidders
Aaron Hoopes
Reconnecting to the Earth
Edin Huskovic
God is a Woman
Patricia Irvine
In Light and In Shade
Kevin Killen
Ghosts and Me
Susan Linville
Blessings from Agnes
Donna Lynn
From Fear to Love
Curt Melliger
Heaven Here on Earth
Where the Weeds Grow
Henry Michaelson
And Jesus Said – A Conversation
Andy Myers
Not Your Average Angel Book
Holly Nadler
The Hobo Diaries
Guy Needler
The Anne Dialogues
Avoiding Karma
Beyond the Source – Book 1, Book 2
The Curators
The History of God
The OM
The Origin Speaks

For more information about any of the above titles, soon to be released titles,
or other items in our catalog, write, phone or visit our website:
PO Box 754, Huntsville, AR 72740|479-738-2348/800-935-0045|www.ozarkmt.com

Other Books by Ozark Mountain Publishing, Inc.

Psycho Spiritual Healing
James Nussbaumer
And Then I Knew My Abundance
Each of You
Living Your Dram, Not Someone Else's
The Master of Everything
Mastering Your Own Spiritual Freedom
Sherry O'Brian
Peaks and Valley's
Gabrielle Orr
Akashic Records: One True Love
Let Miracles Happen
Nikki Pattillo
Children of the Stars
A Golden Compass
Victoria Pendragon
Being In A Body
Sleep Magic
The Sleeping Phoenix
Alexander Quinn
Starseeds What's It All About
Debra Rayburn
Let's Get Natural with Herbs
Charmian Redwood
A New Earth Rising
Coming Home to Lemuria
Richard Rowe
Exploring the Divine Library
Imagining the Unimaginable
Garnet Schulhauser
Dance of Eternal Rapture
Dance of Heavenly Bliss
Dancing Forever with Spirit
Dancing on a Stamp
Dancing with Angels in Heaven
Annie Stillwater Gray
The Dawn Book
Education of a Guardian Angel
Joys of a Guardian Angel
Work of a Guardian Angel
Manuella Stoerzer
Headless Chicken

Blair Styra
Don't Change the Channel
Who Catharted
Natalie Sudman
Application of Impossible Things
L.R. Sumpter
Judy's Story
The Old is New
We Are the Creators
Artur Tradevosyan
Croton
Croton II
Jim Thomas
Tales from the Trance
Jolene and Jason Tierney
A Quest of Transcendence
Paul Travers
Dancing with the Mountains
Nicholas Vesey
Living the Life-Force
Dennis Wheatley/ Maria Wheatley
The Essential Dowsing Guide
Maria Wheatley
Druidic Soul Star Astrology
Sherry Wilde
The Forgotten Promise
Lyn Willmott
A Small Book of Comfort
Beyond all Boundaries Book 1
Beyond all Boundaries Book 2
Beyond all Boundaries Book 3
D. Arthur Wilson
You Selfish Bastard
Stuart Wilson & Joanna Prentis
Atlantis and the New Consciousness
Beyond Limitations
The Essenes -Children of the Light
The Magdalene Version
Power of the Magdalene
Sally Wolf
Life of a Military Psychologist

For more information about any of the above titles, soon to be released titles,
or other items in our catalog, write, phone or visit our website:
PO Box 754, Huntsville, AR 72740|479-738-2348/800-935-0045|www.ozarkmt.com